Digging in the City of Brotherly Love

Yale University Press • New Haven and London

Rebecca Yamin

DIGG1NG

in the City of Brotherly Love

Stories from Philadelphia Archaeology

Set in Galliard Oldstyle type by BW&A Books, Inc.
Printed in the United States of America by Sheridan Books,
Ann Arbor, Michigan.

Library of Congress Cataloging-in-Publication Data
Yamin, Rebecca, 1942–
  Digging in the city of brotherly love : stories from Philadelphia
archaeology / Rebecca Yamin.
        p.   cm.
  Includes bibliographical references and index.
  ISBN 978-0-300-10091-4 (alk. paper)
   1. Philadelphia (Pa.)—Antiquities.   2. Excavations (Archaeology)—
Pennsylvania—Philadelphia.   3. Historic sites—Pennsylvania—
Philadelphia.   4. Archaeologists—Pennsylvania—Philadelphia.
5. Urban archaeology—Pennsylvania—Philadelphia.   6. Archaeology
and history—Pennsylvania—Philadelphia.   7. Philadelphia (Pa.)—
History.   8. Philadelphia (Pa.)—Social life and customs.   I. Title.
  F158.39.Y36 2008
  974.8'11—dc22   2008001585

A catalogue record for this book is available from the British Library.

10 9 8 7 6 5 4 3 2 1

For Dan, who entrusted me with Philadelphia

Contents

Preface

This is not the first book about Philadelphia's archaeological past, nor is it the most comprehensive. John Cotter, along with Dan Roberts and Michael Parrington, published *The Buried Past: An Archaeological History of Philadelphia* in 1992. An impressive work that summarizes virtually every archaeology project done in the city and its environs from the 1950s through the 1980s, *The Buried Past* made a substantial contribution to the urban archaeological literature and is a practitioner's bible. I use it all the time when planning a project or developing a proposal; it is the first place I go to see what came before, who did the work, and what they found.

This book is different. It is about both people in the past and people in the present. I always find myself coming back to this juxtaposition; there is something about combining the two that makes it easier for me to believe in the past. The book begins where Cotter and his colleagues left off, which, not entirely coincidentally, is when I began to work in Philadelphia. Dan Roberts, the head of John Milner Associates' cultural resource division, was busy running a thriving department, and with the completion of *The Buried Past* he was ready to let go of Philadelphia at the moment I was ready to take it up.

When I finished a large project in New York City known as Five Points and came home to Philadelphia, Ed Rendell was mayor and the city was on its way up. Long-ignored blocks of rowhouses were coming back to life, and new neighborhood restaurants with panache created an urban scene that was transforming the dowdy downtown into something not seen for decades, and maybe never, in what locals call Center City. My introduction to Philadelphia archaeology was one of Rendell's pet projects, a sound-and-light show for Independence National Historical Park, a vehicle for keeping out-of-town visitors overnight. The idea for a sound-and-light show originally came from Ed Bacon, the planner who was responsible for the previous renaissance in Philadelphia, in the middle of the twentieth century. Under Bacon's guidance, the run-down blocks in one of the oldest parts of the city, a neighborhood known as Society Hill, were restored to their late-eighteenth- and early-nineteenth-century glory. Empty lots were creatively in-filled with new, but compatible, buildings, and the well-to-do were lured back from Philadelphia's fabled suburbs, the Main Line and Chestnut Hill, with tax breaks on the condition that they restore the dilapidated old houses.

The Society Hill neighborhood abuts Independence National Historical Park, which holds Independence Hall, where the Declaration of Independence was signed, and Carpenter's Hall, the site of the first Continental Congress. The park itself was also part of Ed Bacon's vision, and its creation only slightly predated the rebirth of Society Hill. Beginning in the 1950s, the land around the two famous halls was cleared of buildings dating later than the eighteenth century, and the resulting empty space was groomed into a park just in time for the Bicentennial in 1976. What the sound-and-light show would do, in Bacon's 1960s imagination and Rendell's 1990s realization, was present the story of the fight for independence in dramatic form. Rendell wasn't afraid of glitz, and he entrusted the project to people with Disney experience.

My role was to advise Historic Philadelphia, the city agency charged with developing the show, about their archaeological responsibilities and ultimately develop what is called a 106 Case Report. Our first meeting was in Carpenter's Hall. We gathered in the book-lined library at the top of the stairs, a dark room where prospective members are interviewed for membership in the Carpenter's Company. Rendell wasn't there, but the other major players were, including Ann Meredith, Rendell's handpicked dynamic young manager; Phil Scott, then an architect employee of John Milner Associates and the person who drafted me for the project; Ron Miziker, a former Disney employee who now headed his own business, Miziker and Company, and would serve as creative director; and Ron's right-hand man, Tim Elbourne, who besides working for Disney had managed special events for the Nixon White House. What could be more unlikely? The historic walls of Carpenter's Hall and people from Disney describing how they would sink huge projectors in the ground that would magically rise up to shine images on the sides of historic buildings telling the story of the coming Revolution.

The National Park Service was not enthusiastic, especially about the holes in the ground for the projectors, and archaeology became an important issue. The Park Service argued that the bound-to-be-short-lived program should not be permanently installed in the hallowed ground of Independence National Historical Park, especially in Independence Square, the tree-shaded open space behind the hall that had seen little disturbance since the end of the Revolutionary War (except by archaeologists, but that is another story). Rendell, however, was not to be defeated, and the mayor went so far as to threaten to take the Liberty Bell away from the park if he couldn't have his show. Symbols, you see, carry great weight in Philadelphia, and because the city, not the Park Service, owns the bell—surely one of the weightiest of the symbols—Rendell was at an advantage. Besides threatening to take the bell, he and his project manager were willing to bring in the heavy hitters. They got the distinguished historian Gary Nash on board to review the script for the sound-and-light show and even lured members of the U.S. Congress to Philadelphia to make a site visit. The Park Service ultimately went along with a reversible sound-and-light show. No archaeology was necessary because no holes were dug, but I came away from the project knowing considerably more about politics in the park and the power of symbols in the City of Brotherly Love than I had known before.

Archaeological remains of Philadelphia's past rarely attain even an aura of symbolism, although they might. They are, after all, physical fragments of our heritage, something about which plenty of people are reverent. But archaeological remains are mundane, even when they are things that belonged to famous people. They are bound by their everyday contexts and embedded in a "once upon a time" reality. That is, of course, what is wonderful about archaeology. It makes it possible to believe in a past, not a past constructed for symbolic purposes, but an everyday past. Philadelphia's symbolic past is well known. It is the city's everyday past that this book is about.

Acknowledgments

When I studied archaeology at Penn in the 1960s it was all about Tikal and the Yucatán, Chavín and Peru. We never got around to Philadelphia, and even though I spent almost as much time exploring the city as going to class it wasn't with archaeology on my mind. The Philadelphia I came back to in 1992 was a much different place than in my college days, but I also came back with a new perspective and have been lucky enough to do excavations in the heart of the city. I owe this good fortune first and foremost to Dan Roberts, who hired me as an urban archaeologist even though I really wasn't one, gave me one of the juiciest urban projects (Five Points) of the late twentieth century, and then turned me loose in Philadelphia. He set high standards, wouldn't settle for less, and put up with my idiosyncratic style, for all of which I am grateful. I value my other colleagues at John Milner Associates for their competence as well as their good company: Alex Bartlett and Tod Benedict in the field, Juliette Gerhardt in the lab, Margy Schoettle in West Chester, and Dawn Thomas, Grace Ziesing, Matt Harris, Lori Aument, Courtney Clark, and Doug McVarish in Philadelphia. Grace gets special mention for on-the-spot editing and Dawn for solving my computer problems as well as holding my hand through the final preparation of this manuscript. I am also grateful to Sarah Ruch, director of JMA's graphics department, and her staff, Mary Paradise and Rob Schultz, for their creativity and good work, some of which appears here. Rob, in particular, prepared several new drawings for the book and made old ones publishable. I turned to Neale Quenzel for information on Carpenter's Hall.

Many of my projects have been in Independence National Historical Park, and it has been a pleasure to work with and get to know the professionals there: Doris Fanelli, Jim Mueller, Jed Levin, Coxey Toogood, and Karen Stevens. I thank them all for their knowledge, guidance, and help. Help has also come from other scholars and clients. Ed Lawler, who singlehandedly made us all appreciate the importance of the place where our first two presidents lived, was generous with his time and knowledge. Sally Elk and Sean Kelly at Eastern State Penitentiary inspired me with their imaginative approach to their historic site; Ann Meredith at Lights of Liberty continues to astonish me with her energy and commitment to Philadelphia's past and present; and Dick Tyler has always provided a sense of balance and insight into the real world. Behind the scenes, Reg Pits did much of the historical research for my Philadelphia projects, and Art Washburn and Tom Crist are my sources for anything having to do with physical anthropology. I am grateful to all who were willing to be interviewed, including Dan Roberts, Emily Bittenbender, Tom Crist, Art Washburn, Patti Jeppson, Jed Levin, Dick Tyler, Sally Elk, Coxey Toogood, Jeff Ray, Michael Coard, and, last but not least, Doug Mooney, who told me everything he could about the block on Independence Mall I didn't get to excavate. The interviews were as close as I could get to other people's projects, and it is that personal connection to the past that brings it alive, at least for me.

My Philadelphia friends have been wonderfully patient with my lack of time and frequent complaining. Special thanks go to Andrea McFadden, Ruth Crispin, Coxey Toogood, Maryanne Conheim, Steve Keiser, Dennis Bower, and Chris Hamann. In a category by themselves are Harriette Behringer and Paul Fussell, who have encouraged me, inspired me, and drawn from their depth of experience to advise me. They are my editors in my head. At Yale University Press I had the benefit of beginning this project with Harry Haskell, whose vision it was to do a series of books on urban archaeology. Later in the process I was guided by Laura Davulis, Susan Laity, and Christopher Rogers. Phillip King copy-edited the manuscript with sensitivity and insight. I am also grateful to peer reviewers David Orr and Lu Ann De Cunzo; I only hope I have paid enough heed to their wise suggestions. Susan Drinan at the Atwater Kent Museum, R. A. Friedman at the Historical Society of Pennsylvania, Charlene Peacock at the Library Company of Philadelphia, Andrea Leraris and Karen Stevens at Independence National Historical Park, David Orr, Ed Morin, and Tom Crist helped with illustrations.

Most of all I am grateful to the support I derive from my immediate family: Peter, Eli, Lorraine, Ariana, and Paul. To their children I wish careers as rewarding as my own. The best part about being an archaeologist is that it's so much fun.

Digging in the City of Brotherly Love

CHAPTER ONE

Beneath the Symbolic Surface

The archaeology of cities is the archaeology of building and rebuilding; it is the peeling away of the layers upon layers that constitute the complexity of urban places. It is an archaeology of what makes a city a city in the first place: intense human occupation in a constricted, crowded space. Cities are dynamic places to live and complicated places to dig. They grow and change and transform themselves, but beneath every new surface remains something of the old. This is as true in Philadelphia as it is in New York or Boston or Cairo or Rome. The remains are different, but the general story is the same. Cities hide pieces of their past below-ground and the pieces, often in the most unlikely places, are recoverable. That's what urban archaeologists do. We recover pieces of the city's unwritten past before they are destroyed by its unstoppable future.

In Philadelphia, as in many other North American cities, the pieces have most often been artifacts. When we dig where new buildings have replaced earlier ones, and tenements and factories have filled up former backyards, there is little left but artifacts. They are the trash left behind by people who lived in the buildings that are no longer there. Sometimes they are strewn across old ground surfaces, but more often they are found at the bottom of brick- or stone-lined shafts that once served as privies, cisterns, or wells. Once retired from their original functions, privies and cisterns in particular became convenient places to discard unwanted or broken household goods. Wonderful things have been found in Philadelphia: puzzle jugs and school tokens (Figures 1.1 and 1.2), punch bowls with clever sayings written on them and anthropomorphic pipe tampers in provocative positions. The ceramics alone are noteworthy: sunburst-decorated earthenware (Figure 1.3) and elaborately gilded porcelain, locally made redware (Figure 1.4) and specially monogrammed tewares. Some of these things belonged to the founding fathers, whose efforts are rightly celebrated in Philadelphia, where the Declaration of Independence and the Constitution were conceived, but many more—most of

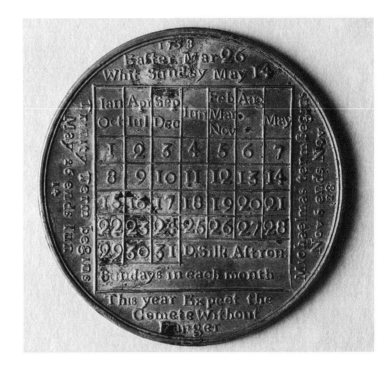

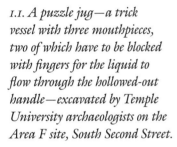

1.1. A puzzle jug—a trick vessel with three mouthpieces, two of which have to be blocked with fingers for the liquid to flow through the hollowed-out handle—excavated by Temple University archaeologists on the Area F site, South Second Street.

(top, right) 1.2. School token from 1758, with a legend referring to Halley's comet. (Photograph courtesy of Kise, Straw and Kolodner and the National Park Service)

(below, right) 1.3. Sunburst-decorated earthenware dish found on the northwest side of Market and Front Streets. (Photograph courtesy of David Orr)

them, in fact—belonged to people whose names are not mentioned in history books. If taken as more than fascinating objects for museum shelves (or unwanted things for overcrowded storage rooms), the artifacts, as the great folklorist Henry Glassie says, lead to history. But it doesn't happen automatically.

Archaeologists need to go beyond the artifacts as objects. We need to know whose things they were, why they had what they had, how it related to who they were or wanted to be. We need to connect the things to whatever else we can learn from every source we can think of: census records, city directories, tax records, probate inventories, diaries. And we need to put the things in the appropriate historical context. We need to read history and pay attention to historians. We cannot get inside peoples' minds, but we can do what historians have always done: string the fragmentary evidence from the past together into narratives that make sense. It is not enough to count the artifacts and describe them in excruciating detail. We have to use them, and everything else we know, to build stories about the past, stories that are not the absolute truth, but are the conceivable

1.4. Philadelphia redware from the middle block of Independence Mall. (Photograph by Juliette Gerhardt)

truth, an approximation, which, after all, is what history always is. By building such stories we discover what we know and, even more important, what we don't know, which leads to more questions, questions we otherwise wouldn't have even thought to ask.[1]

It is a cumulative process. We construct the past; it isn't there to be discovered. We take the fragments—from the ground and from the documents—and weave them into stories of what might have been. It isn't fiction, but it isn't quite science either. It's an interpretive endeavor that seeks to make the most of what we know. In Philadelphia, the challenge is to get beyond what every schoolchild already knows.[2]

Rethinking Independence Mall

It's not so easy to tell new stories in a place as replete with old ones as Philadelphia. The responsibility the city has—along with the National Park Service—for telling the story of

1.5. Independence Hall exterior, south façade. (Photograph by Robin Miller, 2001; Independence National Historical Park)

independence and taking care of its two most important symbols—the Liberty Bell and Independence Hall—influences, in great degree, its openness to less significant remnants of its past. These two great icons have proved to be so flexible that they have served many causes over time, leaving little space for new stories. Indirectly, they have also provided a reason to discover more about the very part of the city where Independence Hall stands (Figure 1.5). When Independence National Historical Park was first created in the 1950s only minimal archaeological work was conducted. The laws requiring systematic archaeological investigations on federal or state property were not yet in place, and the neighborhood adjacent to the hall was considered decrepit and dangerous. In the patriotic postwar 1950s the well-meaning committee of citizens charged with creating a more appropriate context for the hall proposed removing the buildings near it that might catch on fire. To an extent, this was an excuse for taking down everything that didn't date to the eighteenth century, the period they wanted to celebrate in the park.

Demolition of buildings was monitored by archaeologists, but there was neither time nor resources for in-depth research.[3]

After much debate and many alternative plans, the committee also recommended clearing the three blocks in front of Independence Hall to provide a more dramatic frame for what it considered the ultimate symbol of democracy. Over a seven-year period, all of the buildings in the three-block area were taken down (Figures 1.6 and 1.7). The intent was to disconnect the hall (and its mall) from the city. The alleyways that cross-cut the three blocks in front of the hall and connected it to the surrounding blocks were covered up; the new landscape made no reference to the historic configuration of the blocks, and the old buildings' foundations were buried under four feet of fill (Figure 1.8).

With minor modifications that landscape lasted fifty years. In 1976 a pavilion was built to house the Liberty Bell in the middle of the first block. A fountain honoring Judge Edwin O. Lewis, the man who had spearheaded the creation of the mall, dominated the second (middle) block, and a kind of grass garden, designed by Dan Kiley, the preeminent landscape architect of the period, filled the third block. It wasn't a very inviting land-

1.6. *Independence Hall and the blocks to the north before they were cleared to make Independence Mall. (Independence National Historical Park)*

1.7. *Demolition on the block facing Independence Hall, to make way for the construction of Independence Mall, circa 1953. (Independence National Historical Park)*

1.8. The southern block of Independence Mall when it was first created. (Independence National Historical Park)

scape; the second and third blocks were too far from the Liberty Bell and Independence Hall to see much tourist traffic. By the 1990s people complained that the mall was sterile and even dangerous (rats and the homeless, some claimed, were the only inhabitants of the tired setting). The National Park Service began a program to redesign the mall, and by 1995 alternative proposals were under discussion. The final design included buildings along the western edge of the first two blocks and one large structure at the northern end of the mall, all of them intended to reintroduce some of the urban context that had been intentionally removed fifty years earlier (Figure 1.9). Even the long-removed alleys that had once cut across the blocks and continued on either side of the mall were to reappear in the new landscape in an effort to tie the park back into the urban grid. In other words, the new design would attempt to recreate the connections that had been intentionally severed in the 1950s. But before construction could begin, there would have to be archaeology.

Laws passed in the 1960s, and the mandate of the National Park Service to "husband its resources," required that archaeological investigations precede construction that could destroy potentially significant historic remains. As unlikely as it seemed, considering how many buildings had been destroyed to create Independence Mall in the 1950s and how much bulldozing was done to create a landscape where the buildings had been, the possibility existed that significant resources—especially artifact-filled shafts— would be found. In the case of the third block, there was even the possibility of finding

1.9. Aerial view of Independence Square and Independence Mall in 2004, after the Liberty Bell Center, the Visitor Center, and the Constitution Center were completed. (Photograph by Robin Miller; Independence National Historical Park)

never-disturbed historic ground—that is, backyards that had belonged to eighteenth and nineteenth-century residents.

These investigations began in 1999. The middle block came first. Under my direction and under the watchful eye of a client who didn't want to spend one extra dollar excavating an area that didn't absolutely have to be excavated, we removed the concrete cradle that held the 1950s landscape and exposed the basement walls of buildings that had been demolished to create Independence Mall (Figure 1.10). In 2001 we did the same thing on the block across from Independence Hall (Figure 1.11). Beneath the basement floors on both blocks we found multiple artifact-filled shafts that led us to people who weren't part of Philadelphia's narrative of itself—an accountant who worked in the first Department of Treasury, the enslaved Africans and indentured servants who labored in President Washington's household, a family of combmakers who were among the early-nineteenth-century city's growing middle class, and a carriage maker and a cabinetmaker who couldn't decide if they were workers or gentlemen. The next three chapters of this book tell their stories, but they also tell the stories of the excavations, of the archaeologists who did the work, and the politics that swirled around us. The search for the past is never done in a vacuum, and the past that is found is never unrelated to the present in which it is discovered. That process—the interaction of the present and the past—is one of the things that makes archaeology such an adventure. It is not an Indiana Jones adventure—no temples of doom or close brushes with death—but there are dangers and surprises and mysteries to be solved, even in staid Philadelphia.

The third block of the mall—where a building dedicated to telling the story of the Constitution now stands—was the richest of all, because the basements of nineteenth-century buildings had not destroyed all the old backyards (Figure 1.12). Nor had they destroyed the burials left behind when the cemetery for the Second Presbyterian Church was moved. Chapter 5 tells the story of recovering and reburying the bodies that were

1.10. Archaeologists working below the level of the concrete cradle that supported the landscape on the middle block of Independence Mall. (John Milner Associates, Inc.)

hidden under the portion of the mall where the cemetery had been, and it also tells the stories of the diverse population that lived on this block in the eighteenth and nineteenth centuries. There were abolitionists and free blacks, poor Irishmen and maybe even Betsy Ross. The rich and the poor lived side by side, and their possessions led to their stories. But it was not a straightforward path. The Constitution Center planners did not anticipate the extent or expense of the archaeology on the site of their building, and the story of the struggle to analyze the collections appears here as well.

Besides Independence Mall there have been other reasons to conduct archaeological investigations in Philadelphia. Since the passage of the National Historic Preservation Act in 1966 and related legislation, any construction project using federal money, requiring federal permits, or on federal property has required what is called a cultural resources survey. The archaeological portion of such a survey begins with a Phase IA documentary study. A general history of the area is compiled and every map showing the area that will be affected by construction is examined. The maps are the surest indication of what might be found if it hasn't been disturbed by subsequent building episodes. If there is reason to believe potentially significant remains are present in the project area, field testing is done. In urban situations this usually involves directing a backhoe to remove fill under which the potential remains are thought to lie. It is not possible to dig up

1.11. Excavation under way on the first block of Independence Mall. (John Milner Associates, Inc.)

1.12. Overview of excavation on the northern block of Independence Mall. (Courtesy of Kise, Straw and Kolodner and the National Park Service)

whole construction sites, and the archaeologist has to choose carefully where to put the backhoe trenches. Plotting property lines helps. Privies are usually at the backs of house lots; cisterns and wells tend to be closer to the back door. This part of the investigation is referred to as Phase I/II testing and is followed by full-out excavation—Phase III—if significant remains are present that would be destroyed by the pending construction. It is these Phase III excavations that have produced multitudes of artifacts in Philadelphia. But they have not produced multitudes of stories. Descriptive technical reports lie buried in agency files, rarely read and barely readable. In many, if not most, cases the contracts under which the work was done did not allow for interpretive analyses (and certainly didn't encourage them). The consulting archaeologist was responsible for doing background research, finding and excavating what would otherwise be destroyed, cleaning, conserving, identifying, and quantifying the artifacts recovered, addressing some predefined research questions, and writing a report. Tight budgets and time frames made it next to impossible to do much more.

Buried in these technical reports are many more stories—or, at least, potential stories—of Philadelphia's past. At the beginning of the nineteenth century Philadelphia had the largest free black population of any American city, and Chapter 6 tells the story of two projects that relate to that community. A cemetery belonging to the First African Baptist Church at Eighth Street was found during construction of a tunnel in the 1980s, and a second cemetery, this one belonging to an earlier congregation of the same church, was found about ten years later. The analysis of the remains allowed the archaeologists and physical anthropologists working with them to learn about the health of the population, but working with members of the extant congregation taught them even more. These projects paved the way for future studies involving descendant communities, and the story of how that was done is at least as important as the results of the archaeology.

Other construction in the 1980s uncovered remains of Philadelphia's hidden past, and Chapter 7 uses several projects to talk about the waterfront. In Philadelphia, as in many other cities, highway construction cut off the city from the water, in this case the Delaware River. While much of the original shoreline was lost, a lone staircase preserves a small section of the bluff on which William Penn sited his "green country town"; archaeological research near the base of it revealed an early boatyard beneath a parking lot slated for construction that never happened. Another project along the waterfront exposed the large wooden wharves that served Philadelphia's eighteenth-century trade. Before 1800 Philadelphia was the nation's center for international trade, which is reflected in the great variety of imported wares that have been found through digging. It was also a market town, and the analysis of food remains from various archaeological projects suggests that more variety was available in Philadelphia than in any of the other major eastern cities.

No book about Philadelphia could leave out Benjamin Franklin, and in 2005 a project associated with his three hundredth birthday reviewed all previous archaeological work done on his Market Street property. Chapter 8, an archaeological walk through the eighteenth-century city, visits Franklin Court, the site of Franklin's house and shop, but the walk begins farther south in a section of the city once known as Southwark. A whole block was excavated there in the 1970s that included eighteenth-century bakeries, artisans' workshops, and the site of one of the city's early Quaker meetinghouses. Known as New Market, the block abutted one of the city's major trade centers, and the men who developed the block also built the market. A second excavation in Southwark (referred to as Area F), also done in the 1970s and only recently reported, included the properties of a ship's captain, a furniture maker, and a rich china merchant. These two excavations and a third (the Bourse block) on Chestnut Street reveal the past in part of the city that was very close to Independence Hall. Although the people who lived in Southwark may have been invisible to the politicians who were inventing America's democracy, they were the people for whom independence was forged. They were energetically using their talents to do what historian Gordon Wood has claimed was characteristically American: ignoring the old hierarchies, they pursued prosperity, attempting to get rich in any and every way they could.[4]

Between 1800 and 1820 Philadelphia's population grew from 81,000 to 135,637; the city finally spread westward, away from the banks of the Delaware River and toward the Schuylkill River.[5] A walk through the nineteenth-century city, described in Chapter 9, begins at Doctor's Row, now the site of the Pennsylvania Convention Center between Eleventh and Thirteenth Streets, and proceeds to an Irish neighborhood between Fifteenth and Sixteenth Streets and finally to the site of the Magdalen Asylum at Twenty-first Street, now covered by the Franklin Institute's Futures Center. Archaeological excavations in these areas revealed the growing complexity of the city. While the details of residents' personal lives remain a mystery, their very existence adds depth to Philadelphia's story. It is not just a story of great white men; it is a story of ambitious workers, many of them immigrants, carving out new lives for themselves in a new country. The influence of women, so often minimized in standard histories, emerges from artifact assemblages that reflect their choices, their roles in the domestic sphere and as heads of households. In a city still characterized by its distinct neighborhoods, archaeological projects have rediscovered forgotten ones.

The last chapter recounts two projects—two stories—that reveal the phenomenal resilience of the city's physical plan and the irrepressible influence of William Penn. In 2006, one of the squares in Penn's seventeenth-century design for the city got new life. Franklin Square, at the northeast corner of the grid, had faded badly by the 1990s. Its location close to the foot of the always busy Benjamin Franklin Bridge made it seem dangerous, and it appeared that only brave preschool teachers, followed by lines of Chinese-American children, took advantage of its relatively new playground. With the refurbishment of Independence Mall, including construction of the Constitution Center virtually across the street, there was a real need to bring the square back to life. Like the projects associated with the redevelopment of the mall, construction on Franklin Square also required an archaeological study, which led to the discovery of yet another forgotten cemetery.

Another twenty-first-century project encountered a much more recent historical feature, an escape tunnel dug in 1945 by prisoners trying to get out of Eastern State Penitentiary. Although the penitentiary was built almost 150 years after William Penn's time, its genesis came from Quakers wrestling with ideas about prison reform that also concerned Penn. His statue on top of City Hall may no longer dominate Philadelphia's skyline, but his spirit is still with us.

Beneath the Symbolic Surface

Even though a good deal of archaeology has been done outside Center City, this book concentrates on that urban core (Figure 1.13). The purpose is to get beyond the symbols— Independence Hall and the Liberty Bell—from which Philadelphia derives so much of its identity. Recent and not so recent archaeological projects have delved into the city's much more complicated past: the thriving commerce that blossomed after the Revolutionary War and produced a well-heeled middle class; the vibrant free black community that is ancestral to the city's contemporary black population; the ethnic enclaves that nurtured newly arrived immigrants and provided the strong foundations on which future gen-

1.13. Archaeological sites in the present, places in the past, visited in this book.

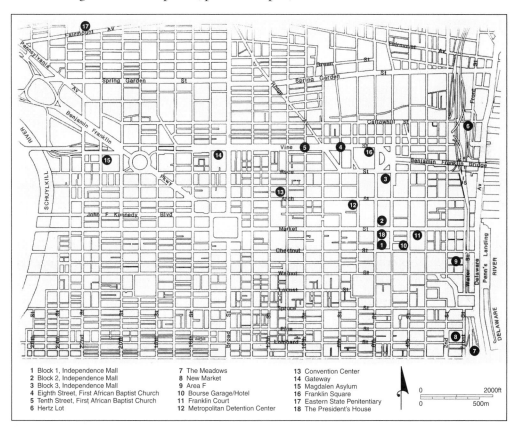

1 Block 1, Independence Mall	7 The Meadows	13 Convention Center
2 Block 2, Independence Mall	8 New Market	14 Gateway
3 Block 3, Independence Mall	9 Area F	15 Magdalen Asylum
4 Eighth Street, First African Baptist Church	10 Bourse Garage/Hotel	16 Franklin Square
5 Tenth Street, First African Baptist Church	11 Franklin Court	17 Eastern State Penitentiary
6 Hertz Lot	12 Metropolitan Detention Center	18 The President's House

erations built successful careers. The city still boasts an outdoor Italian Market and a thriving Chinatown. There are multitudes of gospel churches, and Quakers maintain a conspicuous presence with their pristine meetinghouses and outstanding schools. Philadelphia is a city of differences. Its essence cannot be abbreviated in patriotic symbols; it is far too complex. Its staid exterior hides its many personalities.

It is no wonder that archaeology and archaeologists have struggled to communicate the significance of their finds. They don't fit the city's public persona, but they touch on private ones. Archaeology gets beneath the symbolic surface; it looks at the city from the inside out. Henry Glassie tells us, "the way to study people is not from the top down or the bottom up, but from the inside out, from the place where people are articulate to the place where they are not, from the place where they are in control of their destinies to the place where they are not."[6] As archaeologists, we cannot do what the folklorist does. We can't mingle among the people to know who they are; we can't pass time at their firesides talking about the doings of the day. Our process is different, but it is still people we are after. We begin on the inside, with the artifacts in their archaeological contexts, and weave a historic context until there are no more threads to follow. Ours is a slightly different form of moving from the inside out than Glassie's, but it too moves outward and ends with people whose voices have not been heard.

CHAPTER TWO

Hudson's Square

The Middle Block of Independence Mall

Philadelphia is a city of squares—Rittenhouse, Washington, Logan, Franklin—all four part of Thomas Holme's plan, drawn up for William Penn in 1683 (Figure 2.1). Penn's city was to be a "green country town," a grid of streets stretching between the two rivers—the Delaware on the east and the Schuylkill on the west—punctuated by a large square in the middle (where City Hall now stands) and slightly smaller squares, intended as parks, in each of the four corners. Although Penn saw only one of those squares come to fruition in his lifetime, and that one as a potter's field, the center of the city still looks much as he imagined, anchored, as it is, by the four squares: Washington on the southeast, Rittenhouse on the southwest, Logan on the northwest, and Franklin on the northeast. Hudson's Square, also envisioned by a Quaker gentleman, had a very different fate. In fact, the land between Fifth and Sixth Streets and Market (originally called High) and Arch (originally Mulberry), now the middle block of Independence Mall, may never have been known as Hudson's Square, even though its original owner, William Hudson, specified the name in his will from 1743.

William Hudson began his career as a tanner along Dock Creek (now part of Independence National Historical Park). He was chosen as one of the original councilmen by Penn under the City Charter of 1701; he was a member of the assembly in 1706 and 1724, and the city's mayor in 1725 and 1726. By the time of his death in 1743 he was one of Philadelphia's largest manufacturers, shipping merchants, and shipowners. He lived with his family in a three-story brick house on Third Street, the heart of the city at the time, but among his investment properties was the block between Fifth and Sixth. During Hudson's lifetime the block was nothing but pasture and apple orchards, the city having reached no farther than Fourth Street by the 1740s, but Hudson was a man of vision. He anticipated the growth of the city and designed an urban space that was to become part of it after his death and even after the death of his wife. Like William Penn, Hud-

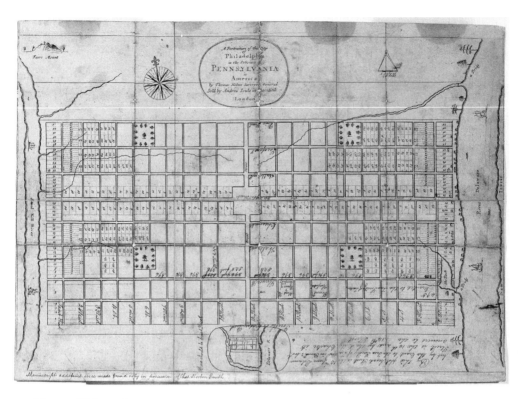

2.1. Thomas Holme, plan
for the city of Philadelphia,
1683 (Historical Society of
Pennsylvania)

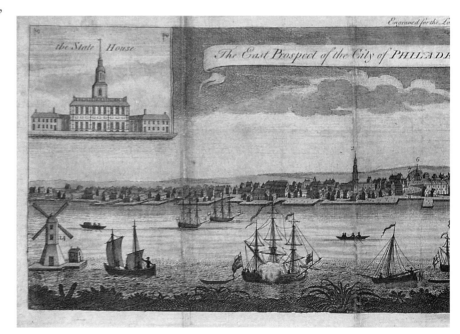

2.2. Philadelphia along
the Delaware River
shoreline, drawn by
Nicholas Scull, 1765.
(Historical Society of
Pennsylvania)

son saw himself as a creator of a new world, albeit smaller than Penn's ideal city of five squares and gridiron of streets, but equally ordered and meant to endure into the future. He was creating yet another piece of Penn's "Eden" and dedicating it to himself.[1]

Although William Penn and Thomas Holme intended the city to develop equally along the Delaware and Schuylkill riverbanks and grow gradually to meet in the center, early commercial activities clung to the Delaware shore, and instead of spreading inward the city expanded north–south (Figure 2.2). By the time Hudson made his long and complicated will in 1741 (probated in 1743), his land on High Street was well beyond the most developed portion of the city. Nevertheless, Hudson must have known it would eventually be absorbed into the urban grid, and following Penn and Holme's model of urban symmetry he specified exactly how what was then pasture should be laid out.

The sketch plan that accompanied Hudson's will called for subdividing the block into three equal parts, created by two thirty-foot-wide public streets (Figure 2.3). These were named, appropriately enough, South and North Streets (later renamed Commerce and Cuthbert, respectively). The mostly long skinny lots facing High Street were to back up on South Street, and the somewhat wider Mulberry Street lots would have their backs on North Street. Between North and South were square parcels with Fifth and Sixth Street frontage and long thin lots in the middle. Hudson's oldest son, also named William, inherited the lot at the corner of Fifth and High (he also took over his father's business and got the house on Third Street); his oldest daughter, Rachel, already married and named

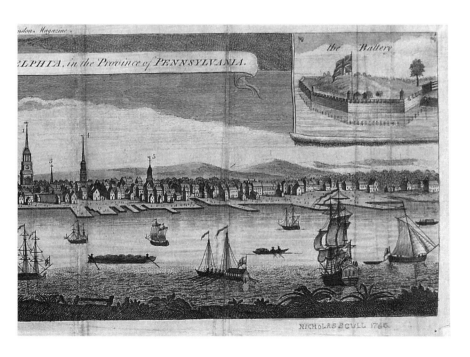

Emlen, received the larger lot at the corner of Sixth and High. The remaining lots, each described as "part of my square," went to other children and grandchildren.

In keeping with Quaker values, grants appear to have been equitable between the sexes, although it is difficult to judge since there were so many more girls than boys in the mix. They didn't receive their inheritance until Hudson's wife, Hannah, died in 1759, and even then the block was barely developed. The heirs, adults by that time, apparently lived elsewhere and eventually sold off their property. What remained as Hudson's legacy was the tripartite organization of the block created by North and South Streets, which he intended "to remain always open to be used as publick streets of the city aforesaid for ever."

When the first Independence Mall was created, the terraced gardens and formal walkways that paralleled Fifth and Sixth Streets made no reference to the original organization of Hudson's Square. Even North (Cuthbert) and South (Commerce) Streets were obliterated by a landscape that took as its focal point a ceremonial fountain honoring the man who spearheaded the movement to create the mall, Judge Edwin O. Lewis. An underground parking garage took up the space that had once bustled with commercial establishments lining Commerce and Cuthbert Streets. In the 1990s redesign, the new Independence Visitor Center, as planned, would extend from where Commerce Street had been to Market Street. The long brick building, completed in 2002, stretches along the east side of North Sixth Street covering an area that originally included six historic lots, three facing Market Street and three facing North Sixth. When we began archaeological investigations within the footprint of the proposed building in August 1999, the first thing we tried to locate was the old alignment of South Street.

If we could find the street, we would know where we were on the ground. We stretched a tape from the edge of Market Street to where the street should have been and began trenching. But the edge of Market Street had moved since Hudson's day, and the distance between its northern edge and the southern edge of the invisible old street

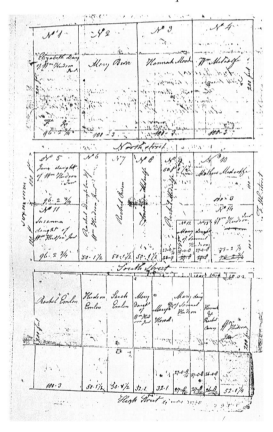

2.3. *Sketch plan of property subdivision from William Hudson's will, 1743. (Courtesy of Anna Coxe Toogood)*

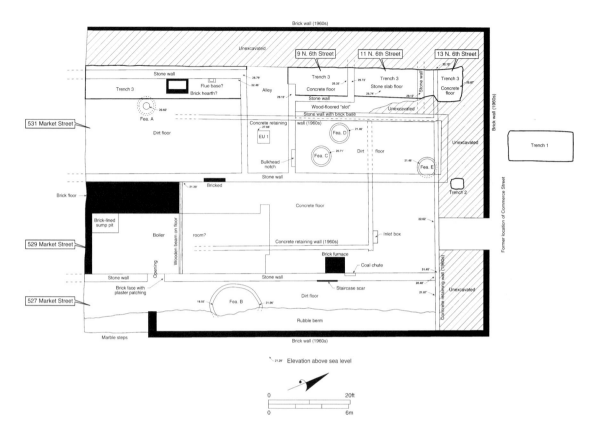

2.4. Plan of archaeological test areas showing backhoe trenches and features on the middle block of Independence Mall.

wasn't quite the same. Our first trench came up empty, the second trench hit a drainage feature for the 1950s landscape, and the third trench—this one placed at the northern edge of where the street should have been—was full of fill. The underground parking garage, built when the mall was first developed, had apparently disturbed a larger area than was shown on the construction plans, and Hudson's alley was completely gone to the south of the garage. We directed the backhoe operator (an enthusiastic young man named Harry Brown who had never worked with archaeologists before) to dig a north–south trench along the western edge of the site. The trench (no. 3 in Figure 2.4) was meant to expose the foundations of the buildings that had faced North Sixth Street before the mall was created. There were three, a small one at what would have been number 13 North Sixth in the 1950s, but was number 11 until 1859; a slightly larger building at number 11 (9 until 1859); and a third at 9 (previously 7). We even found the narrow alleyway that separated 9 North Sixth from the back of the building that faced Market Street at the corner.

We knew from insurance maps and photographs that the buildings that were taken down in the 1950s were not the original structures on the historic lots. If we were to find archaeological features, such as privies, cisterns, or wells, that related to earlier occupation we would have to remove the cellar floors and look underneath. The backyards of earlier houses had been destroyed by the deep basements of nineteenth-century buildings, but portions of features that once reached depths of twenty feet or so could still be present. Unfortunately no such features turned up beneath the North Sixth Street basements.

The most recent buildings on the three lots had reached back about a hundred feet from the eastern edge of Sixth Street. We had not planned to dig behind these buildings, but when no features were found there we changed our plans. Trenches placed behind the Sixth Street foundations initially uncovered three features: a small circular probable privy behind number 11 and two circular shafts behind number 9 (Figure 2.5). These properties belonged to a notary, a painter, a doctor, and an accountant in the eighteenth and early nineteenth centuries, and we looked forward to learning more about the lives of these not so wealthy (or powerful) residents of Philadelphia by retrieving their garbage. But first we had to know what lay beneath the Market Street basement floors.

It was its location on Market, formerly known as High, Street that made Hudson's land so valuable. From the city's very beginning High Street was a major thoroughfare, what Joseph Jackson, Philadelphia's early-nineteenth-century chronicler, called "the most historic highway in America." The city's earliest market was at the base of High Street on the Delaware shore. By 1690 there was a building and bell tower at Second and High that served as both head of the market house and city hall (Figure 2.6). By 1786 the market house had expanded to Fourth Street and by 1816 it reached Eighth. When the properties between Fifth and Sixth Streets were first developed in the late eighteenth century, the market was just a block away, and within the second decade of the nineteenth century it was outside their doorsteps. The first houses along this valuable strip of real estate were substantial three-story brick houses that served as residences and places of business for well-to-do merchants (Figure 2.7). Among them were John Pemberton, a wealthy ironmonger and metal merchant who eventually became a renowned Quaker minister (Pemberton reappears in Chapter 5), Thomas Moore, a "gentleman" owner of a nearby brewery, William Shippen, a delegate to the Continental Congress, and Dr. Caspar Wistar, the celebrated anatomist. Those houses were replaced in the middle of the nineteenth century with warehouses, some of them stretching all the way from Market Street through to Commerce Street. A major fire in 1856 destroyed most of those buildings, and the large structures that replaced them all ran through to Commerce Street (Figure 2.8). It was those buildings that were taken down to create Independence Mall in the 1950s, and it was under their basement floors that we needed to look for privies and cisterns

2.5. Alexander Bartlett and Rebecca Yamin, surrounded by a shoring box, getting ready to map two privies on the middle block.

(below) 2.6. Friends Meeting House (left) at the corner of High and Second Streets and City Hall (right) with the market house extending behind it. (Historical Society of Pennsylvania)

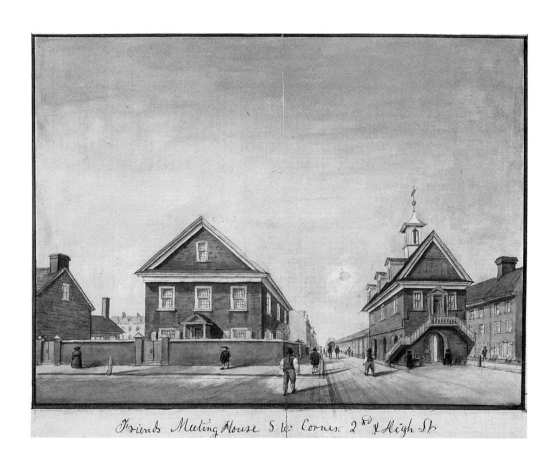

Friends Meeting House S W Corner 2ᵈ & High St

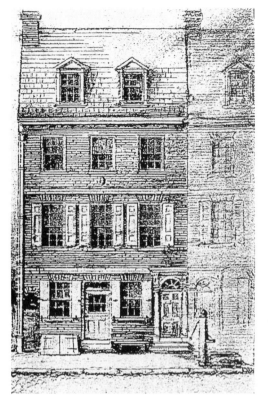

2.7. Drawing of Nathan Sellers house, 231 High Street, 1785–1829. (From Joseph Jackson, Market Street, Philadelphia: The Most Historic Highway in America, Its Merchants and Its Story, *1918)*

related to earlier occupation. The search was more difficult than the one along North Sixth Street. The Market Street basements were deeper and our enthusiastic backhoe driver needed a bigger machine to clear the fill and lift up the floors.

The basement of 531 Market Street, which was an electrical supply store in the 1950s and a silks and fancy dry goods store before that, was about ten feet deep. Cut into the packed dirt floor was a single brick-lined shaft, the reward for an effort that took several days. The basement at number 529 next door, according to the documentary record a hardware store since 1859, was full of iron-lidded troughs, brick platforms, and several coal bins. No shaft features were left there and the function of the troughs remained a mystery, but the next lot, at 527 Market, produced the payoff. A very large cesspool—ten feet in diameter—was found beneath the concrete basement floor of what had most recently been a store for wholesale novelties. Before that it was Arthur Kunkel and Company, clothiers, among other things. The feature was brimming with artifacts. Alex Bartlett, the bottle expert on the project, immediately recognized bottles from the late nineteenth century and we knew, at the very least, we had a historic assemblage. What lay below we couldn't tell without digging deeper.

Finding the Stories

Uncovering the features is just the first step. Next is excavating them, nearly always a challenge in an urban situation. The five shafts we located during the testing were dispersed betwixt and between long buried foundation walls and the concrete framework that cradled the overlying mall landscape. We had to open up a large area, both to remove walls that might tumble unexpectedly, endangering those working on the dig, and to allow heavy machinery to maneuver. We would need the machines to dismantle the features as we went down, four feet at a time, and also, as it turned out, to assist in the construction of wooden boxes—shoring—to hold back the surrounding fill as we

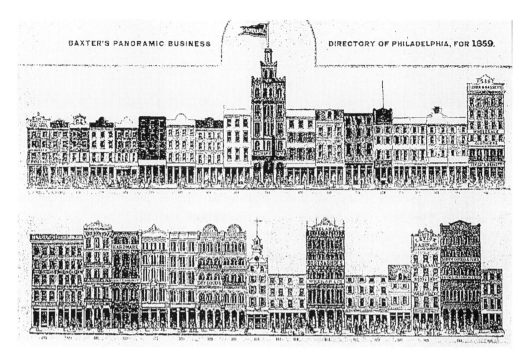

2.8. Market Street between Fifth and Sixth Streets. The upper streetfront shown here is the south side of Market Street; the tall building in the middle is Tower Hall, Philadelphia's first department store. The lower streetfront shows the north side of Market Street. (From Baxter's Panoramic Business Directory of Philadelphia for 1859*)*

excavated the features, the deepest of which reached a little more than eight feet below the basement floor where it was first encountered.[2] In the process of creating space for the boxes, the machine hit additional brick-lined shafts: a privy just north of the one at 11 North Sixth Street, an even larger privy underneath an arch at 9 North Sixth, and an empty domed shaft very close to the large cesspool at 527 Market. Even beneath long-developed (and redeveloped) city lots, in Philadelphia and elsewhere, there still lie buried remnants of peoples' most intimate activities. The problem is to figure out what they can tell us about the people.

As we excavate the artifacts, we speculate. The privy behind 11 North Sixth Street, for instance, the one we called Feature E in the field, contained so many wine and liquor bottles, all dating to the late eighteenth century, that we wondered whether they had belonged to a tavern (Figure 2.9). We envisioned tired politicians ending long days at the State House (which was just a block away) at this Sixth Street establishment. We wondered whether the cesspool, which turned out to hold three assemblages, one dating to the late eighteenth century and two to the first half of the nineteenth century, served two households. Why was it so big and why was it so close to the back of the house at 527 Market Street? The wondering is what makes the digging fun. You never know what will be in the next bucketful. Nightsoil (that is, solid human waste) is generally dense and sticky and more often than not water needs to be used to force it through an archaeological screen. When the glop from the cesspool was delivered to the screen, it was impossible to see anything but the largest artifacts, a teapot, for instance, or a platter (Figure 2.10). It was only with the pressure of a hose (hooked to a nearby fire hydrant) that the multitudes of smaller things—fan parts, fragments of tortoiseshell combs, tiny teacups, cow bones, and watermelon pits that looked as if they had been deposited yesterday—became visible (Figure 2.11). The cesspool was particularly rich and we knew we could tell lots about the people whose possessions these things had been, and even what they ate.

Once the artifacts have been returned to the laboratory, identified, and inventoried, we match the dates of the artifact assemblages with the people who lived on the lot when the things were thrown out. Because styles change over time and manufacturers of ceramic dishes and clay pipes, for instance, can be identified, we assign dates based on the most recently made objects in the assemblage. People may have older possessions, but the most recently acquired ones establish the date after which the things must have been thrown away—what we call the *terminus post quem,* or TPQ. If we are lucky there are census records that tell us something about the households, the number of adults, the number of children, whether there were boarders or servants. City directories supply information on businesses and the tenants on properties whose owners live elsewhere. In the case of the privy we thought might belong to a tavern, we were wrong. William Simmons lived

2.9. Liquor bottles from Feature E, the privy at 11 North Sixth Street. (Photograph by Juliette Gerhardt)

2.10. Alexander Bartlett and Kathryn Wood with a teapot from the Everly cesspool.

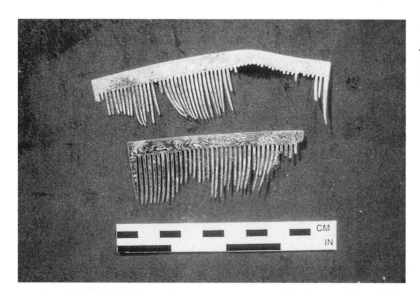

2.11. Tortoiseshell combs from the Everly cesspool. (Photograph by Juliette Gerhardt)

there in the 1790s when the bottles and other things were deposited. According to the 1790 census, Simmons was the principal clerk in the auditor's office of the Department of Treasury during George Washington's administration. Letters included in Alexander Hamilton's published papers recount Simmons's promotion to chief accountant in the War Department during John Adams's administration. The assemblages from the cesspool matched several households. The earliest apparently represented an accumulation of things left by short-term tenants in the first decade of the nineteenth century. They included Joseph Anthony, a director of the First Bank of the United States, two well-to-do merchants who may have been involved in the China trade, and the anatomist Caspar Wistar. Adam Everly moved into 225 (later 527) High Street with his family in 1823, and one of the assemblages appears to have belonged to his household. Everly was a comb manufacturer, which explains the combs that were found, and he also had a fancy goods store. His son, William, took over the store and the third assemblage appears to relate to his household and to the store.

From these assemblages we can tell stories about people who lived on Hudson's Square at two very different times: the 1790s, when the federal government was seated in Philadelphia, and the first half of the nineteenth century when High Street became the city's commercial hub. The stories, however, do not tell themselves, nor do they come from the artifacts alone. They begin with the artifacts and, as described above, with the basic statistics derived from primary documents like census records and directories (also tax records, church records, court cases, diaries, and so on). The next step is to build a broader context, to figure out how these people fit into society, where they fit, and how they expressed who they were in their world. For this step we turn to written history, but we synthesize the secondary historical record as anthropologists and combine it with an interpretive analysis of the artifacts. The result is not an illustration of what historians already know, but rather an elaboration of how specific people lived their lives in periods of history that are known. William Simmons was such a person.

It did not seem that we were going to know more than the bare facts about Simmons, but a serendipitous reference in a book about various departments in the first federal government led me to Alexander Hamilton's published papers.[3] The papers include several letters between Simmons and James McHenry, his boss at the War Department. Simmons complained to McHenry about the special treatment officers were being given, and in his role as chief accountant, he basically refused to grant the requested indulgences. Simmons emerges from the letters as a rigid bureaucrat who was unwilling to bend the letter of the law and was disinclined to favor already advantaged members of society. There is also a letter from Alexander Hamilton to George Washington praising Simmons to the sky and another from John Adams to McHenry concerning Simmons's refusal to do what McHenry wanted.

The artifacts from Simmons's privy included four case-gin bottles, twenty wine bottles, four ale bottles, twelve miscellaneous liquor bottles, two carafes, three decanters, seven tumblers, four flips (a kind of large tumbler), one stemmed wine glass, and a flask. For eating there were two plain dinner plates made of creamware, three saucer dishes, and three soup plates as well as five pie plates with coggled edges, a porringer, a pudding pan, and a tulip bowl, all made of redware and all well worn. The only fancy serving pieces in the assemblage were a fragment of a creamware fruit basket and a wine stand. Also found were twenty white ball-clay pipestems and pipebowls, and ninety-four straight pins, the early bureaucrat's paper clip. Combining the artifacts with the documentary record it was possible to construct a story, in this case what I call a narrative vignette, about Mr. Simmons.

The Accountant and His Discontents

It is not hard to imagine a disgruntled William Simmons trudging up Sixth Street muttering under his breath, "Hyde stole the money, that's what he did, he stole the money and now the soldiers are out their pay. Why doesn't McHenry see it, why doesn't he care?" James McHenry, the secretary of war in John Adams's administration, was Simmons's boss, and they didn't see eye to eye. The issue that was on Simmons's mind that chilly April day in 1799 was one of many. In this case, Mr. Hyde, the paymaster to the First U.S. Regiment, had received a very large sum of money, part of which was intended for the soldiers, but they had not gotten their pay and Simmons was upset about it. The officers, thought Simmons, took advantage of their rank and McHenry turned a blind eye. It was not just, and besides that, it was not legal. He would write a letter, but not tonight. Tonight he would sit by the fire with a comforting glass of gin and try to forget.

Little did he know that the worst was yet to come. In October 1799, the president, no less, wanted Simmons to pay Hugh McAllister, a citizen, a reward for capturing a deserter. Simmons refused, noting that "prevailing custom in effecting settlements here when deserters have been pursued or apprehended, when detachments have been sent in pursuit of deserters . . . their reasonable expenses and not the Premium has been allowed." McHenry considered Simmons's conduct in this matter insubordinate and appealed to the president: "It will be permitted to ask whether in the opinion of the president, the answers of the Accountant [Simmons] to an application on my part, plain, explicit, and definite, and to questions necessary to be answered for the government of the military officers are in a manner respectful . . . and also whether declining, as the Accountant has done . . . the claim of the citizen . . . is not an instance of insubordination, incompatible with the due administration of the Department, with the public interest, and those of Individuals in any manner concerned in business connected with military concerns." We do not know how Adams answered, but McHenry was fired before the federal government moved to Washington, and Simmons kept his job, serving in the department until 1814. However, we are getting ahead of our story.

On April 17, 1799, as the sun was going down and Simmons approached his doorstep at 9 North Sixth Street, he had only one thing on his mind—drink, and maybe a little dinner. He wondered what the cook had in store for him. Would there be an almond pudding, his favorite, before the roast chicken, or would it be the usual corn? Maybe it would not be chicken at all; perhaps the cook had gotten a piece of beef or pork at the market. That would go well with the Madeira he had tucked in the cellar. Ah, yes, a warm glassful and a full stomach would take his mind off Mr. Hyde and Mr. McHenry. He quickened his step.

Last year at this time Simmons would have looked forward to the company of Hezekiah Hosmer, representative from New York, and Senator Samuel Livingston of New Hampshire. Both had boarded with him at 9 North Sixth and had proved amiable drinking companions even though their allegiance to Federalism was a good bit more solid than his own. The trouble with the damn Federalists, mused Simmons, is they are more interested in advancing the rights of their own kind than serving the democratic ideals described so eloquently by Mr. Jefferson—and to think that I owe my present position in the War Department to Alexander Hamilton, the biggest Federalist of them all. He felt guilty about that debt—well, just a little. After all, he had worked hard at Treasury and given up any number of more lucrative opportunities. Even Hamilton recognized that. Simmons could not help feeling proud of the letter Hamilton had written to George Washington on his behalf:

> I have heretofore had occasion to mention to you the merits of Mr. Simmons the writer of the enclosed letter. It is but justice, that I bear in his favour the testimony he deserves. I can with truth give my opinion that he is well qualified for the office in question; insomuch that I believe it will be very difficult to find one who has better pretensions. From long service in the Department he understands thoroughly the course of business in it. . . . His intelligence cooperates with his experience . . . and one may not speak too strongly of his assiduity and integrity.
>
> So necessary was he in the department from his knowledge of the course of the old business that it cost me repeated pains to prevent his leaving it; and as he had a prospect of doing better in the private business than upon a Clerk's salary, one of the means employed was to give him the expectation of a recommendation at some future time to some more adequate station.

He knew the letter by heart; it had been a great tribute for a clerk, but it had not made him into one of them. Of course he lacked the necessary social status, but he did not want it either. What Simmons liked was a plain dinner on plain dishes with a little plain talk. Yes, it was a shame that Hosmer and Livermore were not with him anymore. Those were good evenings around the fire, drinking and smoking until the wee hours (Figure 2.12).

Except for the cockfights Simmons occasionally staged in his own backyard, his major interest was work. He loved numbers and he loved the law. Trained as an attorney, he knew the ins and outs of what was legal, and he knew them considerably better than his

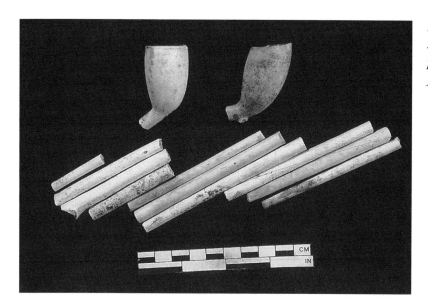

2.12. Pipe bowls and pipe stems from the Simmons privy. (Photograph by Juliette Gerhardt)

boss. When McHenry asked him to grant an allowance for General Macpherson's "table on a late expedition," Simmons said absolutely no. Nor would he grant special moneys to the surgeon of a regiment for attendance on the Indians at the Treaty of Greenville or the expenses incurred by an Indian agent in the execution of his trusts in the Indian nation. It was Simmons's position that "no allowance by my authority or any authority short of Congress can be made by an officer beyond the emoluments fixed to his office by law." One suspects that Simmons's Republican tendencies may have contributed to his adamancy. The already privileged were not to be granted additional privileges. McHenry writhed at the missed opportunities to please his superiors, and in the end McHenry lost. Nevertheless, Simmons's independence finally caught up with him. In 1814, after almost twenty years in the War Department, James Madison fired him "for alleged bitter hostility to the government and rudeness to his superiors." The unbending Mr. Simmons had finally done himself in.

Simmons's years on North Sixth Street may have been his happiest. In Washington there were the obligations of family and many deaths: his wife in 1808, his eldest daughter in 1814, and his mother in 1818. He died in Ohio in 1825 at the age of sixty-eight.[4]

Who Was Mr. Simmons Really?

As with everything else about the past, we can't really know who Mr. Simmons was. We can only speculate from what we do know. To put what we know in a fictional narrative is one way to at least imagine his reality. The narrative combines all the information: the artifacts, the statistics gleaned from primary documents (census records, in this case), and the letters, of course.

Simmons's unwillingness to grant favors to the elite, as recorded in the published correspondence included in Alexander Hamilton's papers, is the basis for speculating that he had Republican tendencies. The tensions between the Federalists and Republicans are well documented in this period, and through Simmons we may imagine how they might have been experienced on a personal level. Simmons's drinking was probably not extraordinary. According to one scholar, "alcohol was ubiquitous in the eighteenth and early nineteenth centuries. . . . Drinking was indulged in by all [including] ministers, doctors, and teachers as well as by clerks, artisans, and workingmen, by young and old, by male and female." It was not even inappropriate to drink at work, which Simmons may well have done, if indeed the flask found was something he habitually had on his person.[5]

That Simmons's dishes were not particularly fancy is also not surprising in light of the documentary evidence for his salary compared with those of others in government employ. When he was principal clerk in the office of the auditor of the Treasury of the United States in 1793, he made $800; the auditor, Richard Harrison, made $1,900. That same year the treasurer, Samuel Meredith, and the comptroller, Oliver Wolcott, both earned $2,400.[6]

We also know where Simmons worked. The Auditor's Office is marked by a brick rectangle just to the north of the First Bank on Third Street, inside Independence National Historical Park. The War Department was in Carpenter's Hall for a short time, but when Simmons worked in the department it was at the northeast corner of Fifth and Chestnut Streets. It is easy to imagine Simmons walking from one or the other of them to his home on North Sixth, which was only two or three blocks away. We know from a descendant of Simmons, Barbara Beckley Chaney, who is writing a book about him, that he married Josephine Bertrand Lapointe in Philadelphia in 1799. He was forty-two years old and she was seventeen. It was perhaps then that his bachelor possessions were deposited in the privy. According to a cousin of Chaney's, Josephine came from Santo Domingo, where her family was killed during the slave uprising of 1798. Josephine was in Paris at the time and returned to the care of an uncle in Philadelphia, where she met and married William Simmons. It is unlikely that she ever lived in the North Sixth Street house. Chaney speculates that their Washington household included eleven persons, presumably Simmons, his wife, and "servants or slaves."[7]

According to other family sources supplied by Chaney, Simmons was born in 1757 in Newburg, New York, and died in Coshocton, Ohio, on April 15, 1825. He entered the Continental Army at age eighteen, rose to the rank of colonel, and commanded a brigade at the Battle of Trenton, New Jersey. This source also claims he was a "trusted friend of George Washington, Greene, and other generals." He apparently moved to Ohio after he left government service. The family papers claim the government gave him 4,297 acres of land at the headwaters of the Muskingum River in Coshocton City "for his services," and he is celebrated locally for having brought with him "the first family carriage, his colored servants, and a solid silver dinner set to set a table for twenty" (quoted from a "True report received from cousin Lucia (Stuart) Welch some years ago" supplied by Barbara Chaney).

While it seems likely that myths have grown up around William Simmons among his descendants, their work and ours has brought to light a person not previously known to history, a person who not only served in the Continental Army but like many others did the important work of the country's first federal government. He lived on Hudson's Square, which probably wasn't called Hudson's Square at all—its creator, William Hudson, having long been forgotten. He lived among artisans and boardinghouse keepers, probably spending time in company with the other civil servants who did the government's work, and the senators and representatives who made the nation's earliest laws. It must have been an exciting time, but it was a short time, only ten years. After the government moved to Washington, Hudson's Square became something quite different. Commerce took over.

The Everlys

No personal accounts of any members of the Everly family were found in the historical records. We cannot even be absolutely sure that Adam Everly manufactured combs at 225 Market Street, but it is more than likely that he did. He listed himself as a "comb manufacturer" at 225 High Street in the Philadelphia Directory of 1825, and in DeSilver's directories for 1830, 1833, 1835, and 1836 he called himself a "comb maker." By 1839 he was just a "gentleman," while his son, William A. Everly, was listed as a "merchant." By 1850, William called the business "W. A. Everly and Company, fancy goods." It is very possible that William gave up the manufacturing part of the operation.[8]

That Adam Everly began manufacturing combs in the 1820s coincides with technological improvements in the industry that made the manufacture of combs more profitable. Enoch Noyes of West Newbury, Massachusetts, is credited with founding the industry, and West Newbury remained a center of comb manufacture for a hundred years. A nephew, David Emery Noyes, apprenticed in the business and then became a journeyman, during which time he went to Philadelphia, where he built the first comb-cutting machine. According to a history of the industry, the machine, which was probably made in about 1820, revolutionized the comb business, since it made two combs from one piece of horn and gave each a better form.[9] In the early 1830s, Noyes made several other inventions, including a machine for cutting, instead of sawing, the teeth. The Noyes connection to Philadelphia is tantalizing and may have stimulated the industry locally. Twelve comb dealers were listed in O'Brien's Wholesale Business Directory of 1844.

The Everly family is documented in census and church records, and several invoices for toothbrushes with William Everly's signature were found in the Winterthur Library. Otherwise, the documents are silent. Adam Everly, however, is mentioned in a publication titled "The Memoirs and Autobiography of Wealthy Citizens," written in 1846. The publication claims there were more than eleven hundred individual fortunes of $50,000 or more in the city at the time, but only ninety-four with $200,000 or more. Adam Everly, identified as a comb and fancy goods merchant, fell into the small group that had $300,000. Having started as a hairdresser on Chestnut Street in the early 1800s, Adam had clearly risen in the ranks by the time of his retirement in 1840.[10]

The artifacts associated with both Adam Everly's household and his son William's suggest a middle-class way of life. Both generations eventually separated their homes from their businesses, and they owned things that indicated a concern with status. Adam and his wife, Mary Everly, for instance, had a Chinese porcelain tea set monogrammed with their joined initials, "AME," that would have been special ordered. They had twelve tea sets, including some for children, as well as several sets of tableware, some obviously for everyday use and some for company (Figure 2.13). The children's tea sets are also indicative of a concern with proper behavior. Middle-class ideas about raising children at the time emphasized gentility; little girls were supposed to learn the skills of a proper lady by playing games that prepared them for their adult roles. Dolls were considered appropriate for girls, for obvious reasons. Boys, on the other hand, were supposed to play

2.13. Chinese export porcelain tableware from the Everly household, middle block of Independence Mall. (Photograph by Juliette Gerhardt)

Middle-Class Markers

The emergence of a middle class in nineteenth-century America brought with it certain material manifestations that are retrievable archaeologically. Although we cannot recover prescribed standards of behavior, we can recover items that relate to applying those standards. At least one scholar has pointed out that by studying the things people possessed we can discover whether they followed the advice found in the prescriptive literature of the time. *Godey's Ladies Magazine,* one of the basic bibles of appropriate middle-class manners, was published in Philadelphia. Through fiction and advice columns it told women how to conduct their lives in accordance with something historians have come to call the "cult of domesticity." Among its precepts were ideas about family conduct, child rearing, entertaining, smoking, and drinking. Many of these changes were directly related to the separation of home and work. As men distanced themselves from home for much of the day, women gained control over the home, creating for their husbands and children a kind of sanctuary, a place where men could find refuge from the competitive world and children could gain the genteel skills and manners necessary to enter that world successfully.

Proper dining etiquette became a major middle-class concern, and its accoutrements are exactly the kind of thing that is recoverable archaeologically. Matching sets of dishes distinguish the middle class from the "lower sort," and more than one set of dishes was considered necessary, one for everyday and one for formal occasions including entertaining guests. These sets included specialized dishes for multicourse meals as well as matching serving pieces. They also sometimes included child-sized dishes, and children were given cups with sayings or their names on them, presumably to indoctrinate them with respect for what was theirs—that is, private property. Children were also encouraged to use gender-specific toys, another thing that is recoverable. Marbles were for boys, dolls and tea sets were for girls. The serving of tea also received a good deal of attention. Historical archaeologist Diana Wall has argued that tea provided an opportunity to communicate a family's social status and make beneficial connections with families of similar standing. Wall thinks the tea sets that matched dinnerware were used for family teas while fancier tea sets were for entertaining. She has also suggested that plain white teawares decorated in the Gothic style communicated a kind of moral, Christian message that was consistent with the cult of domesticity. These would have helped inculcate proper values in children at the family table.

By the middle of the nineteenth century, probably as a result of the temperance

movement, alcohol use was discouraged among the middle class, although it certainly wasn't entirely abandoned. This was also true of smoking, which was considered ungenteel. It is likely that the association of both drinking and smoking with the working class was what made them considered inappropriate for the middle class. The material remains of all these behaviors reveal, at least in part, the process of constructing class differences.

more active games with less delicate toys. Very few toys associated with boys' play were found among the Everlys' possessions.

The artifacts also provide information on the kinds of goods that were sold in the Everly store. Twenty-three cologne bottles, none showing wear on the bottom from use, were recovered (Figure 2.14). Seven of the bottles had the initials "PD" on them, a mark associated with a German moldmaker who lived around the corner from the Everlys on Fifth Street. The many ceramic pitchers in the assemblage may have been for water or some kind of fruit drink offered to customers in the store. Tortoiseshell comb fragments and fans were either thrown out by mistake or were not perfect enough to be sold. Although we cannot be sure if the roach trap found was used in the store or the kitchen, a good businessman would surely have wanted to prevent roaches from appearing in his establishment. Of all the artifacts, the roach trap, perhaps, signifies how urban High Street had already become, a long way from Hudson's imagined legacy (Figure 2.15).

Combining the rich artifactual record with the thin documentary one, it is also possible to imagine the Everlys' lives with a vignette.

Growing Up in the Business

When she was little they lived on High Street, above her father's plain and fancy comb manufactory. Well, it was a manufactory then—now it's a shop, and an elegant one at that. Ann, still Everly, often thought of those days. She was born in the house on High Street, the house that had belonged to rich men before her father, Adam Everly, had gotten the money together to buy it himself. That was 1823, just five years before she was born, the last of the second batch of children. Her sisters, Harriet and Mary, were two and four years older, respectively, but their other sisters—there were four more girls— and a brother were born when the family still lived on Chestnut Street. She guessed her parents had all those children for the sake of the business. Everyone worked, even the little ones. She remembered setting her favorite doll on a chair in the shop while she helped Ann Eliza, her oldest sister, fold handkerchiefs (Figure 2.16). The Everlys did not

2.14. Cologne bottles from the Everly fancy goods store. (Photograph by Juliette Gerhardt)

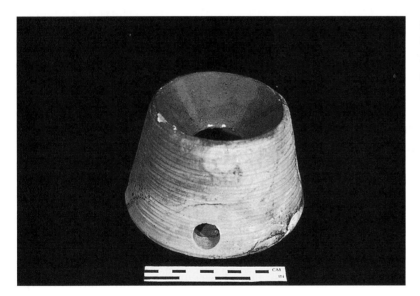

2.15. Roach trap made of local redware from the Everly cesspool. (Photograph by Juliette Gerhardt)

just have combs. There were brushes and looking glasses, perfume and toys, all the same things the other German storekeepers sold. However, not everyone manufactured the combs they sold. That was a serious investment and a lot of work.

Ann remembered how the machines looked when she was a child. There was a comb-cutting machine that made two combs from one piece of horn, and a circular saw for cutting the teeth. Then there was the magical screw press. It consisted of two iron boxes about a foot long by six inches deep and four inches wide that got filled with coal. Then

2.16. Wooden doll parts from a Queen Anne-type doll, ca. 1810–1819, found in the Everly cesspool. (Photograph by Juliette Gerhardt)

the boxes were placed side by side in a frame, with a space between them for the horn that needed to be clarified. The boxes were heated and screwed together, which pressed the horn tight and made it clear—just like magic. That was the fun part. The smell was something else—rotting cattle horns and huge tortoiseshells lying in the cellar waiting to be made into something a lady would want to wear. It seemed almost unbelievable that anyone would wear something that smelled that bad. They did though, and because they did her father made a good living for the family. They lived well on High Street.

There were elegant dinners in the upstairs dining room (the shop and manufactory were downstairs), served on porcelain dishes imported from China. The grown-ups ate all sorts of queer things: quail and pheasant and rabbit. Ann preferred their everyday meals—chicken was good, and meat pie was all right. She even preferred the dishes they were eaten on. It didn't matter if she dropped an everyday plate, since there were piles just like it in the pantry—white with blue around the edges—and serving dishes in every shape and size. It seemed funny that dishes could be so important, that one set of visitors—her mother's friends, for instance—were served tea in the fancy cups with gold rims while the family drank from the ones with pictures of dogs on them (Figure 2.17).

It all seemed perfect until the scarlet fever came. William, the oldest and only living son in the family, was sixteen when they made the move to High Street, and within ten years he was married and a partner in the business. William and his wife, Anna Maria, had two little girls, Mary Denckly, born in 1833, and Anna Louisa, born two years later. Ann loved her nieces, who were not so much younger than she, and they played for hours together, pretending to bake cakes for their dolls and setting the table in the nursery with the miniature tea things that were their prized possessions. She threw the tea sets into the trash when the little girls died of scarlet fever in 1839, one on one day and the other the next. It was too sad to want to play ever again. She even would have thrown her doll away if Ann Eliza had not stopped her. It had been Ann Eliza's doll, too, and she was not ready to part with the beloved remnant of her childhood. In 1840, just a year after

2.17. Pieces from three complementary tea sets decorated in overglaze black transfer-printed patterns popular between 1812 and 1825. (Photograph by Juliette Gerhardt)

Mary Denckly and Anna Louisa's deaths, Adam Everly retired, leaving the business to William. Adam had moved his family to a house at 354 Mulberry Street the year before; William moved with his wife to 398 Mulberry in 1840. The business remained at 225 High Street (the name was officially changed to Market in 1853).

William, Ann noticed, was just as smart as their father, but not quite as interested in manufacturing. With Tower Hall, the city's first readymade-clothing store, just across the street and other specialty shops a short distance away, William wanted to take advantage of the people who came to shop (Figure 2.18). In addition to combs, he chose things that others did not have—especially perfume, toothbrushes, and lovely fans made out of ivory. Ann loved to watch the fashionably clad ladies linger at the counter as her older sisters helped them choose one fan over another and dab their wrists with the sweet-smelling scents. Little did she realize that she would one day resent having to work behind that very same counter. Adam Everly may have retired, but he made sure that all members of the family gave William their full support. In 1850, the still-unmarried Mary L., Harriet, Catherine, Louisa, and Ann Everly were living at home and working in the shop.

Once in the shop Ann realized that, more than anything else, William wished to be known as a merchant rather than a manufacturer. He wanted to belong to the set of progressive merchants that included Colonel Bennett of Tower Hall. Unfortunately the great fire of 1856 stopped William in his tracks. The comb manufactory and shop at 225 Mar-

2.18. Advertisement for Charles Oakford & Son's new store at 826 and 828 Chestnut Street. (The Library Company of Philadelphia; original source unknown)

ket Street were destroyed, and as if that were not enough, William's wife, Anna Maria, died of cancer the next year. Too depressed and drained to rebuild the business from scratch, William gave up, leaving the block between Fifth and Sixth Streets to the already well-established Colonel Bennett and the next generation. Not many years later John Wanamaker opened the department store on the southeast corner of Sixth and Market Streets that revolutionized merchandizing in Philadelphia, catty-corner from what was last known as W. A. Everly and Company, Fancy Goods. For William the closing of the business was a sad end; for Ann and her other sisters it was much yearned for liberation. They turned their minds to other matters.

A Hundred Years of History

The Independence Visitor Center now covers the lots where William Simmons and the Everlys lived. There is a small case in the foyer of the building with artifacts from the privy and the cesspool. Simmons's pipes are there and his wine bottles, his flask, and his simple dishes. The doll that was handed down through generations of Everlys is also there along with the fancy monogrammed teapot, the gaudily decorated pitchers, and the roach trap. The exhibit is called "Beneath Your Feet," but it is hard to bring a hundred years of history to life in a small glass case. Perhaps if the outlines of the privy and cesspool were marked on the floor of the Visitor Center it would be easier to imagine the people who owned the things that are on display. In the presence of material remains, the past becomes more believable, especially when the remains are still connected to the ground. As archaeologists we are privileged to experience that connection when we first uncover them. The challenge is to figure out how we can let other people in on the excitement. That challenge was directly confronted on the next block we excavated, where a new building housing the Liberty Bell now stands.

CHAPTER THREE

An Icon and an Icehouse

The First Block of Independence Mall

We began testing the site of the proposed new pavilion for the Liberty Bell in November 2001. Working in the shadow of Independence Hall, we wanted above all to find something that related to the heady days of creating the nation. Just the stables would do, the ones we knew were behind the State House Inn, which stood directly across Chestnut Street from the State House (now called Independence Hall) and was surely the site of many an important debate (Figure 3.1). What we didn't bank on was anything relating to the president's house at the other end of the block (Figure 3.2). The new home for the Liberty Bell was to stretch along South Sixth Street between Chestnut and Market Streets. Only a small part of the proposed building—the location of the mechanical room—would require deep excavation, and we needed to test for shaft features only in that area, as anything else would not be disturbed by the proposed construction. We began as we had on the middle block: we looked for the cross-cutting alleys that had subdivided the block before it became the mall. Once these were found we could focus on the backs of the historical lots where the privies, cisterns, and wells ought to be.

This block had alleys running in both directions, one east–west, parallel to Market Street, and another oriented north–south behind the properties facing South Sixth Street. There were stables on South Sixth that backed up on the north–south alley, and there was also a stable at its terminus, just to the east of the State

3.1. The State House (Clark's) Inn, across from the State House on Chestnut Street. (The Library Company of Philadelphia)

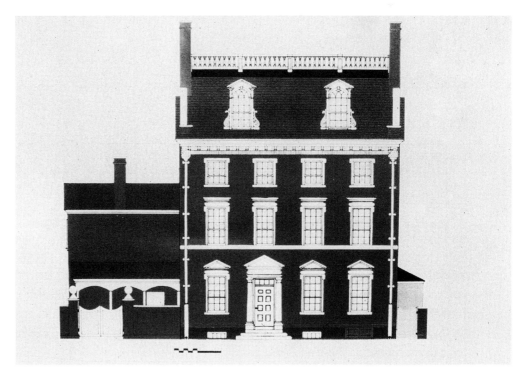

3.2. Rendering of the president's house at 190 High Street by Edward Lawler Jr.

House Inn. We imagined visiting politicians "parking" their horses at the stable and crossing the street to tend to important affairs of state. Unfortunately, once the alley was located it became clear that it had been bulldozed when the mall was created, as had the properties that bordered it. Nothing was left of the stables, so we turned our attention to the other end of the block.

The first published street map of the city, created by Matthew Clarkson and Mary Biddle in 1762 (Figure 3.3), shows the east–west alley, called Minor Street, dividing the block into two not quite equal parts. Minor Street ran behind the generous lots that faced High Street, among them one belonging to the Revolutionary War financier Robert Morris, who rented his house on the property to the federal government for the use of the first two presidents of the United States. Only the very back portion of the lot fell within the project area, but on it was a curious feature unlike any other found in Philadelphia. It was made of stone blocks apparently arranged in the shape of an octagon (Figure 3.4). The octagon measured thirteen feet in diameter, way too big for a well and of unlikely construction for a privy or cesspool. A small excavation inside the feature

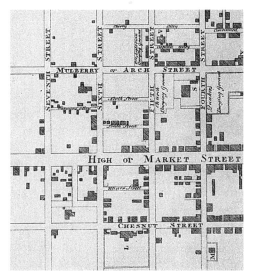

3.3. Detail from the Clarkson and Biddle map of 1762, showing the area between Race and Walnut Streets. (Historical Society of Pennsylvania)

(right) 3.4. The remains of the icehouse in the southwest corner of the president's house property, southern block of Independence Mall.

produced nothing but fill with no artifacts, and in consultation with the Park Service we decided to have the backhoe remove the rest of the fill in the hope that the feature's function would become obvious once its walls were exposed.

The shaft was constructed of unmortared blocks of schist. It reached a depth of nine feet before ending in a gravel "floor." There was no concentration of artifacts at the bottom or in the fill that might suggest the function of the feature, and we were as mystified when it proved empty as we had been when it was first uncovered. We didn't know whether it had been built in the eighteenth century or more recently. We didn't understand why it was octagonal, and we couldn't figure out why it was located at the back of the yard, where there should have been a stable in 1787, according to a map reconstruction of the property by National Park Service historian Anna Coxe Toogood.[1] One possibility was that it could be the pit beneath an icehouse, and we turned to the documentary record for confirmation.

I found an insurance policy dating to the early nineteenth century that listed an icehouse in the backyard of Morris's lot, at 190 High Street, but provided no exact location and no details except that it had a "roof and door." Tod Benedict, John Milner Associates' field director for the project, found something much better on the Library of Congress Web site: a letter from George Washington to Robert Morris asking how to build an efficient icehouse. On June 2, 1784, Washington wrote, "The house I filled with ice does not answer—it is gone already—if you will do me the favor to cause a description of yours to be taken—the size—manner of building, & mode of management, & forwarded to me—I shall be much obliged." Morris responded on June 15 with the following detailed description of his icehouse, presumably the same one we were investigating:

> My Ice House is about 18 feet deep and 16 Square, the bottom is a Coarse Gravell & the Water which drains from the Ice soaks into it as fast as the Ice melts. This prevents the necessity of a Drain which if the bottom was Clay or Stiff Loam would be necessary and for this reason the side of a Hill is preferred generally for digging an Ice House, and if needful a drain can easily be cut from the bottom of it through the side of the Hill to let the Water run out. The Walls of my Ice House are built of Stone without Mortar, which is called a Dry Wall, until within a foot and a half of the Surface of the Earth when Mortar was used from thence to the Surface to make the top more binding and solid. When this wall was brought up even with the Surface of the Earth I stopped there and then dug the foundation for another Wall two foot back from the first and about two foot deep, this done the foundation was laid across so as to secure the whole of the Walls built on the inside of the Hole where the ice is put and on this foundation is built the Walls which appear above ground and in mine they are about ten foot high. On these the Roof is fixed, these Walls are very thick, built of Stone and Mortar afterward rough case on the outside. I nailed a Ceiling of Boards under the Roof flat from Wall to Wall, and filled all the Space between that Ceiling and the Shingling of the Roof with Straw, so that the Heat of the Sun cannot possibly have any effect on the bottom of the Ice House. I placed some Blocks of Wood about two foot long and on these I laid a platform of Common Fence Rails Close enough to hold the Ice & open enough to let the Water pass through, thus the Ice lays two foot from the Gravel and of course gives Room for the Water to Soak away amazingly. The upper Floor is laid on Joists placed across the top of the Inner wall and for greater security I nailed the Ceiling under those Joists and filled the Space between the Ceiling & Floor with Straw. The Door for entering this Ice House faces the north, a Trap Door is made in the middle of the Floor through which the Ice is put and taken out. I find it best to fill with Ice which as it is put in should be broke into small pieces and pounded down with heavy Clubs or Battons such as Pavers use, if well beat it will after a while consolidate into one solid mass and require to be Cut out with a Chizell or Axe—I tried Snow one year and lost it in June. The Ice keeps until October or November and I believe if the Hole was larger

so as to hold more it would keep until Christmass. The closer it is packed the better it keeps & I believe if the Walls were Lined with Straw between the Ice and the Stone it would preserve it since The melting begins next the Walls and Continues round the Edge of the Body of Ice throughout the Season.[2]

To the extent that we can compare the icehouse found at the site of the new Liberty Bell Center with Morris's description, they appear to be identical. The excavated ice pit was also built of unmortared stone, and it, too, had a gravel "floor." Our icehouse was only nine feet deep, but it was truncated, cut off at the top by the approximately nine-foot-deep basement of the nineteenth-century building that stood on the lot until demolition began for the mall in the 1950s. What was lacking, of course, from Morris's description was the shape, which was perhaps incidental or too eccentric to mention.

Robert Morris, who had been a friend of Washington's since before the Revolutionary War, was fascinated by technology. Besides the icehouse, his house at 190 High Street had marble and wooden baths with a copper boiler and bath apparatus. At the Hills, Morris's country estate on the Schuylkill River, he had built a greenhouse with an elaborate hothouse and vault beneath it for preserving plants in winter. Even more indicative of his interest in technology were his mills in New Jersey. When all of Morris's property was being assessed in 1797, at least seven mills were included. Located on an island about one mile south of Trenton, they served many different purposes. There were grist and saw mills, a slitting mill for making iron into nail rods, a rolling mill for rolling bars of iron into sheet-iron hoops, a mill for snuff, and even one for stamping or grinding plaster of paris. In 1794 Morris began construction of an ornate mansion on Chestnut Street designed by Pierre Charles L'Enfant, the architect and urban planner who laid out Washington, D.C., but the building was never finished, and it came to be known as "Morris's Folly." As described in John Watson's recollections of old Philadelphia in 1857 and repeated twenty years later by Thompson Westcott, a local historian, the house had two and sometimes three stories underground, with arches, vaults, and labyrinths. Although Watson described the four sides as covered with marble adorned in expensive relief, Westcott claimed the building was "actually of red brick, ornamented with marble window-heads, lintels and sills, and pilasters." Bas-reliefs were prepared for the decoration of the mansion but were never used, so they were incorporated into other buildings. Whether the house's grandiosity was a product of Morris's encouragement of L'Enfant or vice versa is unclear. Morris ended up making some large investments that went bad and bankrupted him, and he was thrown into debtor's prison before the house could be completed.[3]

The icehouse, apparently one of many experimental projects, was built within a year of

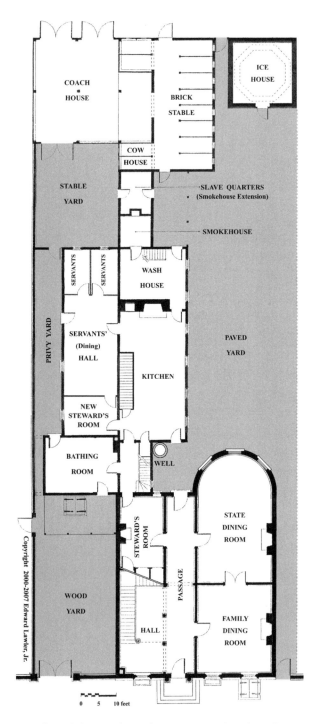

3.5. Plan of the president's house property by Edward Lawler Jr. (Reprinted from www.UShistory.org)

when Morris acquired the High Street property in 1781. A contemporary diarist, Jacob Hiltzheimer, mentions it in February 1782: "Loaned Robert Erwin a wagon and two horses to assist bringing ice from the Schuylkill to the ice house of Robert Morris in the rear of his house on Market Street." An article about the president's house in the *Pennsylvania Magazine of History and Biography,* based on exhaustive research by local historian Edward Lawler Jr., includes a ground plan of the property as it looked when Morris first acquired it, and the icehouse fits nicely into the otherwise empty southwest corner of the backyard (Figure 3.5). A rendering of the icehouse drawn by Tod Benedict and Rob Schultz combined what was learned from archaeology with Morris's written description to show how it probably looked when the presidents were in residence (Figure 3.6).[4]

The President's House

Before George Washington brought his family to Philadelphia he made significant changes to the house that Robert Morris rented to the government for the president. The renovations were discussed in correspondence between Washington and his secretary, Tobias Lear, and these letters provided much of the information that Lawler included in his article about the president's house. Washington's most dramatic change was to add a two-story bow to the western half of the south facade. The inside of the bow was semicircular (thought by some to be the model for the Oval Office), but the outside might well have been semi-octagonal as were such features on other houses of the period. The shape would have echoed the octagonal icehouse that stood in direct view of the window in the southwestern corner of the yard.

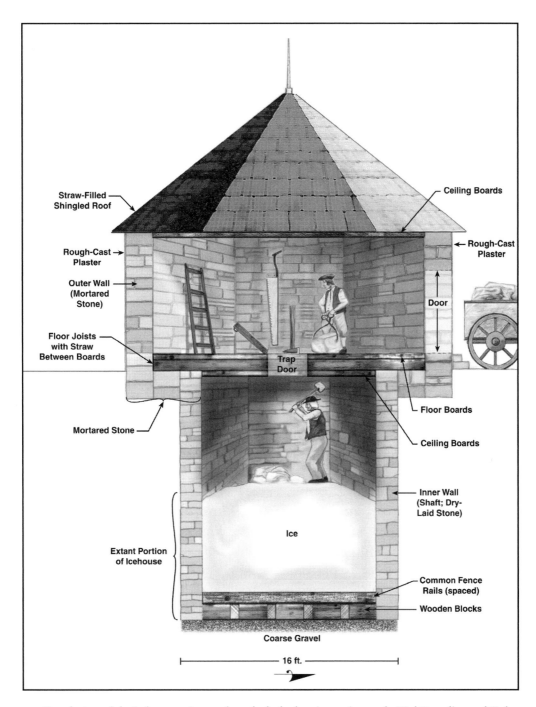

Straw-Filled
Shingled Roof

Ceiling Boards

Rough-Cast
Plaster

Rough-Cast
Plaster

Outer Wall
(Mortared
Stone)

Door

Floor Joists
with Straw
Between Boards

Trap
Door

Floor Boards

Mortared Stone

Ceiling Boards

Inner Wall
(Shaft; Dry-
Laid Stone)

Ice

Extant Portion
of Icehouse

Common Fence
Rails (spaced)

Wooden Blocks

Coarse Gravel

16 ft.

3.6. Rendering of the icehouse as it may have looked when it was in use, by Tod Benedict and Rob Schultz.

Washington converted the upstairs bath into his study, added a servants' hall along the eastern side of the kitchen, and made the smokehouse between the washhouse and brick stable into two good rooms "for the accommodation of the Stablepeople."

According to Lawler, the "stablepeople" were enslaved Africans from Mount Vernon. Washington's domestic staff of twenty or so included nine slaves at the beginning of his presidency and two at the end. Among them were Ona Judge, Martha Washington's body servant, who escaped to freedom in June 1796, and Hercules, the cook, who escaped to New York in 1797. The others, who were shuffled back and forth between Mount Vernon and Philadelphia, included Ona's older brother, Austin, who worked as a waiter, carriage footman, and stableman and may have slept in the converted smokehouse, and Giles and Paris, who probably also worked in the stables and shared quarters with Austin. Also in the household were Christopher Sheels, Washington's body servant; Joe Richardson (also known as "Postilien Joe"), the president's coach footman and stable worker; Moll, the nanny to Martha's two youngest grandchildren; and Richmond, Hercules's son who was a kitchen worker and chimney sweep.[5]

Even before the federal government moved to Washington, Morris's house was sold to Andrew Kennedy, who continued to rent it to the federal government for use as a presidential mansion and subsequently to John Francis, who ran the Union Hotel there. In 1832 Nathanial Burt bought the property, demolished the house, and replaced it with three commercial buildings. The only remnants of structures dating to the period when the first two presidents lived at 190 High Street are archaeological. Besides the icehouse, we found a well that may have been built when Washington added the bay window to the back of the first floor. Several unidentified wall fragments were uncovered during the creation of the mall in the 1950s and many more were uncovered in the spring of 2007.[6]

The icehouse, now partially buried under the Liberty Bell Center (Figure 3.7), might have been used to tell the stories of life at 190 High Street when Washington and Adams were in residence. President Washington held state dinners and levees on Tuesdays and Thursdays. For the levees he placed himself in front of the bay at the back of the state dining room (sometimes called the reception room) and formally received guests. Martha Washington's Friday night levees were more informal, but for all of these events plus the open houses held on holidays and on the president's birthday, there would have been a flurry of activity in the kitchen and yard as enslaved Africans and indentured servants made the necessary preparations. During hot Philadelphia summers there would be a need for ice to cool the punch and confections, and it is easy to imagine slaves and servants scurrying between the icehouse and the back kitchen. There was an opportunity here to use the icehouse as a focal point to talk about life at 190 High Street from the perspective of the members of the household who were essential to its success but have been ignored by history.

The Park Service, however, was uninterested at the time, arguing that introducing something besides the Liberty Bell into the site's interpretation would only confuse visitors. At a press conference called to announce the finds on a snowy day in February 2001 (Figure 3.8), a stubborn reporter kept asking the Park Service representative why they were not going to incorporate the features into the new landscape, but the representative held firm. There was no room for stories about anything but the Liberty Bell in the Liberty Bell Center, he said, and besides, it wasn't the Park Service's job to interpret every archaeological feature that was found; it only had to protect them. It would also have cost more money to make the architectural changes necessary to avoid the icehouse. And it would have taken some imaginative thinking about how to interpret a feature that began nine feet below grade in the landscape. Nevertheless, I believe it would have been worth it. The size of the ice pit, its unusual shape, and its connection

3.7. *The completed Liberty Bell Center. (Photograph by Robin Miller, 2003; Independence National Historical Park)*

to a piece of Philadelphia's treasured past from a refreshingly different perspective caught the public's imagination. There were letters to the editor of the local paper in favor of interpreting the icehouse, and a direct descendant of Robert Morris (also named Robert Morris) tried his best to convince the Park Service. His pleas, the reporter's pleas, and my pleas, however, fell on deaf ears. The Park Service lined the icehouse with plastic, filled it with gravel, and buried it (Figure 3.9). There would be no interpretation of life at 190 High Street from the perspective of the back door. Something else happened, though, that did lead the Park Service to alter its plans for the Liberty Bell Center. It began with an attack on archaeology.

In March 2002 the eminent historian Gary Nash appeared on Radio Times, a local talk show hosted by Marty Moss-Coane. Nash complained that the Liberty Bell Center exhibits, as planned, avoided any reference to the fact that George Washington brought slaves with him to Philadelphia and kept them at 190 High Street, the site of the new Liberty Bell Center. In addition, he claimed that the archaeological investigations on

3.8. Jed Levin and Rebecca Yamin during a news conference held at the Liberty Bell Center site on February 23, 2001. (Photograph by Michael S. Wirtz, reprinted by permission from the Philadelphia Inquirer)

(below) 3.9. Icehouse being filled with gravel by the National Park Service.

the site had failed to find the slave quarters behind the house and that, too, was probably intentional since he characterized the investigation as a "once over lightly" job. Nash, who has written many distinguished books on Philadelphia's history, was not actually familiar with our archaeological investigation (he lives in Los Angeles), but he apparently assumed there ought to be remains of the slave quarters because Ed Lawler's diagram of the outbuildings showed one.[7] What Nash didn't understand was that when Burt demolished the house in 1832 and replaced it with three commercial buildings, their basements destroyed all aboveground structures, leaving only deep shafts—the well and ice pit that we found, and cellar foundations that were discovered much later.

What Nash did accomplish was to call attention to the fact that the exhibits in the new Liberty Bell Center would not say anything about the enslaved Africans in Washington's household, even though the entry to the building was virtually at the same location as the converted smokehouse in which some of them lived. The irony was not lost on anyone, and the African-American community got involved. How could an exhibit about the Liberty Bell, that icon of independence, possibly leave out such an important truth? The *Philadelphia Inquirer,* the city's major newspaper, began coverage of the story in April 2002 and didn't let up until the new center opened to the public in October 2003.[8]

The Park Service initially met Nash's challenge by assuring the press in April 2002 that "in the walking tours and accounts given by the park rangers at Independence Mall, the Park Service had made sure slavery and its connection to the founding fathers was assigned a prominent role in the narrative of the fight for independence and the symbol of the bell." African-American columnist Acel Moore, however, wasn't convinced. Moore visited the park, read all the brochures, and listened to the guides, but it left him feeling "very little that humanized the story of my African ancestors—or those of millions of other Americans." Even the *New York Times* picked up the controversy, and on April 20, 2002, the paper ran a big article titled "Slave Site for a Symbol of Freedom; Critics Say Park Service Is Burying History." The *Times* described Gary Nash's efforts on behalf of the coalition that was trying to pressure the Park Service into representing the house where George Washington had lived with his slaves, and to depict slavery more extensively in the exhibits inside the new center. The Park Service, the article said, had refused, "saying an elaborate floor plan and detailed information outdoors would be confusing for visitors"—the same argument that was used for the icehouse. The Liberty Bell Center, the officials insisted, needed to be about one thing and one thing only, the bell.

By May 2002 the Liberty Bell story had made it to the *Inquirer*'s front page, above the fold. A story by Stephan Salisbury (a reporter who became fascinated with the African-American part of Philadelphia's story being uncovered by archaeology on the mall) announced that the controversy was over: "National Historical Park officials said that exhibits in and around the new Liberty Bell Center will discuss slavery as it once existed in Philadelphia and the nation." Salisbury noted that this represented "a major departure from the current bell story told by park rangers, which focuses almost exclusively on the bell's presence during the Revolutionary War era, as a symbol taken up by abolitionists prior to the Civil War, and as an international symbol of freedom." But the controversy wasn't really over, and just twelve days later Salisbury published another article, titled "Liberty Bell's Symbolism Rings Hollow for Some." This story talked about rumors of slaves buried on the site that were circulating in Philadelphia's black community and of Temple University professor Charles Blockson's concern that there were not enough African Americans involved in the Liberty Bell discussions and decision making for the Park Service.

Symbol of Freedom

Things have a way of embodying ideas, but the ideas don't always remain the same. The Liberty Bell has meant different things to different generations and even to different groups within the same time period. Charlene Mires has brilliantly explored this issue in her book *Independence Hall in American Memory,* showing how the Liberty Bell's particular strength was its detachability from place. Unlike Independence Hall, the bell could be moved, and in the late nineteenth century it covered thousands of miles. According to Mires, the bell took seven rail journeys between 1885 and 1915, with 376 scheduled stops in thirty states. Each stop was an event, with inspirational speeches, lofty sermons, and ritual bell touching. "Children presented flowers to the bell, sang patriotic songs, and waved American flags," she writes. No longer just a remnant of the Revolutionary era, the Liberty Bell became "an instrument" through which Americans imagined themselves as one nation. At the same time, it provided a symbol of heritage for groups like the Daughters of the American Revolution (DAR), and it brought newer citizens, immigrants, into the fold. It was also used to sell causes and even to sell products. Suffragists carted around a replica of the Liberty Bell to symbolize women's struggle for the vote. Businessmen attached its image to products as various as flour, banks, department stores, rail companies, home furnishings, and movie theaters. There was money to be made in souvenirs, and the aura of the bell's significance was attached in the unlikeliest of places, becoming, for instance, the logo for the Pennzoil Company in 1916.

All of this enhanced the value of the bell and Philadelphia's attendant responsibility to take proper care of such an important symbolic object. Through the first half of the twentieth century it "lived" in Independence Hall, but by the 1960s there was pressure to create a special structure. Designed by Mitchell/Giurgola Associates, the new pavilion was ready in time for the Bicentennial, and the bell was moved to its new home at midnight on December 31, 1975. Although the pavilion protected the bell (even if many people complained about the aesthetics of the building) and at the same time made it completely accessible to the visiting public, it did not successfully keep someone from hitting it with a sledgehammer in 2001. An initial article in the local newspaper reported that a self-described wanderer from Nebraska had pulled out a small sledgehammer and struck the symbol of American freedom four times, shouting "God lives!" with each blow. By the next day some people were expressing concern that the event would lead the Park Service to put the bell behind glass, out of reach. Little did they know that just a few months later, all sorts of security measures would be instituted in response to the attack on the World Trade Center on September 11. Now no one enters the new Liberty Bell Center, or Independence Hall, without going through a security check. Although the bell isn't under glass, it hangs out of reach in its new home.

Sacred, and now untouchable, the Liberty Bell continues to be exploited as well as revered. A full-page ad in an August 16, 2005, issue of the *Philadelphia Inquirer* shows the bell with a Band-Aid across its infamous crack. The ad is for United-Healthcare, a New York insurance company, and the copy reads, "A new kind of freedom in health care is coming." No longer allowed on the road, the bell is safely guarded in its new home, but its image is as exportable as ever.

Next came a push for the excavation of the slave quarters. On a hot day in June a small group calling itself the African People's Solidarity Committee appeared on the Liberty Bell site and "denounced the Park Service for refusing to excavate the site of the former slave quarters." The rumors were clearly getting out of hand, and Salisbury felt the need to tell the story from the beginning. In July 2002 he wrote an article that described Ed Lawler's search for information about the first president's house in response to a visiting relative's question about where the president had lived in the early years of the nation. When Lawler began, wrote Salisbury, "he didn't know that Washington quartered slaves there. Nor did he know that movers and shakers tore most of the building down 170 years ago, or that the city and state unknowingly finished the job in the 1950s when they created Independence Mall." In the same issue of the *Inquirer,* Salisbury's byline appeared above another article, "A Protest Today Seeks Memorial to Slaves." The story reported that a group had met at the office of U.S. representative W. Curtis Thomas to plan a demonstration at the construction site of the Liberty Bell Center, seeking "to memorialize the fact that our ancestors in and around Sixth and Chestnut were brought there, forced there by a white man, George Washington. . . . He brought them, body and soul, and we want to memorialize them, not just as our ancestors, but as people." Although the article went on to say that the Park Service had already agreed to "expand its discussion of slavery at the Center and throughout the Park," the group, which called itself Avenging the Ancestors, wanted to be called upon to plan the monument and remembrance.

Avenging the Ancestors came into being in the spring of 2003.[9] According to Michael Coard, a dynamic, fast-talking trial lawyer who has been involved since the beginning, local African Americans found the move of the Liberty Bell from the pavilion to its new home interesting but not relevant to their community. When there was discussion of the president's house, that also didn't seem terribly important to black Philadelphians. However, when it was disclosed that George Washington had kept slaves there, and they were quartered five feet from the front door of the new Liberty Bell Center, it was time to act. Coard had the students in the course he was teaching in criminal justice at Temple University write letters to Martha Aikens, then the superintendent of Independence National Historical Park. The students also told their families and friends, which resulted in a couple hundred letters crossing Aikens's desk. A petition followed, asking for the story of enslaved Africans to be told at the site. No fewer than fifteen thousand people signed, a number that surely got the Park Service's attention.

Besides the petition, Coard spread the word by talking about George Washington and his slaves on his weekly radio show, and involved African Americans began to meet about the issue. At one meeting a young law student from Nigeria suggested they call themselves ATAC, an acronym that stands for Avenging the Ancestors Coalition. The group embraced the name and quickly grew to a membership of just under 500 with about 150 members attending monthly meetings, "rain or shine," Coard says. Their mission is "to tell the truth, the whole truth, and nothing but the truth." ATAC has no officers, but in addition to Coard the steering committee includes two history professors, another lawyer, and a board member of Art Sanctuary, an organization for African-American artists headed by Lorene Cary.

Coard comes to activism with a good deal of experience. As a college undergraduate at Cheyney University, the only all black state-sponsored university in Pennsylvania, he was president of both student government and his fraternity; he served as the one student on the Board of Trustees, and also served on the student judicial board. When he realized that students coming before the board didn't have representation he left the board to provide legal aid to students, probably the beginning of the end of his intended career as an English teacher. Coard loves the English language and many of ATAC's key talking points are his invention: "As you enter this heaven of liberty you have to cross the hell of slavery" is one, and "from denying to designing" is another. His article on the project is titled "The 'Black' Eye on George Washington's 'White' House," a piece he intends to develop into a book.

While ATAC was mounting its campaign to recognize the slaves on the president's house site, Independence National Historical Park came under the direction of a new superintendent, Mary Bomar, who reached out to the African-American community. By October 9, 2003, a golden autumn day that could not have been more perfect for the Liberty Bell Center's outdoor opening ceremonies, the conflicts were nowhere in sight. Rabbi Ira Stone of Beth Zion Beth Israel blew the shofar to celebrate freedom, and Father Martini Shaw of St. Thomas's African Episcopal Church offered the invocation (Figure 3.10). A parade of politicians thanked the people who had provided the money to make it all possible, especially Mrs. Walter Annenberg, who sat regally on the podium. Only Joe Hoeffel, a state senator, reminded the well-heeled crowd that the issue of how to memorialize the slave quarters on the site had not been settled, and security measures under consideration by the Park Service threatened to lock away our most precious symbols of freedom. St. Thomas's gospel choir sang to the heavens as a curtain ceremonially opened to reveal the bell in its new home. The sun-drenched guests were then invited into the building to view the much-discussed exhibits. Written in response to the controversy, the exhibit script takes care to cover George Washington's slaves, and there is even a larger-than-life portrait of Hercules, his enslaved cook.[10] In the end, the Park Service came around and produced exhibits that satisfied pretty much everyone. The fight for a memorial, however, continued, and Lawler persisted in a campaign to outline the president's house in the pavement where it actually stood.[11]

Bomar, the new park superintendent, wisely invited the African-American community to participate in discussions about how to memorialize Washington's slaves and the president's house. At public meetings members of the community argued that they wanted the memorial to be designed by an African-American firm, they wanted to take part in the decision-making process, and they wanted to be assured that African Americans would be involved in its construction. A design competition held in 2006 produced five finalists whose plans were publicly displayed at the Constitution Center and at the African-American Museum. The advisory committee, which included Mayor John F. Street, judged the design presentations and finally chose Kelly/Maiello Inc., the only

3.10. Rabbi Ira Stone and Father Martini Shaw at the opening of the Liberty Bell Center, October 9, 2003. (George Feder, Top Guns Photography; Independence National Historical Park)

3.11. Winning design for the president's house site memorial. (Kelly/Maiello Inc.)

minority-headed firm in the competition. The winning design represents the president's house with wall fragments and chimneys; a translucent box marks the location of the slave quarters, and video screens will be used to tell stories of all members of the house-hold, enslaved and free, presidential and plebian (Figure 3.11). An archaeological excavation of the memorial site was to precede construction, not because anyone believed there was anything of the president's house to find, but because the attention to the site had made it into a kind of sacred ground. No expense would be spared.

The Lost Archaeological Battle and an Unexpected Discovery

The archaeological features that we had previously found were already lost, not to posterity (they are protected underground), but to the public. What is curious is how park personnel came to recognize the mistake they had made. That icehouse, they realized, might have worked as a focal point for discussing George Washington's slaves. Conflicts with the public might have been avoided if the Park Service had taken advantage of an actual remnant of the past to tell the whole story of life in the president's house. No matter how informative exhibits are, they are necessarily a construction of the present. Physical remains of the past are something different. They are powerful in their authenticity, and in this case that authenticity could have been effectively connected to the story of the workers who supported the elite household of our first president.

This project also had an unexpected impact on my understanding of my own past. I was already accustomed to having archaeology politicized and exploited for other peoples' purposes. I had, after all, seen it happen on the sound-and-light show project at the beginning of my work in Philadelphia, and I had also seen how inflammatory archaeology could be in situations involving racial politics. The African Burial Ground project in New York City was under way in 1992 when I joined John Milner Associates, and the firm was dealing with very complex issues surrounding the excavation of an eighteenth-century burial ground and the interests of the local African-American community whose ancestors were being dug up and subjected to analysis. But my insights did not result specifically from the sound-and-light show or from New York; they came from a photograph in the exhibit inside the new Liberty Bell Center.

The photograph shows Frederick Douglass, flanked by other abolitionists, at a rally in Cazenovia, New York (Figure 3.12). The caption reads, "Cazenovia Fugitive Slave Law Convention, second day, August 22, 1850. Grace Wilson's orchard, Sullivan Street, Cazenovia, N.Y. E. G. Weld, daguerreotypist." I grew up in Cazenovia, and I had never heard

3.12. Daguerreotype that appears in the Liberty Bell Center exhibit, taken by E. G. Weld at the Cazenovia Fugitive Slave Law Convention, August 22, 1850. Frederick Douglass sits with his elbow on the table and Gerrit Smith stands behind him. (Madison County Historical Society, Oneida, New York)

of the convention. There were virtually no African Americans in Cazenovia when I was young there in the 1950s. We didn't learn any black history, and in fact we didn't learn any Cazenovia history to speak of. I had generally assumed there wasn't anything special to know about my idyllic hometown in the heart of the Finger Lakes region. I certainly didn't know that a major abolitionist convention had been held there in response to the U.S. Senate's approval of the Fugitive Slave Act in 1850. The act provided for the appointment of special federal commissioners to facilitate the reclaiming of runaway slaves. These commissioners could appoint marshals to arrest fugitives, and these marshals could in turn, when making an arrest, "call to their aid" any bystanders, who were "commanded" to "assist in the prompt and efficient execution of the law." Slave owners could "pursue and reclaim" fugitives without a warrant and the commissioner would judge the case without a jury. Fugitives would not be allowed to testify, but if their identities were proven the slave owner was authorized to use all "reasonable force" to return them to the place of escape.[12]

Cazenovia is just ten miles from Peterboro, which was the center of operations for Gerrit Smith, a well-to-do white man who was an active abolitionist and apparently a close friend of Frederick Douglass. He stands behind Douglass in the photograph, and it was he who drafted an incendiary document, "A Letter to the American Slaves from Those Who Have Fled from American Slavery," that was introduced at the convention. The letter, which purported to be written by fugitive slaves, encouraged those who were still in bondage to escape even if it meant "resorting to physical force." It reassured the still enslaved that they would find help in the abolitionist community, especially from members of the American Anti-Slavery Society, or the Liberty Party, as well as from their already free brethren. Douglass apparently felt strongly that the letter "put into the mouths of the fugitives language [that] was not theirs," but after a good deal of debate the fifty or so fugitive slaves present at the convention adopted the letter, which was subsequently published in national abolitionist newspapers, including *The North Star,* the paper Douglass edited in Rochester, New York. In spite of these efforts, the act was signed into law just one month after the convention.[13]

Cazenovia's Fugitive Slave Law Convention attracted two thousand people, so many that it had to be moved from the Free Church on Lincklaen Street, where it opened on August 21, to an apple orchard belonging to Grace Wilson, a leader in the Cazenovia Ladies Anti-Slavery Society, the following day. The Free Church was formed in 1836 as an antislavery offshoot of other churches in the village; the local antislavery society began a year earlier. Although the village newspaper, *The Whig,* painted the convention as the work of outside agitators and assured its readers that "there are few abolitionists here, and their meetings occur almost unnoticed and with the exception of a few idle women and children quite unattended," an anonymous letter to the editor stated otherwise. According to the person (assumed to be a woman) who signed it "S.B.S.," a large number of people showed up for the meetings, and "the women and children who attend [them] are, many of them, the wives and daughters of farmers of this and adjoining towns." Cazenovia apparently had an active antislavery society, although this has been largely forgotten in its history. A picture of the Free Church included in a book about the village published in 1993 identifies it as an abolitionist offshoot of the Presbyterian Church that was subsequently converted into a concert hall. The book does not mention the convention.[14]

In addition to the Free Church, Cazenovia had a hotel, something Peterboro didn't have and probably the reason the convention was held in Cazenovia, because it could accommodate out-of-town attendees. The hotel, called the Linklaen House and still in operation, opened in 1839 next door to the Free Church. Although it took me a trip to Peterboro in the summer of 2006 to figure out why the convention was not held there, the editor of *The Whig* who claimed it was the work of outside agitators also said Cazenovia was chosen for its hospitality. On this point he was obviously right.

Even today we continue to leave out unsavory parts of our history unless a determined effort is made to include them. Gary Nash and others felt it would be unconscionable not to mention that George Washington kept slaves on the very site where the Liberty Bell would be displayed. He publicized the issue and put pressure on the Park Service to rescript the exhibits for the new building to include a discussion of slavery as well as the abolitionist movement, which used the Liberty Bell as a symbol of freedom deserved by all. Even though it was very unlikely that anything archaeological remained of the smokehouse that had been converted into slave quarters, the possibility excited the public. Nash suggested on the radio that we, the archaeologists who investigated the site for the Park Service, had missed remains relating to slaves on the site, or intentionally avoided them. Although that wasn't true and left out what we did find from the period when slaves were part of Washington's household, it was a powerful way to make a point. Nash succeeded in influencing the Park Service to change the exhibits where we had failed, and his success benefited us all.

As I found out, too, museum exhibits can lead to unexpected insights about one's own life. The suppression of information about slavery has been so prevalent for so long that most of us were taught very little about this part of our history. The discovery of an African burial ground in New York City in the early 1990s confronted New Yorkers with the reality of slavery in their city's past. An educational program was initiated in the city's schools as part of the African Burial Ground project, but two exhibits about slavery mounted at the New-York Historical Society in 2005 and 2006 continued to provide revelations. It seems that the fact that slavery was not limited to southern plantations continues to surprise northerners. To its credit, Philadelphia instituted a required high school course on black history in 2005, and the memorial that will eventually be built on the site of the president's house will provide a locus for contemplating the meaning of slavery, in the past and in the present.

There is also a lesson in democracy here. It was a citizen—Ed Lawler—who brought the issue of the president's house and George Washington's slaves to the attention of the Park Service and ultimately to the public. Lawler is a professional singer, not a professional historian, but his passionate interest and willingness to do exacting historical research without remuneration led to insights he believed could not be ignored. He took on the Park Service, a federal agency, he presented the facts to professional historians, he communicated with the African-American community, and he educated us all along the way. Without his persistence and the activism of the African-American community, the president's house site might be marked as innocuously as it was before construction began, with a wayside that stated only the basic facts:

> When Philadelphia became the temporary United States capital in 1790, the city rented an elegant residence at this site for the nation's first president, George Washington. Washington held cabinet meetings here and hosted receptions, dinners, and celebrations in a manner befitting the presidency.[15]

The real story was a bit more complicated, so much so, in fact, that it inspired a thought-provoking play produced in Philadelphia in the winter of 2007. Called *A House with No Walls,* by Thomas Gibbons, the play focuses on five characters: Cadence Lane, an African-American university professor with Republican sympathies who believes it is time to stop portraying African Americans as victims; Salif Camara, a radical African-American organizer (loosely based on Michael Coard) who is continuing the struggle; Allen Rosen, a white former boyfriend of Cadence's who is trying to figure it all out (the Ed Lawler character); and Ona and Austin Judge, enslaved members of George Washington's household. "Locked" inside the "walls" of the minimalist set, Ona and Austin make slavery real and the argument between Cadence and Salif is dramatically framed in the context of their shared past. The issues raised by the play—and by the president's house site—are among the most important of our time, and there is perhaps no better example of how embedded archaeology and history are in the politics of the present.

CHAPTER FOUR

Artisans in a Changing World

John Adams became president in 1797, and he and his wife, Abigail, lived at 190 High Street for the few years that the federal government remained in Philadelphia. In 1800 the government moved to Washington, and the president's house became a hotel, not a particularly illustrious fate for the precursor of the White House. Philadelphians, however, were thriving and the businesses along South Sixth Street continued to service the politicians and clerks who frequented the line of buildings that had become known as State House Row (Figure 4.1). The State House didn't have a special function in those days (Lancaster had been made the temporary seat of the Commonwealth of Pennsylvania in 1799), and it actually fell into disrepair, but the building on the southwest corner of Sixth and Chestnut Streets, known as Congress Hall since Congress had met there, reverted to its original function as the county seat, and the building at the other end of the row, which had housed the federal, supreme, and district courts, again became City Hall.

Among the businesses on Sixth Street were the cabinetry and coach shops of Alexander Turnbull and Thomas Ogle. Their properties fell within the archaeologically sensitive part of the Liberty Bell Center site, and John Milner Associates excavated the privies associated with them under contract to the National Park Service in 2002. Both Turnbull and Ogle lived with their families on the premises for at least most of the first two decades of the nineteenth century, and both left household goods in their privies that provide clues to how such artisan businessmen dealt with the turbulent times (Figure 4.2).

The position of artisan-businessmen was unsettled between the Revolutionary War and the flowering of the Industrial Revolution. Artisans like cabinetmakers and coachmakers tended to still be categorized as manual laborers, even though as masters of their own shops many no longer worked with their hands. They also made a good deal more money than the journeymen and apprentices who actually

4.1. John Lewis Krimmel, painting of State House Row on Election Day, 1815. (Courtesy, Winterthur Museum)

did the manual work, but as historian Gordon Wood has pointed out, money did not automatically translate into "self-esteem and self worth in the face of age old scorn in which their occupations were held." By the 1820s the "market revolution" was in full swing and conspicuous consumption was on the rise. Among artisan-businessmen, however, there was also a movement to organize into associations of mechanics for the betterment of their trades. These men looked to science rather than material goods to give them respectability. Without dispensing completely with a connection to the manual work upon which their trades depended, they achieved higher status by associating with the very thing that was propelling society into the Industrial Revolution.[1]

We do not know exactly how Thomas Ogle and Alexander Turnbull dealt with these tensions, but their material possessions, at least, reveal how they identified themselves at home. Lacking documentary records of people's everyday lives, historical archaeologists have learned to squeeze all sorts of information from their material possessions. Diana Wall, for instance, used the tea- and tablewares left in backyard privies in New York City's Greenwich Village to explore the participation of women in the middle-class rituals that came to characterize their changing roles as wives and mothers in the early decades of the nineteenth century. My colleagues on the Five Points project and I found in the material culture a whole different perspective on a neighborhood traditionally characterized as New York City's most notorious slum. The artifacts recovered from the Ogle and Turnbull privies on the Liberty Bell Center block provided an opportunity to see how two artisans conducted their lives in a time when their place in society was in flux.[2]

Thomas Ogle, the Coachmaker

Thomas Ogle took over David Clark's coachmaking business at 7 South Sixth Street in 1794. Clark had repaired George Washington's carriage while he was staying with Robert Morris in 1787, and Ogle was clearly inheriting a classy clientele. He remained in business on South Sixth Street until 1830, although he moved the family residence to nearby Sansom Street in 1816. It was becoming customary for businessmen to separate their homes and places of work in this period, and the Ogles were in the vanguard in Philadelphia. Ogle had a succession of wives: Patience, who bore three children; Elizabeth, who also had three; and Catherine, who had five. In 1810

4.2. Archaeologist Mark Tobias excavating the Ogle privy at 9 South Sixth Street.

there were fifteen people in the household: two white males under ten, one white male under sixteen, seven white males under twenty, one white male, presumably Thomas, over forty-five, two white females under sixteen, and one white female, Thomas's wife at the time, under forty-five. At least six of the men in this mostly male household may have been apprentices.[3]

The only specific records of Ogle's coachmaking business were a series of receipts for work done for Thomas Butler, Esq., who lived at 309 Chestnut Street. Although some of the words are illegible, the receipts dating to 1815 and 1816 mention "mending [illegible] front spring, cutting the tires of wheels and putting on with [illegible] nails, cleaning and oiling carriage, and commission for sale of coaches." In 1825 Butler paid $300 for a "secondhand coach with patent accessories" and $5 for "chair strap plaits." In 1827 he paid $395 for the price difference in an "exchange of carriages," and in 1830, the year Thomas Ogle died, Thomas Ogle Jr. billed Butler for "a new plate in the hind spring of coach, taking off all the wheels cleaning and oiling the brass, lining the [illegible], fitting in the front and [illegible], the scrubbing and varnishing the roof of body of two coaches, varnishing and polishing the sword case and polishing the body, new binding for a blind, and a new hind plate glass in coach." Thomas Ogle Jr., along with his brother, William, followed their father into the coachmaking business, and by the 1820s William had a successful partnership with George W. Watson. Ogle and Watson's factory, run by waterpower near the falls of the Schuylkill, was considered a "marvel of ingenuity and efficiency," and they shipped their products as far as South America and Scotland.[4]

While there are no descriptions of the older Ogle's coach shop on South Sixth Street, nor of Clark's before him, the daybook of a contemporary of Clark's has been studied in depth. Richard E. Powell Jr.'s study of George and William Hunter's daybook provides some insight into the coach business in the Federal period. The book covers twenty-five months from December 1788 to January 1791. Ogle was younger than the Hunters and may even have apprenticed in their shop. The general information on the Hunters' shop provides at least some understanding of what Ogle's operation was probably like (Figure 4.3).[5]

Coachmaking required "knowledge of prevailing fashion, engineering, and animal draft power." As represented on a float in the Grand Federal Procession of July 4, 1788, coachmaking used the skills of a carriage maker, a wheelwright, a trimmer, a harnessmaker, and a painter as well as a smith and an upholsterer. The Hunters apparently employed them all, and in addition George Hunter, a chemist by training, made copal varnish, which he also sold to other firms. Approximately eighteen journeymen

4.3. A typical urban coachmaker's shop, circa 1800. (From Carl Bridenbaugh, The Colonial Craftsman, New York University Press, 1950)

and ten apprentices worked in the Hunters' shop. Apprentices received board, clothing, a freedom suit, medical attention, and some formal schooling in return for their labor. According to Powell, the Hunters operated as shop masters and surrogate parents, taking legal and financial responsibility for the actions of their apprentices.[6]

Journeymen brought well-honed skills and their own tools to the shop. They were paid in a variety of ways—by the piece, the job, the day, or the month—and were hired as needed. Philip Schuman, for instance, made lace, his most utilitarian project being girth and straining webs (presumably for horses) and his most esoteric being tasseled silk fringe. Other journeymen specialized in the forging of iron and steel vehicle parts, and still others were tailors hired to make clothing to sell to apprentices or journeymen. The firm purchased dry pigment to create paint and depended on William Healy, another shop owner, for brass and silver harness furniture. Although the tasks in the shop were varied and required very different skills, Powell claims that "workers remained united by the cooperative production of vehicles and by location as well as by leisure time activities," including the drinking of wine, which the Hunters sold to their employees by the gallon.[7]

Powell's account of the factory building, or several buildings, as he says, is perhaps the most tantalizing clue to what Ogle's shop may also have looked like. In Powell's description:

> The business depended on ample room outdoors and facilities resembling warehouses, in which few manufacturing activities took place. Open spaces were required for heating and setting tires and, probably, a protected yard in which freshly varnished carriages could be washed and sun dried to harden the finish. Perhaps the greatest allocation of space was for storage. On one occasion the Hunters had ten used carriages for sale, and at most times they had at least a few vehicles in long-term storage for absentee owners or unsettled estates.
>
> Inside the factory building . . . were roughly thirty workers and their benches, three or four new carriages under construction, and local vehicles awaiting repair or refurbishment. The workers operated forges, a small loom, and at least one lathe, clouding the air with smoke, fibers, and dust. Painting and varnishing demanded an environment free from the pollution of other work processes and protected from rapid temperature fluctuations. Upholstering also needed relatively clean work spaces. These activities were almost certainly separated from the smithing and woodworking. Confirmation of segregated shops within the Hunters' coachmaking complex comes from the reference to candles for the paint shop and the purchase of "a bucket for [the] stable & Tub for [the] smith shop." In sum, the stages of work were conducted in designated areas where each employee assumed a regular place.[8]

This kind of operation would have been possible on the double lot that Ogle occupied on South Sixth Street, and it is not unlikely that his shop looked much the same. In fact, the receipts for services to the Butler family suggest that Ogle's shop conducted the same variety of activities that the Hunters did, perhaps on a smaller scale. At least one of the artifacts recovered from Ogle's privy might have been specific to the shop. This was a fragment of a netting mesh, a narrow flat tool made of bone that was used to make loops for nets, perhaps mesh pouches to hang on coach doors for holding things. Net pouches used to hang next to the bunk beds on sleeping trains, and it conceivable that these were a holdover from earlier days.

Although the evidence for the appearance of Ogle's shop is circumstantial, the artifacts from the Ogle privy provide clues to how family members saw themselves and wanted the world to see them. The material record suggests that the Ogles were more interested in spending their resources on maintaining a large household and a thriving business than on impressing their peers. They took their meals on a well-worn set (actually several compatible sets combined) of blue shell-edge-decorated dishes that included dinner-size plates and smaller, octagonal shaped dessert plates (Figure 4.4). Such dishes were the least expensive English ceramics you could buy during this period, and although they made a perfectly respectable table, they were certainly not fancy. In the Ogle household, the edge-decorated flatwares appear to have been combined with blue printed serving dishes. The printed wares would have been slightly more expensive, but the Ogles chose common patterns—Willow and English pastoral scenes, all in standard blue and white.

4.4. The Ogles' blue edge-decorated plates. (Photograph by Juliette Gerhardt)

There was also an even plainer set of dishes, undecorated creamware, that may have been used for breakfast or, perhaps, in the kitchen. It was more worn than the edged sets and is further indication of the Ogles' lack of interest in keeping up to date. For drinking there were a few undecorated wine glasses and plenty of tumblers, probably for alcohol.[9]

Alcohol consumption in the early decades of the nineteenth century was widespread. According to one historian, the average man consumed more than five gallons per capita per year, a larger amount than ever before or since. Gordon Wood speculates that excessive drinking reflected the stresses of the times: "Everything seemed to be coming apart, and murder, suicide, theft and mobbing became increasingly common responses to the burdens that liberty and the expectation of gain were placing on people. The drinking of hard liquor became an especially common response."[10] Drinking was also seen as an expression of independence in the post-Revolutionary period and was not stigmatized or believed to interfere with productivity. In fact it was rampant in the workplace, as workers felt increasingly exploited and frustrated. The practice was actually encouraged by shop owners who supplied alcohol to their workers, presumably to keep them happy and productive. While some of the Ogles' tumblers may have been for consuming beer and cider at the table, others were surely for harder spirits (whiskey, gin, and brandy were the drinks of choice) in the shop.

It is not difficult to imagine the Ogle table at an evening meal. As many as fifteen may have sat down together in 1810, Thomas at the head of the table and his wife at the foot, with the children tucked between strapping shop apprentices who received room and board as at least part of their pay. There was usually a roast—beef or mutton, more rarely a ham—and plenty of side dishes. Sometimes there would be chicken and even a duck, but workmen required hearty meals and the roast was the mainstay in the Ogle household. If there was fish it was mainly in spring and summer, when salads flavored with mackerel and anchovies were served. For dessert there were puddings, some sweet, some savory, served in the well-worn redware dishes they were baked in. It was a diet of everyday fare, for a family and its employees, not for fancy company.

Tea at the Ogles, however, may have been different. They owned twice as many tewares as tablewares—or, at least, twice as many tewares were discarded in the privy. This is the opposite of the usual pattern and requires an explanation. In addition to bits and pieces of a variety of porcelain and hand-painted teaware, the Ogles had two sets, possibly used together, that were decorated with transfer-printed designs, but it is also possible that one set was used at home and the other was used in the shop. Other archaeologists have speculated that tea was served in the workplace. On the Barclay Bank site in Manhattan, for instance, an assemblage of unmatched porcelain tewares was interpreted as a group of vessels that might have been used in Van Voorhis's silver, gold, and jewelry shop.[11] The rest of the artifact assemblage included crucibles and other items

Making Food Remains Talk

Claudia Milne analyzed the food remains from the first two blocks of Independence Mall. Using skills honed on the Five Points project in New York City, she identified every recognizable bone. Her specialty is fish, an expertise she gained from creating a type collection by boiling down the leftovers she picked up in Chinatown on her way home from the Five Points lab at the World Trade Center to her tenement apartment on East Ninth Street. While domesticated animals (cow, pig, sheep) made up the largest part of most people's diets by the mid-nineteenth century, the presence of lots of fish and particularly wild birds suggests that a taste for these hunted creatures continued, at least among the well-to-do.

Faunal remains are quantified in several ways. The relative abundance of a given species is calculated by adding all the fragments identified together. The resulting number is referred to as the number of identified species per taxon, or NISP. This method, however, doesn't account for multiple bones from a single animal or for variability in the survival of certain elements. A second calculation, the minimum number of individuals, or MNI, attempts to eliminate this problem, but it has the potential to underestimate the number of animals represented because meat bought at market is purchased in individual cuts. For historical assemblages the most meaningful method of analysis is the minimum number of retail cuts. Milne's analyses use all three measures, and she also calculates the biomass—the potential meat weight based on the weight of the archaeological bone.

Milne's ability to identify the enormous variety in the faunal assemblages from Philadelphia has made it possible to envision what was being placed on the tables of the people whose privies we have excavated. By combining the identification of the bones to the species level with research into contemporary cookbooks, she is able to reconstruct probable meals. The Ogles, for instance, appear to have eaten mackerel and anchovies in the spring and summer as a first course, but in the other months they would have had small chops and cutlets or a meat-based soup. They preferred beef rib and round roasts to mutton or pork, using the latter for flavoring rather than for the major meat course. The Ogles ate some wild birds (pheasant, duck, goose), but more often they ate chicken. The Turnbulls, on the other hand, probably served lots of different kinds of fish (Atlantic cod, black sea bass, striped bass, bass, mackerel, shad, herring, and lobster were all identified) for the first course, and a variety of wild birds—roasted pigeon, snipe, duck, pheasant, and turkey—for the second. They preferred mutton for the main course, but also ate standing rib roasts of beef and veal roasts from the leg and loin (thirty-eight different roasts were identified in the assemblage). Both families would have served vegetables, and they undoubtedly indulged in the steaming pies and puddings of all kinds that take up large sections of period cookbooks. In her book *Savory Suppers, Fashionable Feasts,* Susan Williams speculates that pies "may have supplied an element of surprise . . . [which] served to lighten up an otherwise dull event."

Pies may not have been the only thing that livened up the table. The number of wild foods in the Turnbull and Everly faunal assemblages suggests a good deal of variety, and they also suggest something else. The wild birds, which were undoubtedly purchased at the High Street market, may have been a reminder of the man's role as hunter in earlier times. Game had masculine associations, which were conspicuously displayed in dining-room furniture, and it is likely that putting game on peoples' plates would also have recalled the head of household's role as breadwinner in the family. By the middle of the century every respectable dining room had a sideboard elaborately decorated with wild animals, plants, and the tools of the hunt.

What is wonderful about faunal analysis is that it provides so much information. This includes information about nutrition, of course, but also about ethnicity and class based on what foods people prefer and how they cook them. By telling us how the bones were butchered and how they were cooked (for instance, fried on the stove top, simmered for hours in a stew, roasted in the oven), Milne tells us things about people that relate to who they were and who they wanted to be. Because of the way ceramics and glass were marketed, differences between assemblages can be very subtle, but the variety in food remains tells many different stories. It also counters the conformity that the dishes reflect. People may have bought the same dishes, but they put different things on them, which their garbage reveals.

relating to the work done there. It is certainly true that in many other cultures, and even in our own, making a large purchase involves more than a commercial transaction. Buying a rug in Turkey, for instance, requires hours of tea drinking, polite haggling over price, and the expenditure of enough time to get a good bargain. The purchase of a car in twenty-first-century America also generally entails a good deal of coffee drinking and chatting about more than just the price.

The Ogles' Chinese porcelain tewares, though fragmentary (a few cups and saucers only), were fancy, decorated in hand-painted overglaze floral patterns, and they also had an English bone china set. It is clear that wherever these things were used they were given more importance than the dishes on which everyday meals were served. But that does not necessarily mean that the Ogles spent a lot of time on social events. They don't even seem to have belonged to a church; a concerted effort to discover where they worshipped turned up empty. Even funerals and weddings were held at home. When Thomas's third wife, Catherine, died in 1826, after "a severe and lingering illness of several months," the funeral was held at her home on Sansom Street, and when her daughter, also named Catherine, died, she too was mourned at home. Another daughter, Sarah, was married in 1821 in a civil ceremony conducted by Mr. Robert Wharton, who was mayor of Philadelphia at the time. If church membership was more a social obligation than a spiritual experience in this period, as some scholars have suggested, it would not be surprising that it was eschewed by the Ogles, whose possessions show such a lack of concern with appearances.

Alexander Turnbull, the Cabinetmaker

Alexander Turnbull opened his cabinetmaking shop at 5 South Sixth Street in 1801, and his residence remained there until his death in 1826. He and his wife, Margaret, had three children baptized in the Second Presbyterian Church: Alexander, born November 10, 1799; Margaret, born August 17, 1804; and Henry Christy, born November 17, 1809, but there were probably more, because Alexander Sr. was already thirty-six when Alexander Jr. was born. In 1810 the household consisted of one white male under ten, two white males under sixteen, two more white males under twenty (probably apprentices), and Alexander himself, who was over forty-five. There were also two white females under ten, one under twenty (an upholsterer, perhaps), and Alexander's wife, Margaret, who was still under forty-five.

There are no documents describing Turnbull's cabinetry shop, but an insurance policy dating to 1813 describes a first-floor front room as a cabinet wareroom, and directory entries for 1818–19 mention "furniture stock for sale."[12] Like his neighbor Thomas Ogle, Alexander Turnbull also owned a double lot, which in his case was probably used to store seasoned wood. There were many cabinetmakers in Philadelphia in Turnbull's time—768 between 1785 and 1820 plus 121 joiners, and as many turners and chairmakers.[13] Although we don't know how many men Turnbull employed, another cabinetmaker in the period employed 13 in a typical year, up to 8 at a time (Figure 4.5). They worked eleven hours a day, six days a week, and were sometimes paid by the piece but more often weekly. The paternalistic practice of providing room and board for apprentices as payment for their labor continued right up into the 1820s, but journeymen would have been paid by the piece or by the week. Of the purchase price for a piece of furniture, 33 percent paid for the labor that went into its fabrication, 20 percent went to materials, and the rest, less incidental expenses and overhead, belonged to the master of the shop. Owners were thus exploiting their workers, and by the mid-1820s journeymen were beginning to organize. They formed the Pennsylvania Society of Journeymen Cabinetmakers in response to the

4.5. A typical cabinetmaker's shop, circa 1800. (From Bridenbaugh, The Colonial Craftsman*)*

refusal of masters to adjust wages for inflation and to the practice of substituting un-skilled for skilled labor. The society issued a constitution, organized a strike for higher wages, and for a brief period opened its own wareroom. Apprentices, likewise, began to strain under a system that virtually kept them bound until the age of twenty-one (for boys) and eighteen (for girls), and some of them ran away.

It is not known where Turnbull stood on these issues, but his son Alexander Jr. edited a newspaper aimed at journeymen called *The Journeymen Mechanics' Advocate.* He began publication in the spring of 1827, the year after his father's death, but the paper lasted only a few months. Edmund Morris acquired Turnbull's subscription list and began publica-tion of *The Mechanics Gazette* in November 1827. Both Turnbull's and Morris's papers were aimed at organized, or, more accurately, organizing, labor.[14]

There is no way to know whether the young Turnbull was rebelling against his fa-ther's labor practices, but through the artifacts we can picture the household he grew up in. The Turnbulls appear to have set the table differently for different occasions. For everyday meals it would not have looked unlike the Ogles' next door. The Turnbulls also used shell-edge-decorated plates in several different sizes, but, unlike the Ogles, they also had matching vegetable dishes, sauceboats, and platters. In addition, their edgewares came in both blue and green, perhaps used together, perhaps not. Like the Ogles, the Turnbulls also had blue printed serving pieces, which may have been used alongside the edge-decorated ones. But for special occasions they had something the Ogles did not: a very elegant set of Chinese export porcelain dinnerware decorated in the Fitzhugh pattern (Figure 4.6), and another set decorated with a Chinese landscape motif. The Fitzhugh set included three different sized plates and a large platter. Such a set would

4.6. Blue Chinese export porcelain tableware set decorated in the Fitzhugh pattern. (Photograph by Juliette Gerhardt)

4.7. Children's mugs with sayings and names. (Photograph by Juliette Gerhardt)

have impressed any guest in the Turnbull household, and there were also other vessels that would have communicated something about the family's values. A matching plate and tureen displayed the patriotic image of General Lafayette landing in New York in August 1824, his first return trip since the Revolutionary War, and on the lighter side, another plate depicted the popular literary figure named Dr. Syntax arguing over a bill with his landlady. There were child-size cups with sayings on them like "For a Good

4.8. Decoratively etched decanters and other drinking paraphernalia. (Photograph by Juliette Gerhardt)

Girl," obviously meant to reward good behavior and, perhaps, inculcate a sense of private ownership (Figure 4.7).

Elegant wine glasses went with the fine china, and there were huge numbers of glass tumblers (one hundred were recovered), presumably to use for the significant amount of alcohol that was being consumed in the Turnbull household and also in the shop (Figure 4.8).

Just eight people would have sat down at the Turnbull table on a daily basis, half of them children under sixteen, in 1810. The two apprentices in the household were also very young men (between seventeen and twenty), and when Alexander Turnbull looked down the table he saw practically all young faces. Even Margaret, his wife, was more than ten years younger than the already aging cabinetmaker. Unlike the Ogle table, everything matched at the Turnbulls: there were different-sized dishes or plates for each course (even for children) as well as serving dishes in all sorts of shapes and sizes.

The Turnbulls needed all those dishes for the huge variety of food that was put on the table. Some meals surely started with soup, ladled carefully from one of the family's many covered tureens, presumably by Mrs. Turnbull. On other family occasions, the first course probably consisted of fish, but when there were guests there would have been many choices. The Turnbulls' diet was notable for the number of birds it included, many of them wild species. In addition to chicken they ate turkey, pheasant, quail, grouse, snipe, pigeon, duck, and goose, all of which would have impressed company as a second course. For the main course there was roast beef and steak, a good deal of veal, and lots of mutton (Figure 4.9). Philadelphia's market—just around the corner on High Street—

4.9. Faunal (food) remains, including large mammal and fish bones.

was famous for its plentitude of "animals and vegetables . . . beyond the wants of the inhabitants," and the Turnbulls clearly took advantage of the market's proximity. Along with their fancy dishes the Turnbulls used meals to display their social standing, which seems to have been more of a concern in their household than it was at the coachmaker's next door.

For serving tea they were even more extravagant. They owned nineteen different tea sets, almost three times as many vessels as tableware. Surely some of these sets were reserved for the shop, but the problem is, which ones? Would Alexander Turnbull have wanted to impress his potential clients with elegant Chinese porcelain teawares used in the context of a showroom full of elegant furniture? Or would he have reserved the fanciest for the entertaining that is suggested by the household's other dishes? There were nine sets of Chinese export porcelain, three of them with matching teapots, one with both matching tea and coffee pots (Figure 4.10), and one with a slop bowl. It is useful to place this assemblage in the context of what was considered adequate at the time. The standard composition of tea and coffee service in the late eighteenth and early nineteenth centuries consisted of twelve teacups and saucers, six to twelve coffee cups, a teapot with a cover and stand, a covered sugar dish with stand, a slop basin or bowl with stand, a covered tea canister, milk pot or cream jug, spoon tray, and two bread-and-butter or cake plates. Clearly, the Turnbulls met and exceeded the standard. There were twenty teapots in the assemblage, a coffee pot, fourteen slop bowls, seven creamers, and four sugar bowls.

There were also child-size dishes in the Turnbull assemblage including three mugs

4.10. One of the Turnbulls' blue Chinese export porcelain tea sets. (Photograph by Juliette Gerhardt)

4.11. Doll-size dinnerware set (left), dominoes, clay marbles, and a writing slate (behind the marbles). (Photograph by Juliette Gerhardt)

with sayings: "For My Dear girl"; "For a Good Girl"; and "Present from Carolina." A cup with a child's name would have distinguished it from things belonging to his or her siblings and thereby developed a sense of ownership appropriate to the emerging competitive capitalist economy. A small plate with an entertaining design of a dancing cat and accompanying poem suggests that children were invited to eat at the table. The poem itself reflects changing attitudes. With its play on drunkenness—"The wine got up in Pussy's head, she would not go to bed, but purr'd and tumbled leap'd and danc'd, and stood upon her head"—it points to the dangers of alcohol, at least for cats and maybe also for children. According to Karin Calvert's study of the material culture of childhood, it was not until the first half of the nineteenth century that many mothers stopped using alcohol to quiet their babies, turning instead to patent soothing syrups, and they may also have discouraged young children from partaking, although another scholar claims that even children drank in excess in the early decades of the nineteenth century.[15]

A twenty-one-piece set of doll-size dinnerware is unusual in an archaeological context and surely indicates a concern in the Turnbull household with educating the next generation in the niceties of meal presentation (Figure 4.11). This is not surprising since the adult-size dishes associated with the Turnbulls were also unusually elegant. Calvert argues that children were encouraged to use gender-specific toys at the same time they were being dressed androgynously. She claims that androgynous dress kept children from noticing the differences of the sexes, "a circumstance which would deprive them, at an early age, of their innocence and happy ignorance." At the same time, parents believed that supplying them with gender-stereotyped toys would "bring out what was considered to be their inherent nature," and parents were also confident that suitable gender-specific toys would give their children the most pleasure.[16]

The set of dinnerware with its many specific serving pieces would surely have allowed a little girl to practice the art of genteel table setting and service with her dolls. Parents who supplied such a toy, the Turnbulls in this case, were preparing their daughter for what they expected would be her adult role in life: to carry on the genteel manners that were so important in their own household. There is also the possibility that this set wasn't used by a child at all, but was instead part of someone's collection, perhaps a young girl's or even a not-so-young girl's. This does not lessen the meaning of the set. It represented what was considered proper, and we know it was consistent with what the Turnbulls actually used in their home.

Other toys in the Turnbull assemblage were a slate game board and eight marbles. Board games were among the only toys allowed to both boys and girls, but marbles were strictly for boys.

The assemblage from the Ogle household did not include any child-size dishes, but there were two miniature transfer-printed willow-decorated plates probably meant for dolls and one miniature redware jug. The only other toys recovered were two marbles. When the Ogles moved to Sansom Street in 1816 the family included young children, and it is probably telling that so few toys were found in the privy they left behind. The Ogles apparently did not put much emphasis on training the next generation. Perhaps they did not yet subscribe to new ideas about child rearing and did not yet see the proper guidance of child development as a major family responsibility. They seem to have been less concerned than their fashionable neighbors with imposing adult expectations on the younger members of the household.

Artisans in Conflict

The subtle differences in the Ogle and Turnbull artifact assemblages suggest differences in lifestyle, even though there is no reason to believe that one household was better off economically than the other. According to tax records available for the years between 1800 and 1825, Ogle and Turnbull were assessed at the same rate in 1810; Ogle was assessed for slightly more the next year, but in 1817 and 1818 they were again identical. While both the coachmaker and the cabinetmaker appear to have been successful at their crafts, they clearly took different approaches to dealing with the contradiction in status they faced in the early decades of the nineteenth century. Turnbull balked at the limitations of his station and used material culture, and the manners that went with it, to establish himself above the position of a laborer. Ogle followed a more modest style, continuing a tradition of usefulness, or "decent competency," as it was called. He probably stood with other local men who defined themselves as "mechanics" and looked to science to achieve the status they lacked because of their association with manual trades. The Franklin Institute, Philadelphia's major science museum, was founded in 1824, and it would not have been surprising to have found Ogle among its early supporters, especially since its first headquarters were in City Hall at the corner of Chestnut and Fifth Streets, just a block away from Ogle's shop. But Ogle was just six years away from death when the institute was founded, and perhaps he was too ill to participate. Surely his son would have supported it. Among the institute's earliest activities were annual exhibits that encouraged manufacturing and fine craftsmanship, and in 1825 it offered prizes for the best specimens in eighty-two branches of manufactures.[17]

Either in imitation of the elite of an earlier period or assuming the pretensions of the newly emerging middle class, Turnbull used his prosperity to live like the rich. Whichever it was, Turnbull was clearly willing to spend his resources on fancy entertaining, on eating extravagantly, and on providing the children of the household with things that would prepare them for a genteel future. Americans were already very concerned with the material trappings of status, and Turnbull's choice was not at all out of step with what others in similar businesses would do in the next generation. In that sense, he was ahead of his time, but interestingly it was his business, not Ogle's, that disappeared from the records. Alexander Turnbull's son attempted to start a newspaper that supported labor's growing complaints, and he may well have disapproved of his father's approach to the problem of status and wanted instead to side with the workers. The younger Alexander unfortunately disappears from the records, however, and we do not know how his life turned out.

The view from archaeology is a view from the inside out. We begin with tangible pieces of the past and work outward. In the case of the icehouse on Robert Morris's property, we went from an unusual stone-lined hole in the ground to the first president's household, and the struggle to recognize the work that was done by black slaves and white servants to support it. An archaeologist's endeavor is never concerned only with the past: it is about what we can know of the past in the context of where we are in the present.

The artifacts belonging to the Thomas Ogle and Alexander Turnbull households, retrieved from neighboring privies on the block where the Liberty Bell Center now stands, brought to light another struggle. Artisan businessmen did not have a clear place in America's emerging class system in the early decades of the nineteenth century. No matter how successful they were financially, artisans were denigrated because of their association with manual labor. The material possessions of these two households, and even the food they ate, were different, not because one household was better off financially than the other but because they chose to deal differently with their place in society. Through their things we have glimpsed the complexity of their lives and the tensions inherent in the culture of American capitalism. An imagined conversation between the two aging artisans brings those tensions to life.

A Vignette of Thomas Ogle and Alexander Turnbull in Old Age

[A golden October day on South Sixth Street, 1824. Two old men approach each other on the street.]

"So don't you even say hello to your old neighbor?" It was Mr. Thomas Ogle speaking, but he had to repeat his words. Alexander Turnbull, the neighbor who had just passed him on the street, was a bit hard of hearing. "Good morning, Mr. T.," Ogle repeated.

"Oh, oh, sorry, old man, I didn't see you."

Nose too high in the air, thought Ogle, but he didn't let on. He greeted his old friend heartily; he was truly glad to see him, for it had been a while and they had both been unwell over the summer. "So what have you been up to?" he said.

"Well, you know Margaret," Turnbull said. "She still insists on the most up-to-date dishes. I've had to go over to High Street to look at yet another set—a beauty, I must admit, but what I liked even more were the ones for little girls. We have grandchildren now, you know, and it's never too early to start training them to be proper young ladies."

"Ah, yes," said Ogle, "we are getting on. My son has set up his own shop down on the Schuylkill—he's making fancier carriages than I ever could with all that newfangled equipment and using waterpower besides. Going to be a rich man, I suspect. What a waste."

"What ever do you mean?" said Turnbull. "We can't be workers forever. It's good to get a little class—I never could understand why you didn't . . . well, I don't mean to criticize, but we artisans need to show the world who we really are."

"No, you never did approve of us, did you, Alex? You with your fancy guests eating off all those fancy dishes and what was it they ate—quail and pheasant, for heaven's sake. What ever for? Give me a good roast any day, sturdy dishes to eat it on, and the company of my men. Why, you know, we often sat down to dinner with fifteen at the table, at least half of them apprentices."

"Of course, I know you did," said Turnbull huffily. "What a racket came from those rowdy fellows."

"I wouldn't talk," responded Ogle, sounding more than a little agitated. "It wasn't my boys who did all that drinking. I always wondered how those drunkards could fill your orders for bedsteads and bureaus without cutting off their fingers. Maybe they did."

"Well, uh, uh—anyway let bygones be bygones. What have you been up to, Thomas?"

"So glad you asked, so glad you asked. I've been looking into this new organization that's being talked about—the Franklin Institute of the State of Pennsylvania for the Promotion of the Mechanic Arts. They're meeting in City Hall right down the street, you know."

"No, I didn't know, as a matter of fact. And I'm not interested in going about with men dressed like hoodlums worrying about educating the masses. I've got enough to worry about with my silly son writing those newspaper columns about journeyman's rights."

"These are complicated times, Alex. Fancy tea parties aren't going to make us gentlemen. It's knowledge that counts. It's decent competency that matters. That's how our kind will get respect."

"So be it, Thomas, each to his own, as Benjamin Franklin used to say. Well, maybe it wasn't Ben Franklin. Anyway, a good day to you."

That was the two old neighbors' last encounter. Turnbull died two years later, at age sixty-three, and Ogle died at the same age four years after that. Their old-fashioned shops died with them, as industrialization transformed both the cabinetry and the coachmaking businesses.

CHAPTER FIVE

"We the People"

The Free Black Community, Native Americans, and the Celebration of the Constitution

The National Constitution Center, a museum dedicated to increasing awareness and understanding of the U.S. Constitution, opened on July 4, 2003. The *Philadelphia Inquirer*'s architecture critic described the building as "neither a puffed-up federal edifice nor a modern building in colonial drag . . . but a thoughtful work of architecture that distills our core national values into easy-to-read physical form."[1] The NCC, as it has come to be known, spans practically the entire width of the mall on its northernmost block, encompassing an area of 160,000 square feet, 130,000 of which were examined archaeologically. But first the opening.

It was a gorgeous day. Philadelphians were out in full force, and those who hadn't been invited to sit in the cordoned area immediately in front of the NCC's porch, "the stage," lolled on the lawn beside the Visitor Center on the middle block of the mall. There were many events that day: a bell-ringing ceremony, with young descendants of signers of the Declaration of Independence symbolically striking the Liberty Bell; presentation of the Liberty Medal to Sandra Day O'Connor, the first woman justice of the Supreme Court; and finally the ceremonial opening of the NCC's main entrance. Speakers were brief: Joe Torsella, the president of the NCC who had seen the difficult project to completion; Governor Edward Rendell, who, as mayor, had done a good deal to promote the Constitution Center, including hiring Torsella for the job; Senator Arlen Specter, a supporter from the beginning; Philadelphia's mayor, John Street. As Justice O'Connor finished her talk, she joined the dignitaries on stage to ceremonially pull the ribbons and open the curtain in front of the forty-foot-high glass entryway. They did more than that, though, as the massive piece of stage scenery that held the curtain came tumbling down (Figure 5.1). Fortunately no

5.1. Justice Sandra Day O'Connor at the opening of the National Constitution Center, July 4, 2003. (AP Images, photograph by Chris Gardner)

one was seriously hurt, although Mayor Street's elbow was hit and Torsella got knocked in the head. Torsella of all people.

It was Torsella's day. He had done the impossible, taking what was a moribund project in 1997—Rendell called it "floundering"—and brought it to fruition in six short years. He had raised an astounding $185 million, recruited three Supreme Court justices (O'Connor, Antonin Scalia, and Stephen Breyer) and a distinguished history professor (Richard R. Beeman) as advisers, hired top architects and exhibit designers—Pei Cobb Freed & Partners and Ralph Appelbaum Associates, respectively—developed a nationally recognized educational program, and forged partnerships with major institutions including the National Park Service and local hotels and restaurants. He had also learned to live with the National Historic Preservation Act, which required an archaeological evaluation of the proposed building site and follow-up excavations as appropriate. Fearing anything that might prevent finishing the project on time and within budget, Torsella would have avoided the archaeology if he could have, but he couldn't and the building got done anyway, much to the credit of National Park Service guidance and consultants who put their all into the project.[2]

Kise, Straw and Kolodner (KSK), a Philadelphia architecture and planning firm, did the historical background study in 1999. KSK began archaeological field investigations on June 5, 2000, and finished on September 10, 2001. By the time they were done, the firm's archaeologists had excavated 98 burials, sampled 110 historic house lots, identified 279 historical features, and recovered artifacts from 135 shafts. Although the collection is yet to be analyzed it appears to include as many as a million artifacts and probably more. This block, which since the 1960s had been a kind of grass garden, was silently hiding a surprisingly undisturbed record of an entire eighteenth-century neighborhood. It is probably the richest site ever investigated in Philadelphia.

KSK, as any consultant would be expected to do, set out to develop a sampling strategy that would retrieve enough information to address three basic research themes: eighteenth-century lifeways; ethnicity and consumption patterns; and consumer choice among different socio-economic groups. The archaeologists knew they couldn't dig up the whole block, so they also recommended monitoring during construction. To monitor, an archaeologist stands on the site while building proceeds and stops any activity that appears to be destroying something significant from the past. Needless to say, this is not the way to do careful archaeology. It also has the potential to cost the contractor money by shutting down construction activities for as long as it takes the archaeologist to record what is about to be destroyed.[3]

The north block of Independence Mall, between Arch and Race Streets, was different from the other two blocks on the mall. Unlike the first two, this block—at least the northern half, where the NCC would stand—had never been disturbed by nineteenth-century buildings with deep basements (Figure 5.2). In fact, in some areas there had never been any buildings at all. There was a chance that large areas of intact ground surface—that is, historic period backyards—might lie beneath the fill that supported Kiley's landscape, which would provide a unique opportunity to learn about the lives of the artisans and laborers who lived there in the eighteenth century.

According to KSK's background study, the earliest houses on the block were built in the middle of the eighteenth century. In 1756, for instance, the *Pennsylvania Gazette* advertised a two-story house with kitchen and cellar on the north side of Arch Street between Fifth and Sixth Streets, and in 1760 Thomas Bartholomew was selling three new two-story brick dwellings on Fifth Street and a three-story brick dwelling on Arch. In 1764 Caleb Cresson, who appears to have owned the entire north half of the block, was subdividing his property for sale; by 1774 he had built five new adjoining two-story brick "tenements" on the south side of Cresson Alley, which ran east–west and divided his holdings in half. But it was in the 1790s that development really took off. By 1795, 168 heads of household and 133 dwellings were recorded within the project area. Residents were tavernkeepers and blacksmiths, watchmen and tallow chandlers, carpenters and

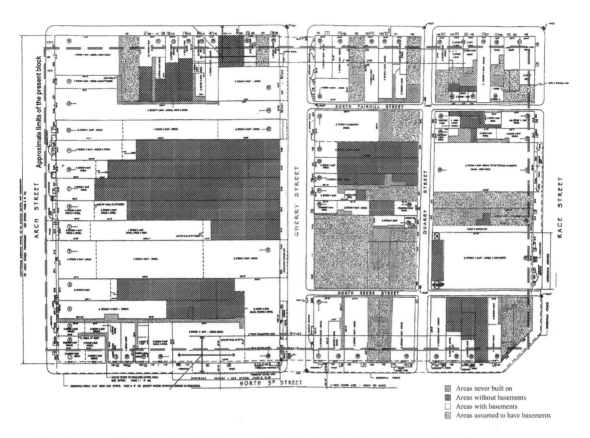

5.2. Kise, Straw and Kolodner's sensitivity map of the Constitution Center site on the northern block of Independence Mall. (Adapted from Kise, Straw and Kolodner, Inc.)

bricklayers. There were tailors, shoemakers, wheelwrights, laborers, brewers, and bakers. And there were scriveners, schoolmasters, merchants, and gentlewomen. Although artisans, construction tradesmen, and laborers made up nearly three-quarters of the heads of household, the presence of merchants and gentlemen among them suggested to the researchers that the neighborhood included a mixture of social ranks. In addition, six of the listed heads of household were African American, which meant the block was at least somewhat racially mixed.[4]

Besides a record of life in an eighteenth-century neighborhood, the archaeological investigation of this block had the potential to produce a record of death. In the 1750s the Second Presbyterian Church purchased a lot on Arch Street at the southeast corner of the block for use as a burial ground. The 50-foot-wide lot stretched from Arch Street north for 360 feet and was in use from around 1750 to 1864. When Cherry Street was built in around 1761, burials were removed from the 17 feet of the cemetery that extended that far north; fifteen hundred bodies were "reportedly relocated" when the cemetery finally closed in 1868. KSK's principal investigator, Tom Crist, had experience with supposedly relocated burial grounds in Philadelphia, and from the start he believed there was a chance that the Presbyterians, like others, would have left some burials behind.[5]

Crist had worked on the First African Baptist Church Burial Ground project in Philadelphia in the 1990s and also on the African Burial Ground project in New York City. He was pursuing a Ph.D. in bioanthropology at Temple University at the time and was also on call with the Philadelphia medical examiner for forensic cases. Crist, who has gone on to an academic position at Utica College in upstate New York, has been involved in virtually every burial ground excavation in Philadelphia in the past decade, and he couldn't help but think that burials from the second half of the eighteenth century would add to the comparative data base.

With all this potential, the question was how to begin testing what we call the impact area, the ground inside the footprint of the proposed building that would be disturbed by construction. According to Jed Levin, the National Park Service's designated archaeologist for all the work on Independence Mall, the NCC (and its consultants) wanted the archaeological testing done one way and he wanted to do it another. The battle that ensued is a story in itself.[6]

Levin, who had been working for the National Park Service in its Maryland office for about ten years, was transferred to Philadelphia for the mall project because Alan Cooper, the Park Service archaeologist in charge at the time, needed someone with urban experience. Levin had plenty. Raised in Brooklyn, New York, he went to City College in the heady days of open admissions and abandoned his intended major of marine biology for anthropology after taking an introductory course. He joined forces with two other New York natives—Ed Staski and Bill Askins—and for their senior project they excavated Jed's mother's backyard. She was planning to re-landscape the yard behind her circa 1844 Brooklyn townhouse, and before she began, the budding young archaeologists removed the paving with sledge hammers, sampled the underlying ground surface, and excavated an artifact-filled cistern. Nourished by the materialist theory they were studying, their analysis focused on the changing use of space. In the early days the yard mainly served utilitarian purposes, for trash disposal and the like, but later, in keeping with middle-class ideas about private space, it had more recreational uses, including as a place for children to play. Levin was fascinated by the fact that some of the things they found were his own toys. He was hooked and went on to graduate school.

At the graduate school of the city's public colleges, Levin studied with Bob Schuyler, a historical archaeologist who was then excavating a site on Staten Island. It was the early 1980s, urban archaeology was coming into its own in New York, and Levin got to work on practically all the major projects in downtown Manhattan.[7] With colleagues Roselle Henn and Bill Askins he excavated inside a building at 209 Water Street (part of the South Street Seaport) and found portions of a ship in the underlying fill (scuttled ships have been identified as supports for fill deposits in several places in the city). He was the lab director for the Telco project, a block that included side-by-side historic lots, several with their waste (privies) and water supplies (cisterns) right next to each other, and he was also the lab director for the Barclays Bank site. Foreshadowing things to come, Levin didn't think the budget for the Barclays Bank lab effort was adequate and he complained to the overseeing agency, the New York City Landmarks Preservation Commission. From the very beginning, Levin set high standards for archaeology and stuck to his guns no matter what (in the case of Barclays Bank it meant leaving the job).

In Philadelphia, Levin's high standards and depth of experience came fully into play on the NCC site. The potential for undisturbed backyards and shaft features was so great that he thought the only way to know how to sample them was to remove all of the overlying fill and then make decisions about where to excavate. The NCC wanted to put the test trenches in from the surface, an approach that Levin was sure wouldn't provide the archaeologists with enough information, and they would have to remain on the site during construction to prevent important archaeological resources from being destroyed. The NCC was clearly thinking about money (and time), but so was Levin. If the archaeologists had to monitor during construction, he argued, they would have to keep closing down the work to recover the archaeological remains, surely not an efficient way to get a building built. Emily Bittenbender, who joined Torsella's team as manager of design development in January 2000, remembers a year of screaming matches. The NCC, she says, started out with a development mentality, determined not to let anything get in the way of constructing the building.[8]

Bittenbender was in a difficult position. She came from a family of history buffs and had grown up in a house filled with the very stuff the archaeologists would eventually dig up. Torsella also had a background in history: he was a Rhodes scholar working toward a Ph.D. in history when he got sidetracked into politics. He didn't understand what archaeologists could possibly learn from animal bones—food remains—but he surely did know that the study of an entire eighteenth-century neighborhood including a diverse population of artisans, laborers, gentlemen, and possibly Native Americans and African Americans would be of value. He just couldn't afford to have the study get in the way of his deadline (and bottom line), and Bittenbender was the one who had to fight the battle for him.

Although Bittenbender was only in her early thirties, she already had plenty of experience in the world of construction. She had taken over as project manager for the $42 million renovation of the Municipal Services Building for the City of Philadelphia. Next she was hired to assist Mayor Rendell's cabinet in a real estate consolidation program, which evaluated seven candidate buildings for purchase and entrusted Bittenbender with overseeing the $56 million renovation of the eighteen-story one they bought. She then became capital programs tsar, with responsibility for spending $454 million over three and a half years, representing the mayor at Independence Mall working meetings and getting to know all the major players. When Rendell left office, she called Joe Torsella. The two had gone to high school together, and he hired her to take over from a key person who was leaving his team, just in time to do battle over the archaeology.

In the end, the Park Service won the battle. Levin convinced Dave Rupp, the head of the construction management firm handling the project, that stripping first would save everyone time and money, and Rupp convinced the NCC. Stripping began in early June 2000; the archaeologists opened the first of their five test trenches on the fifth. Within an hour Tom Crist's suspicions were confirmed. There were still bodies in the Presbyterian burial ground.

That first scoop came from a trench at the back of where Concordia chapel once stood. The chapel, which appears on nineteenth-century maps, was on the south side of Cherry Street, but the street itself had once been part of the burial ground. Tommy Williams, the backhoe driver who had honed his skills on the middle block of the mall, rolled a skull right out on the ground in front of Doug Mooney, KSK's field director. Crist was on the site within minutes, and the process of removing leftover burials continued for many weeks (Figure 5.3). Because press helicopters constantly buzzed overhead, physical anthropologist Art Washburn conducted an initial inventory of the bones as they came out of the ground under the cover of a tarp. A total of 150 separate remains were identified, but it was not possible to determine the minimum number of individuals represented. Coffins were stacked, in one instance seven deep, preservation was generally not good, and in some cases remains were commingled. The best-preserved burials were the forty-five found under the old alignment of Cherry Street. The street was laid out in 1761, which means the burials beneath it dated to the first decade of the cemetery's use.[9]

Once removed from the field, complete skeletons were taken to KSK's laboratory in Pennsauken, New Jersey, for recording; Washburn looked at the commingled remains in the Temple University archaeology lab. According to him, the most extraordinary find was the skull of a man with a bullet in his head, apparently a homicide, maybe the city's first. There were also some newborns, but not even a basic demography was ever completed. Because reporting has not yet been funded for this part of the project, the data remain unanalyzed.[10]

Following a precedent set on the earlier First African Baptist Church project, Crist recommended that the recovered remains be reburied in a ceremony presided over by

5.3. Excavating a grave that was left behind when the Presbyterian burial ground was moved. (Courtesy of Kise, Straw and Kolodner, Inc., and the National Park Service)

5.4. Reburial ceremony at Woodlands Cemetery in West Philadelphia. (Courtesy of Kise, Straw and Kolodner, Inc., and the National Park Service)

the minister of the descendant congregation. In the winter of 2001, less than a year after they had been excavated, the remains were reburied at Woodlands Cemetery in West Philadelphia (Figure 5.4). With a dusting of snow on the ground, they were cere-moniously driven from the Pennsauken Laboratory in New Jersey, across the Benjamin Franklin Bridge into Philadelphia, and up Walnut Street to pass the present-day Presby-terian Church. The archaeologists who had worked on the cemetery served as pallbearers and the minister read from an ancient Presbyterian Book of Prayer. Each set of remains was placed in an unmarked brown bag, intended to be as biodegradable as the original wooden coffins had been. The bags were placed in three vaults. Crist later gave an informal lecture on what might be learned from the remains to interested members of the Presbyterian congregation.

Beyond the Burial Ground

Once the demolition rubble had been stripped away from the entire footprint of the proposed Constitution Center building, the archaeologists placed their exploratory trenches in areas they thought were the most likely to contain intact ground surface. Guided by their own sensitivity map, they knew exactly where the property lines should be, where the backyards had been, and which backyards hadn't been disturbed by later construction. The area between Quarry and Cherry Streets on the north and south, and Starr Alley (called North Fairhill on the map) and Hoffman Alley (called North Reese on the map) on the west and east, turned out to be the least disturbed, and it was there the archaeologists focused their efforts. Ultimately, they investigated four thousand square feet of amazingly well preserved ground surface, or backyard. In profile, the old backyards looked like a band of dark organic soil approximately half a foot thick (Figure 5.5).

Among the most notable finds were two parallel lines of postholes and trenches at the back of the yard that belonged to the house at 55 Cherry Street. Israel Burgoe, an African-American wood sawyer, lived in a house that sat midway between Cherry Street and Cresson Alley (later Quarry Street) for twenty years. Benjamin Cathrall owned the lot from 1791 to 1801. Cathrall was a prominent Quaker who lived with his family in the house at the front of the property. Burgoe was one of 264 founding members of St. Thomas's African Episcopal Church in 1794, but the artifacts he left behind, and even his house, suggest that he and his small household of three identified with their African roots.

Burgoe's house, apparently built with posts in trenches, may have resembled houses that have been identified elsewhere as belonging to both enslaved and free Africans. At Parting Ways, a tiny community of free blacks near Plymouth, Massachusetts, for instance, one of the structures identified consisted of postholes at two of the four corners of a shallow rectangular pit and a posthole at the midpoint of each long side. Traces of mud walls suggested post-in-ground construction reminiscent of West African building methods. The earliest house remains (1740s–90s) at Yaughan and Curriboo plantations in South Carolina consisted of narrow trench features excavated into subsoil. Posts standing in the trenches would have supported mud-walled structures. The later houses at Yaughan and Curriboo (1780s–1820s) were post-in-ground frame structures. All of these types, and even their measurements, have African correlates and it is believed that they represent traditional African prototypes.[11]

Among the artifacts associated with the Burgoe household were twenty-six ceramic gaming pieces. Similarly reworked pottery sherds have been found on a number of sites identified with African Americans. For instance, Douglas Armstrong found Delft pottery sherds shaped into circular disks in the slave quarters at Drax Hall Plantation in Jamaica. Burgoe's were made of redware sherds that had been smoothed out on the edges. Also found in Burgoe's yard were ankle bones from a small animal that were incised with the Roman numerals I to XV. Although Mooney has not been able to identify the specific game or other activity these relate to, he wonders if they might have been used for divination, or as dice. Sixteen cowrie shells in the assemblage also suggest an African connection, as do the multitudes of trade beads (upward of three hundred) that were found (Figure 5.6).[12]

The multicolored trade beads are made of a variety of materials, including glass, bone, stone, and ceramic. Similar beads were traditionally sewn on women's and children's clothing, woven into waist belts, and made into necklaces, bracelets, and anklets. These, too, have been identified with African Americans elsewhere. At the Calvert House in Annapolis, for instance, a hundred beads were recovered from under the floorboards. Anne Yentsch, who wrote a book on the excavations, interprets their presence to mean that the enslaved Africans in the household did not have to hide expressions of personal identity on an everyday basis. She believes beads were thought to have magical qualities and that, made into jewelry, they conveyed information, distinguishing older and younger persons, for example, or mothers of twins from mothers of single births. A waist belt of beads found in association with a female burial at the African Burial Ground site in New York City

(top) 5.5. Stratigraphic profile showing the buried ground surface, formerly a backyard, present on the northern block of Independence Mall. (Courtesy of Kise, Straw and Kolodner, Inc., and the National Park Service)

5.6. Sherds of Colono Ware (at left), cowrie shells (center, above), trade beads (center, below), and gaming pieces (right) associated with Israel Burgoe's house lot. (Courtesy of Kise, Straw and Kolodner, Inc., and the National Park Service)

was interpreted as probably related to fertility. The woman buried was of childbearing age, and the waist beads may have emphasized her procreative powers. She also had modified teeth suggesting that she had been born and come of age in Africa.[13]

More mundane artifacts from Burgoe's yard included sherds of pottery that have been tentatively identified as Colono Ware. Colono Ware, a utilitarian ceramic type that has been found on sites from Maryland to Georgia, is believed to have been made by African Americans. Some of the vessel types are identical to containers made in West Africa and others are imitations of European types, including three-legged pipkins, milk pans, porringers, punch bowls, chamber pots, and teapots. One scholar has noted that certain pieces made in Ghana are indistinguishable from those made in South Carolina. Some of the vessels identified as Colono Ware were flat-bottomed, burnished, grit-tempered, and had incised X's on their bases. The ones studied by Leland Furguson from South Carolina, however, have rounded bottoms, as if to balance on a three-stoned hearth. The pieces found associated with Burgoe's household have not yet been examined closely.[14]

Burgoe's was not the only African-American household in the vicinity of Cresson Alley in the late eighteenth century. According to research done by Anna Coxe Toogood, there were five African-American households grouped together along the alley between number 6 and number 18, including twenty-five individuals. A second possible post-in-ground house was investigated several lots to the east of Burgoe, and many trade beads were found there too. Even farther east was the home of James Oronoko Dexter, another founding member of St. Thomas's African Episcopal Church. His yard was not part of the original NCC project area, but when it was discovered that a bus drop-off would be built on top of Dexter's house site, members of Philadelphia's African-American community requested that an archaeological excavation precede construction. The Dexter excavation took place in the winter of 2003 and the analysis of the finds was completed in 2006.[15]

James Oronoko Dexter, enslaved until 1767, rented a house at 84 North Fifth Street from Ebenezer Robinson, a brushmaker and Quaker abolitionist, from 1790 to 1799. According to recently discovered documents, the first organizational meeting for St. Thomas's African Episcopal Church was held in that house on December 12, 1792, which is one of the major reasons the site has such importance for African Americans. The man himself also piqued the curiosity of the archaeologists, especially Doug Mooney, who also directed the excavation of the site.

The site included Robinson's own house lot and the one he rented to Dexter immediately to the north. A small portion of one stone foundation wall of Dexter's house was uncovered, but the remainder of the foundation, if it still exists, lies under Fifth Street, which was widened by thirty-three feet when Independence Mall was created in the 1950s. Six archaeological features were found behind where Robinson's and Dexter's

The Pursuit of James Oronoko Dexter

Large construction projects, conceived to serve needs in the present, have a way of leading to people in the past who would otherwise remain unknown. There could be no better example than James Oronoko Dexter. Identified as one of several African-American heads of household on the north block of the mall in Kise, Straw and Kolodner's preliminary research, it was Anna Coxe Toogood's discovery that Dexter was a founder of St. Thomas's African Episcopal Church that made him seem particularly significant. Jed Levin knew immediately that the descendant community needed to be contacted and, with the blessing of the church, Dexter became the object of an intense search to learn everything possible about his life from the documentary record. Doug Mooney, often with Levin at his side, spent Wednesday evenings at the Historical Society poring over any source that might yield information about the former slave who became a leader of Philadelphia's free black community.

One of the earliest records—a testimonial by Isaac Zane—describes how "James Oronoque Dexter a black Freeman" gained that freedom in 1767. He was apparently hired out by his "master," also named James Dexter, to the keeper of a tavern, and when the master died in debt Oronoko became the property of his creditors; from them, he purchased his freedom, with fifty pounds that he earned himself and another fifty pounds contributed by the tavernkeeper. Although Joseph Yeates may have been the tavernkeeper for whom Oronoko worked, Mooney speculates that James Dexter's mother, Eleanor, who held a tavern license, is another possibility. If it was she who paid half the amount Oronoko needed to gain his freedom, he might have taken her son's name in gratitude after his death in 1781.

James Dexter had inherited Oronoko from his father, Henry Dexter, in 1749. Oronoko's history before that remains a mystery. The name itself is curious. In his Manumission Record, from 1767, he is referred to as "Oronoke royal Slave." According to research by Daniel Rolph, a "said-to-be-true anti-slavery novel of 1688 by English author Aphra Behn [was] entitled *Oroonoko, or The Royal Slave*." Even after taking Dexter's name he continued to use the name Oronoko on occasion. He signed "Oronoko Dexter" to a 1782 petition to "fence in the Negroes Burying ground in the Potter's field," and a letter from Phineas Bond in 1784 is addressed to "Oronoko at Mr. John Pemberton's."

Oronoko worked for the Pembertons in the 1780s and seems to have lived in the Pemberton house for at least part of that time. In his will, drawn up in 1784 and probated in 1795, John Pemberton granted "unto James Oronoko Dexter (a black man who lives with me) twenty pounds a year to be paid by my executors and after the decease of my wife the said twenty pounds a year to be paid to him by the overseers of the Public School under the Society of Friends." In addition he bequeathed "unto James Oronoko Dexter and Absalom Jones or the survivor of them the sum of ten pounds in trust to be paid to the treasurer of the Society of black people to be added to their stock for the support of their poor being willing to encourage them in things commendable." One final mention in the will grants another "fifteen pounds a year during his life and a further sum in case my dear wife departs this life without will, I do hereby will unto him after the decease of my wife the sum of £30 Pennsylvania currency on and besides the first sum of £15 making in the whole £50 Pennsylvania money yearly and every year during his natural life." Clearly, Dexter's well-being was important to Pemberton, as well as to Pembertons' friends. Elizabeth Drinker, one of those friends, mentions him numerous times in her journal, more often than not calling him "Noke." On August 10, 1799, she wrote, "John Drinker called here—Oronoko is dead, our Jacob went to his funeral, many a pleasant ride have I taken with his Mistress under his care and protection, poor Noke."

In city directories dating from 1794 to 1798 the man the Pembertons called Oronoko or Noke was identified as James Dexter, coachman. Dexter was married twice, first to Priss, whose freedom he had bought "in consideration of the sum of sixty pounds" from William Jones in 1767, the same year he himself was manumitted. According to information recently gleaned from Pemberton letters by Mooney, Priss died in 1784 and their son died a year later. He had remarried by 1789, and it was evidently with this second wife that he lived at 84 North Fifth Street. They rented the house from Ebenezer Robinson from 1790 until 1799, and it was there that the first organizational meeting for St. Thomas's African Episcopal Church was held in 1794. Dexter was one of several deacons or elders who guided the construction of the church. His particular responsibility appears to have been the procuring of stone for the foundation. By 1796 Dexter was a vestryman. A ledger covering church business from 1791 to 1796 shows Dexter managing financial affairs between 1795 and '96. As indicated in the ledger, he and others advanced their own money for various tasks and were later reimbursed by the church. A single repayment of £270 from the church to Dexter suggests that he had plenty of money to lend, and Doug Mooney speculates that he may have been one of the wealthier members of the black community. A ledger reference in 1807 mentions money being moved into Dexter's account, perhaps to repay an outstanding debt. Dexter had died by that time, but it is possible that he left money to the church that remained in an account under his name.

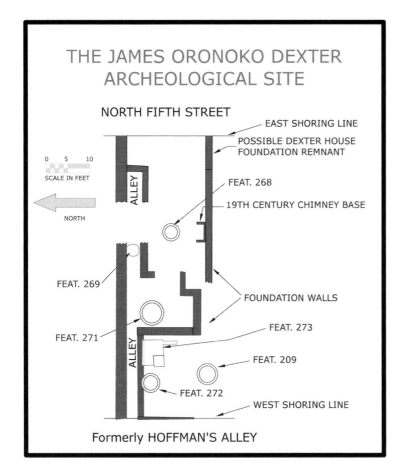

houses would have been (Figure 5.7). They included four privies, a wood-lined pit that may have been a root cellar or icehouse, and a barrel, apparently embedded in the ground and used for sweepings from the yard and occasional trash. Only the fill from the barrel could be unequivocally associated with the Dexter occupation.

The micro-strata in the barrel suggest recurrent sweeping, a practice that has been traced to West Africa. The approximately four thousand artifacts recovered from the many layers dated to the right time period, and the alley that was eventually built over the barrel sealed its contents. Many of the artifacts were small ceramic sherds, but there were also several Chinese porcelain saucers, a colorful Whieldon teapot, and a green Wedgewood plate (Figure 5.8). There were glass beads like the ones found on the Burgoe lot, but not in great enough numbers for Mooney to be confident they related to African

5.8. Green-glazed Wedgewood plate recovered from fill associated with the Dexter household. (Photograph by Jed Levin)

customs. Other artifacts included fragmentary white clay pipe bowls and pipe stems, a toothbrush, buttons, straight pins, and even the hook for a hook and eye, leading the investigators to think that someone in the house may have been working as a seamstress. The Dexter household included nine individuals, but it is not known whether they were all related, if some were boarders, or even how many were men and how many women.[16]

The food remains suggested that the household ate well. Beef, pork, mutton, chicken, duck, pigeon, turkey, and plenty of fish bones were all recovered. A more unusual find was a cluster of pigs' feet in the middle of the barrel, deposited in what the faunal analyst for the project, Marie-Lorraine Pipes, thought was a single event. Pipes speculated that the pigs' feet represented some kind of communal feast, perhaps associated with Dexter's role as an organizer of St. Thomas's African Episcopal Church.

The close relations between white Quaker abolitionists and African-American Philadelphians is one of the important things the NCC project brought to light. It's not that it wasn't known that black and white abolitionists were working together toward a common goal, or even that African Americans lived on properties owned by Quaker patrons, but the details of these living arrangements and their physical record goes beyond what was known previously. As already noted, Israel Burgoe's house was on a lot owned by Benjamin Cathrall. Cathrall was a schoolteacher who had purchased his property from Thomas Smith, another Quaker, in 1791 and remained there until at least 1801. Cathrall and Smith, along with fellow Quakers (and neighbors) Ebenezer Robinson and Joseph Hewlings, signed a petition to the Continental Congress in 1783 asking the nation's new leaders to "discourage and prevent so obvious an Evil" as the slave trade with Africa. They were members of the Philadelphia Meeting, which in 1776 required that all Philadelphia area Friends relinquish their slaves or their membership, and they undoubtedly also supported the gradual emancipation law, passed by the Pennsylvania legislature in 1779–80. The emancipation law, the first such passed in America, allowed owners to hold in servitude the children of slave women until they reached age twenty-eight, when they were to be freed.[17]

Scholars have claimed, however, that in spite of their activism even these Quakers treated blacks paternalistically. They did not welcome former slaves as full-fledged members of the Quaker congregation until the 1790s, and except for one light-skinned black named Robert Purvis they did not admit blacks into the Pennsylvania Abolition Society during the entire period of its existence. We cannot know exactly what the relationship was between Benjamin Cathrall and Israel Burgoe, but we do know that trash from both their households was deposited in the privy that straddled the line between the Cathrall property and the Smith property next door. Mixed with trade beads and gaming pieces were two wine bottles with Benjamin Cathrall's seal on them (Figure 5.9).[18]

We also know that the free black community was coalescing in this period. James Dexter was working with Absalom Jones to found St. Thomas's African Episcopal Church (which opened in 1794) at about the same time others, including Richard Allen, founded Mother Bethel, eventually the independent African Methodist Episcopal

5.9. Cathrall wine bottle seal. (Photograph by Jed Levin)

Church. Free blacks were creating a community of their own, and the connection between the white property owners and the blacks who lived in their backyards may have been a good deal less important than those among all the blacks on the block. According to Gary Nash, Philadelphia had the first gathering in one American community of a large number of former slaves, and beginning with the founding of the Free African Society in April 1787 they were joining with other free blacks to found their own institutions.

A telling document that turned up in KSK's research on the Constitution Center block suggests that some Quakers' efforts for abolition had more to do with their own salvation than with ensuring African-American dignity. The record, now in the Historical Society of Pennsylvania, was the journal of Caleb Cresson, the Quaker gentleman who originally owned the land where Burgoe and Dexter lived. Cresson's journal reveals a kind of obsessive concern with cleansing his own soul and a lack of interest in local African Americans, whom he mentions only when they die: "Cousin S. Emlen's black lad, Jim, fell through the ice in the Schuylkill and was drowned," and "deceased, Dubree's black man, Ishmael, an honest creature, whom I have known many years." He does describe a revolt on the island of Hispaniola, however, where "the blacks and mulattos" have armed themselves "and being filled with indignation and despair are carrying fire and sword through to different settlements in order to recover that personal liberty which, unquestionably, was intended by the Great Author of Nature as a right unalienable to the human species." Cresson was an observant Quaker; he was active in the Society of Friends, held gatherings to discuss business in his own home, and went to meeting as many as three times a day. He was committed to righteous behavior and dutifully sat by the bedside of his dying aunt who had raised him.[19]

Perhaps African Americans were so much a part of city life by the 1790s that they attracted little notice, a condition that was clearly not true for Native Americans. Cresson was fascinated by the Indians who visited the city. About fifty members "of the Six Nations" came to town in March 1791, and he wrote, "How earnestly is it to be desired that they may be instrumental in bringing about a peace with their country folks to the westward, where so much blood hath been lately shed." He was apparently not alone in his fascination. When there was a funeral for an Indian "in the ground opposite our door," he says that several thousand spectators attended "from motives of curiosity and were very disorderly, much, I think, to the discredit of our city." Another Indian, called Big Tree, was buried in the Friends' ground at the request of his companions, and according to Cresson many Quakers were present.[20]

Cresson's house faced Quarry Street. Two and maybe four privies were found within his property, but it is not yet clear whether their fills relate to Cresson's occupation. There was also a shell midden in his backyard that included enough historic-period trash to discount the possibility that it related to pre-contact Native American activity. Knapped glass found among the huge (some as long as a foot) oyster shells and trade beads suggested to Mooney that the midden might have been left by Indians who visited in historic times, but more analysis is needed to determine whether that is likely. Indians knapped glass the same way they did stone, and similar artifacts have been found at contact-period sites elsewhere.[21]

Native American artifacts were found in the most deeply buried stratum on the Burgoe lot and on the three lots to the east (Figure 5.10). Together they constituted a probable hunting camp dating to the Archaic or Early Woodland period (ca. 1000 B.C.). According to a geomorphological analysis of the soils, the area was once swampy and would have been ideal for hunting waterfowl. The artifacts found included rhyolite, jasper, and quartz debitage from making or repairing projectile points, at least one identifiable point, and a piece of mica schist that had been drilled, perhaps used as a gorget.[22]

Although stories of Indians coming into town to meet with William Penn are standard Philadelphia lore, very little evidence has been found of prehistoric activity in what became the city's core. Exceptions are the site of the Sheraton Hotel at Front and Dock Streets and more recently on the Old Bookbinder's site next to the Ritz movie theater on Second Street. At the Sheraton Hotel site, 137 prehistoric artifacts were recovered. Although most of these came from historic fills, three of them—a fragment of chipped stone, one ceramic sherd, and one piece of fire-cracked rock—were found in alluvial and swamp soil deposits sealed beneath the historic-period ground surface. The ground has been greatly altered in this area, but in prehistoric times there was a high sandy bluff at the point where Dock Creek flowed through swampy ground into the Delaware River. Most of the prehistoric artifacts recovered were probably originally deposited on the

National Constitution Center Site Plan Map

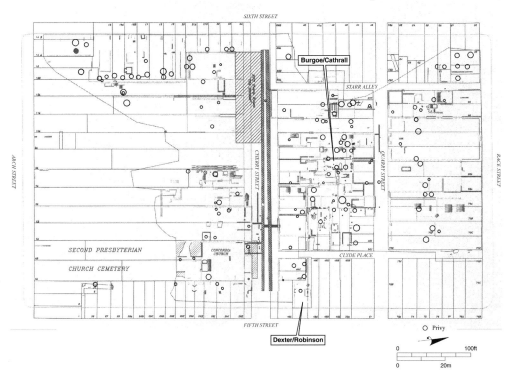

5.10. Site map showing features (privies and wells) excavated on the National Constitution Center site, including the Burgoe–Cathrall and Dexter–Robinson lots. (After Kise, Straw and Kolodner, Inc.)

bluff. When the bluff was cut down to fill the swamp below, the artifacts were incorporated into the soil. They included portions of at least six projectile points, two drills made out of chert, at least one cobble fragment that had been used for chopping, many flakes, most of them showing use wear, and nineteen ceramic sherds. Using standardized typologies, the investigators grouped the artifacts into three periods, the Transitional/Late Archaic period (ca. 3000–1400 B.C.), the Early/Middle Woodland (ca. 1000 B.C.–A.D. 1000), and the Late Woodland (ca. A.D. 1000–1600). The finds at the Old Bookbinder's site included stone debitage, a few tools worked on both faces, a single stemmed point, and a pottery sherd probably dating to the Early Woodland period. There was an intact ground surface at the site, but the construction was not publicly funded and therefore did not require an archaeological excavation. KSK archaeologists watched as most of the ground surface was destroyed.[23]

Building the City and Excavating the Evidence

The African-American and Native American finds on the Constitution Center block received particular attention because they were so unusual, but most of the features and finds were related to white workers and their families. As is evident from Cresson's journal, the block buzzed with construction in the 1790s and many of the workers lived in the neighborhood. In November 1791, Cresson "agreed with Nathan A. Smith to build several tenements for men on Cresson's Alley having a piece of ground there which I think may be yet for me to improve," and in December he again talked about "building some tenements on a vacant piece of ground I have yet remaining." In January 1792, "neighbor Robinson began his new building near my dwelling," and Cresson himself was "much taken up about by my new building." By the 19th "the masons began to lay stone in my new building" and on the 3rd of February a well burst "near the one I was causing to be dug." In May, he says, "Building in most parts of the city goes on with great spirit." In June, "our workmen have got to the top story, so we made them welcome, in the evening, to a small repast." But there was work yet to be done and at the end of the month Cresson notes the tiling of "several chimneys in my new tenements . . . 8 in all" and the finishing of the plaster work. All of these workers—carpenters, masons, well diggers, and chimney builders—probably lived nearby, and it is their household possessions and those of others like them that will eventually be analyzed.[24]

5.11. Privies exposed during the excavation of the area where the Constitution Center now stands. (Courtesy of Kise, Straw and Kolodner, Inc., and the National Park Service)

Cresson's descriptions recall the clatter of ongoing construction, not so unlike the noise of excavating the block, much of which he once owned. The excavation also involved a variety of skilled workers, sixty field archaeologists at its height (September to November 2000), but there were also construction workers. Huge machines swirled about the site, moving backdirt piles from one place to another, dismantling brick shafts as the archaeologists removed their fill, and delivering bucketfuls of dirt to the water-screening operation set up in an area at the edge of the site. The field director, Doug Mooney, fresh from a huge prehistoric project

5.12. Interior photograph of the laboratory in the Living History Center where artifacts from the Constitution Center site are laid out for mending and analysis. (Photograph by Jed Levin)

in the Susquehanna Valley, relished having everything happen in one place—the excavation, the construction, the field lab.

Since the excavation ended Mooney has given no fewer than seventy-five talks to all kinds of audiences. His presentation shows a long line of privies—seventy were excavated—and the wonderful things recovered from them (Figure 5.11). Among them were shoes with the laces still tied, plates of hardboiled eggs, a coconut shell modified into a wine goblet, four gold coins, and a calendar token minted in 1758 that read, "This year expect the comet without danger." A single privy yielded five thousand marbles, and another, two flintlock rifles. There was knapping debris associated with making gun flints that probably belonged to the gunsmith who lived on Cresson Alley, and there was a privy (not excavated) that belonged to John Harper, a saw maker who made the dies for the first coins minted as United States currency. The artifacts are not the "art mobile" that Mooney studied on a Fulbright scholarship in England, but they are intriguing in their variety and will eventually be used to tell stories not even imagined yet.[25]

Mooney, along with everyone else who worked on the Constitution Center project, is still excited about uncovering remnants of a whole neighborhood. This is unique in Philadelphia and it has presented special problems for the people paying the bills. In late 2003 an agreement was negotiated in which the National Park Service would share the cost of completing the artifact processing and analysis with the NCC and would have direct responsibility for seeing the project to completion. In anticipation of the task, the Park Service allotted space for an archaeological laboratory in its newly opened Independence Living History Center on Third Street. Open to the public, the laboratory has already been used to process the Dexter collection. The light-filled space is perfect for mending ceramics broken into many pieces, and its tables are covered with newly reconstructed vessels from one of the late-eighteenth-century features (Figure 5.12).

5.13. *Jed Levin talking to schoolchildren in the laboratory. (Photograph by Charles Fox, reprinted by permission of the* Philadelphia Inquirer)

For Jed Levin, who is directing the effort, it is "the project of a lifetime": the story of "we the people." As he guides the project, which may extend well into the next decade, he is determined to do justice to an assemblage that, because of its associations, may be the most important ever recovered in Philadelphia. He is also determined to let the public in on the process of constructing the past (Figure 5.13). School classes stream into the center daily and tourists are treated to lectures on demand. The Constitution Center tells the story of the document and the politics it engendered, but the archaeology tells the story of the people. Both have added immeasurably to Philadelphia's cultural landscape.

CHAPTER SIX

Life and Death in the Nineteenth-Century City

Philadelphia's African-American mayor John Street chose *The Price of a Child* by Lorene Cary as the first book for the "one city, one book" program. It was 2003 and there was renewed interest in the underground railroad, at least among scholars, and Cary's book was a painless way to introduce the topic to a wider audience. The story, which is loosely based on an actual case, takes place in 1855 in Philadelphia.[1] An enslaved woman named Ginnie, and two of her three children (she has left one behind), are being forced to accompany their "master," Jackson Pryor, to Nicaragua, where Pryor is to become ambassador. Left in a hotel room in Philadelphia, Ginnie manages to contact Philadelphia's Vigilance Committee, which dramatically wrests her away from Pryor just as they are about to depart on a steamer for New York. Ginnie is taken in by the Quicks, a sprawling family of educated free blacks who have made a good living as caterers and urban property owners. Through various legal negotiations Ginnie, renamed Mercer Gray, is exposed to a coterie of Quaker ladies who convince her to give lectures for the abolitionist cause to audiences in New England. Leaving her children behind with the Quicks, Mercer sets off on an extended tour on which she tells tales of slavery and displays her scars to dramatic effect. She returns to Philadelphia, survives a fugitive-slave trial (held, incidentally, in Congress Hall, the building immediately west of Independence Hall), and she and her children finally flee to Canada.

What is most interesting about the book is the portrait of the Quicks, an extended family with all the quirks of a real family: an unfaithful patriarch; a drunken aunt (with money in the mattress); an accomplished aunt who runs a school for African-American children; an unhappily married son who falls for Mercer; and his dead brother who squandered the family's money on the Africa Society, a back-to-Africa movement that ultimately led to the founding of Liberia. Cary brings to life the complexity and vibrancy of free black life in mid-nineteenth-century

Philadelphia, albeit from the perspective of one family on one block of Pine Street, just south of Independence Hall.

Another picture, not inconsistent with Cary's, was revealed by two archaeological excavations in another part of the city. Besides the black community and its churches that began in the eighteenth century to the south of Market Street, another black neighborhood developed a little later on the north side of Market. The First African Baptist Church, founded by black members of the Baptist Society in 1809, was located at Tenth and Vine Streets, and an offshoot of the church, formed seven years later, worshipped at Eighth and Vine. Both churches had cemeteries and both cemeteries were impacted by twentieth-century construction projects (Figure 6.1). The Tenth and Vine Street cemetery, the earlier of the two, was in the path of the Pennsylvania Department of Transportation's construction of the Vine Street Expressway and was excavated by John Milner Associates in 1990. The Eighth and Vine Street cemetery, the later one, was found first, during construction of the Center City Commuter Rail Tunnel in 1980. It, too, was exca-

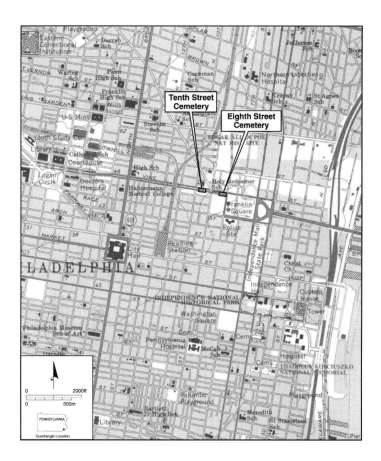

6.1. Map showing the location of both First African Baptist Church cemeteries along the Vine Street Expressway.

vated by John Milner Associates, and it was the first experience for the firm and its chief archaeologist with an African-American cemetery. The project was important, not just because it was significant archaeologically, but also because it was a delicate situation that needed to be handled sensitively. Dan Roberts, director of the firm's cultural resource department, took the challenge very seriously and developed an approach that has served as a model for all subsequent excavations of African-American cemeteries.

Roberts graduated from Beloit College in 1971. Infatuated with the Egyptian mummies at the University Museum in Philadelphia, where he grew up, he went to Beloit to study archaeology. His first field experience was digging an ossuary—a mass grave including the bundled skeletal remains of forty to fifty Native Americans—in the woods of northern Wisconsin. After college he returned to Philadelphia and found himself at the bottom of deep brick-lined wells and privies at Franklin Court. Benjamin Franklin's home and yard were being developed into a historic site by the National Park Service, and Dan was part of Barbara Liggett's field crew. Liggett was a cigar-smoking lady archaeologist who did a good deal of digging in the city during the 1970s. Still thinking he would be a prehistoric archaeologist, Roberts got a master's degree at Idaho State, and when a museum job didn't work out in Idaho he again returned to Philadelphia. What he thought was a two-week job with the National Heritage Corporation (John Milner Associates' predecessor) in West Chester turned into a thirty-year career.[2]

There were other twists and turns along the way, but the most significant one came in November 1980 in Philadelphia. During construction of the Center City Commuter Rail Tunnel, a coffin containing skeletal remains was unexpectedly found protruding from the east slope of the tunnel near the southwest corner of Eighth and Vine Streets. Although construction did not proceed in the immediate area for another two and a half years, the problem of what to do about it posed a challenge for Roberts that would ultimately lead him, in his own words, "to question some of the fundamental scientific underpinnings of my anthropological and archaeological training."

Initial research determined that the coffin came from a burial ground used by an offshoot of the First African Baptist Church between 1824 and at least 1841. The First African Baptist Church was formed in 1809 by African-American members of the First Baptist Church of Philadelphia. According to historian Reginald Pitts, many African Americans found the Baptist and Methodist faiths appealing alternatives to the staid Anglican Church, and in both the North and the South they joined existing white congregations or started their own. The group of African Americans who founded the First African Baptist Church in Philadelphia was apparently led by John Harris, who lived on Cherry Street between Sixth and Seventh Streets when he first arrived in the city sometime before 1794. Although much of the city's African-American population lived south of Market Street, where the first two black churches were established, W. E. B. Du Bois claimed that as much as 25 percent of them (538 people) lived north of Market and south of Vine.[3]

John Harris, sometimes a waiter, sometimes a wood sawyer, married Eleanor Callendar (later changed to Kelly) in 1795. The Pennsylvania Abolition Society hired her to teach in its schoolhouse on Cherry Street below Sixth in 1793, and in 1796 she was in charge of "forty scholars all of her own color."[4] The society's minute book called her "a well qualified tutoress of children" and "a black woman of considerable parts" who had "been for several years employed as a teacher of white children in England." Eleanor Harris died in 1797, however, and when her husband, John, joined the church founders he lived with his second wife, Sarah Barber Harris, on Smith's Court near Eighth and Vine Streets, as did many of the other early church members.

Edward Simmons, a carter, and his wife, Jane Gibson, were members of the group of thirteen who founded the church, as were Hannah Cole, Nancy Cole, washerwoman Phillis Dorcas, Zilpha Rhees, Betsey Jackson, Jane Riddle, Samuel Johnson (once a sailor who sported a mermaid tattoo and a coat of arms on his left arm), his wife, Sarah, and yet another Sarah whose last name was Bentley or Bartley.[5] All of these people were members of the First Baptist Church of Philadelphia, but they held prayer meetings and separate services in one of their houses—probably John Harris's—for two years and finally appealed to the Baptist Church for permission to start their own congregation. All were officially "dismissed" from the church on June 12, 1809, whereupon they formed the First African Baptist Church. They purchased property on Tenth Street, south of Vine, and built a frame meetinghouse that measured twenty-six by thirty feet. Henry Cunningham, a slave preacher from Savannah, came to Philadelphia to be the minister of the First African Baptist Church, but he could not be ordained until he was free, so a white man, John W. King, served as the first official minister. King, it turned out, had two wives, one in Philadelphia and another in New York, which led to his removal after a year.

It wasn't long before the new church split in two, and although the reason is not absolutely clear it appears to have had something to do with the fact that some of the members, including acting deacon Edward Simmons, had been slaves and were relatively recent arrivals in Philadelphia. Simmons was expelled from the church for an unspecified cause, and the disputes between congregants escalated from name calling to physical threats. Former slaves from Virginia and Georgia, who had arrived in Philadelphia after 1800, were apparently pitted against the native-born members of the congregation who looked down on the country ways of the new arrivals. There were also fights over the appeal of John King to return as minister, Edward Simmons or his brother, Henry, was shot in the thigh, and nineteen worshippers were forcibly removed from the meetinghouse during a Sunday service. Whatever the underlying reason, Henry Simmons left the church in 1817 to found an alternative congregation, confusingly also called the First

African Baptist Church, where he served as pastor for twenty years (Figure 6.2). He was described in the Abolition Society census as a preacher and old clothes dealer. This second congregation lasted until the late 1830s, but it was the original congregation, the Tenth Street Church, that received the Philadelphia Baptist Association's official blessing and is the one that has endured into the twenty-first century.[6]

Roberts sensed that digging up the remains of African Americans who belonged to this lively free black community under the noses of their descendants was a far cry from digging up anonymous bones in the backwoods of Wisconsin. There was no precedent to follow and he and Dick Tyler, then the head of the Philadelphia Historical Commission, held long discussions about how to approach the problem. Most important of all, they felt, was accountability to the community that would care, local African Americans. Tyler leaned toward working with the nearby Afro-American Historical and Cultural

6.2. *Reverend Henry Simmons. (Historical Society of Pennsylvania)*

Museum; Roberts thought it was essential to include the living congregation. Ultimately both were involved.

Before beginning the excavation of the Eighth Street cemetery, John Milner Associates made two presentations, the first to the Orphans Court of Philadelphia and the second to the board of directors of the Afro-American Museum. The purpose of the Orphans Court presentation was to request "leave to remove human remains from the First African Baptist Church Cemetery and re-inter them in Eden Cemetery in Delaware County, Pennsylvania, after suitable analyses had been performed."[7] In addition to John Milner Associates, the Philadelphia Redevelopment Authority and the Afro-American Museum gave expert testimony. After no more than an hour the court granted the requested permission and the project was legally cleared to proceed. The museum presentation went equally smoothly. A few questions were asked, but no one seemed to have a problem with what was being proposed. Roberts remembers only one instance in which someone made a demand of the archaeologists. Barbara Potts, a young African-American lawyer who worked for the city, wanted to be sure that blacks would be hired for the project. "If not," she said, "you will have problems with me."

Elvis Turner, the First African Baptist Church minister, and the descendant congregation were less demanding, although they thoroughly appreciated that their ancestors would eventually be reburied. Roberts stayed in contact with Turner throughout the project and kept him apprised of the progress of the excavation. Turner and his congregation apparently trusted that their ancestors would be treated with respect. Unlike the turmoil that surrounded the excavation of the African Burial Ground in New York City a decade later, there was no effort by these Philadelphians in the mid-1980s to politicize the project.[8] This may have been because John Milner Associates was so careful to be inclusive from the beginning, or, perhaps, the political potential of such a project was not yet appreciated. The hands-off attitude of the church did not prepare Roberts for the enormous interest generated by the African Burial Ground excavation in New York City, a project John Milner Associates took over in 1992 in great part because of the firm's experience with the First African Baptist Church cemeteries. In New York, concerned African Americans not only wanted to be informed, they wanted to have decision-making power. They wanted to dictate where the bones would go, how they would be handled, and who would do the handling. They wanted accountability every inch of the way, which they fundamentally got.

In Philadelphia the community got more than it asked for, but the investigators, Roberts most of all, got even more. In a well-attended talk he gave at the Afro-American Museum in 2003 "on the occasion of the rites of ancestral return dedication ceremony in honor of the ancestors originally interred in the Eighth and Tenth Streets First African Baptist Church Cemeteries," Roberts summarized what he learned under three categories: values, passion, and privilege.[9] By values he meant that "human remains are not specimens, but ancestors who, in the course of their lives and deaths, inherited, practiced, and passed on cultural values that are still being inherited, practiced, and passed on." He also described the passion individuals have for understanding their own history. He said to the audience, "You have a passion, a hunger, really, to know your past, to directly connect with and come to know those who came and suffered before you, that has heretofore been denied." There is an irony in that, he said, for "in the case of burial grounds, at least, it is only through disturbance of the dead and subsequent scholarly inquiry that much of that knowledge can be obtained." Last he talked about privilege, the honor he felt that "the fragile remains of your ancestors were entrusted to us." The almost completely black crowd of hundreds gave him a standing ovation.

The Results of the Excavations

Although the original Eighth Street find—the lone coffin sticking out of the side of the commuter tunnel trench—was at the edge of construction and had been covered over for protection, a new plan in 1983 for an office building on the site required excavation of the cemetery, assuming more than one burial was still there.[10] With a field crew of about eight, at least half of them black (Barbara Potts's words were not forgotten), and in public view (a wooden viewing platform was built alongside the excavation), 146 skeletons were excavated from the Eighth Street site in 1983–84 (Figure 6.3). The burials were crowded into an area no more than fifty-five feet north–south and twenty feet east–west (Figure 6.4). Some burials had been disturbed when the land was used for housing after the

6.3. Public viewing platform built for the Eighth Street First African Baptist Church excavation.

6.4. Diagram of burials found in the Eighth Street cemetery.

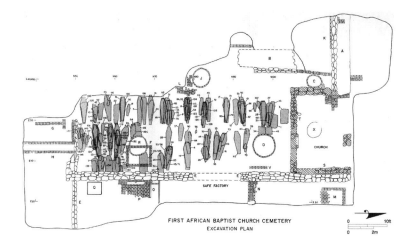

FIRST AFRICAN BAPTIST CHURCH CEMETERY
EXCAVATION PLAN

offshoot of the First African Baptist Church dissolved in 1838. In one instance a cranium and two long bones had been reinterred in what the excavators interpreted as a skull and crossbones position, presumably by a workman who found them while digging a privy through the grave (Figure 6.5).[11] Undisturbed interments were generally in supine position, oriented east–west with the head to the west and hands at the sides. Presumably because of lack of space, or lack of records, or both, many burials were superimposed on top of one another, with as many as nine in a single pit.

Only 135 of the 146 skeletons excavated from the Eighth Street cemetery were sufficiently intact for study; the late Larry Angel of the Smithsonian Institution in Washington led the analysis. Seventy-five (56 percent) of the skeletons were adults, and the remaining sixty were children younger than sixteen, including infants.[12] Infants under six months represented 19 percent of the interments. The average age of death for adult females was thirty-nine, and the average for males was forty-five, with only 19 percent of the adults in the burial population having lived beyond the age of fifty. Thirteen individuals from Eighth Street had bone fractures of one kind or another, none of them related to gunshot wounds, although six (a broken nose, a depressed parietal lesion, and four wrist fractures) may have resulted from interpersonal violence. There was one broken leg (a healed midshaft break to the right femur in a male forty-five to forty-nine years old), but more than half of the fractures were minor ones involving fingers and toes. One female between twenty-five and thirty had been subjected to an autopsy that cut through the cranium.

Close analysis of the infant remains was perhaps the most telling.[13] Sixty-eight percent of the infants (0.3–1.9 years of age) were affected by pathologies, some of which suggested dietary iron deficient anemia and possibly sickle cell anemia. There were also in-

dications of vitamin C–deficient scurvy and vitamin D–deficient rickets. All the observed lesions
indicated widespread nutritional deficiencies associated with a starchy diet, an absence of fruits
and vegetables, and poor-quality protein. Faults
in the formation of the deciduous teeth in one of
the infant skulls could have resulted from infantile
tuberculosis, and faults in others appeared to relate to bacterial infections of one kind or another.
In general, the infants appeared to have suffered
severely inadequate nutrition combined with
chronic infections during the age of weaning.

The investigators thought the symptoms exhibited by the First African Baptist Church infant
grouping fit the profile of a syndrome defined in
the late 1960s for Third World data as "weaning
diarrhea." As described, the condition resulted
when an infant who was developing normally
on breast milk alone had its milk supplemented
at three to six months with other foods. If the
supplementary food was low in protein, the child
would slowly approach protein malnutrition. As
a result the child's resistance to infection would
decline and the condition would be exacerbated
when complete weaning occurred. As a result, a

*6.5. Redeposited bones found lying in what
appeared to be a skull and crossbones pattern.*

cycle of diarrhea and infectious disease would quickly sap a child's resources and cause
death.

The death certificates for infants in the burial ground recorded that 42 percent of
them died of infectious disease, 8 percent from respiratory disease, 33 percent from
diarrheal disease, and 17 percent from diseases of infancy. Although this information
complemented the excavation data, the certificates alone do not reveal much about the
nutritional status of the population. The death certificates do communicate other things
about these individuals though, and the table from the original project report, modified
slightly, is included here (Table 6.1). First are the names. These were real people, not just
laboratory specimens, even if their lives are something that we unfortunately can know
very little about. What we do know is there was suffering. Daniel Bloxom, for instance,
lost not one but two babies, one in June 1828 and another in 1832. That same year John
Edwards appears to have lost his wife, Sarah, and their eleven-day-old baby, both to

Table 6.1. Board of Health Records, 1825–42, for Interments in the First African Baptist Church Cemetery, Philadelphia, Pennsylvania (from Parrington et al. 1987)

Date	Name	Age	Sex	Cause of death
June 1825	Sara Johnson	6 mos.	F	Cholera infantum
June 1825	Nancy Johnson	40 yrs.	F	Liver inflammation
February 1826	Margaret George	26 yrs	F	Lung inflammation
February 1826	Isaac White	20 yrs.	M	Catharral fever
February 1826	Julia Johnson	32 yrs.	F	Consumption
February 1826	George Cooper	3 days	M	Hemorrhage
March 1826	Amelia White	17 yrs.	F	Consumption
April 1826	Amelia Lee	51 yrs.	F	Lung inflammation
April 1826	Ann Buller	49 yrs.	F	Mania a patu
April 1826	Eliza Shelds	45 yrs.	F	Epilepsy
June 1826	Lewis Johnson	32 yrs.	M	Consumption
June 1826	Emery Warren's infant daughter	1 yr. 5 mos.	F	Pertussis
July 1826	Mary Wood	53 yrs.	F	Dropsy
July 1826	Maria Ferrel	34 yrs.	F	Consumption/phthisis
July 1826	Helen Jane Johnson	3 mos.	F	Cholera
July 1826	Mary Keel	6 mos.	F	Cholera
August 1826	Mary Eliza Mitchell	3 yrs.	F	Atrophy
October 1826	Peter Aberdeen	62 yrs.	M	Scrofula
October 1826	Moses Bayard	30 yrs.	M	Mania a patu
October 1826	Male child of Louisia and Louis Napoleon	—	M	Stillborn
October 1826	Male child of Louisia and Lewis Napoleon	3 wks.	M	Debility
October 1826	Sarah Hagerman	49 yrs.	F	Colic/Crampcolic
December 1826	Clarissa Warmley	30 yrs.	F	Consumption
December 1826	Henry Thompson	6 mos.	M	Debility
February 1828	Elizabeth McKell	3 mos.	F	Enteritis
March 1828	Joseph Poulson	90 yrs.	M	Variola
June 1828	William Barger	2 1/2 yrs.	M	Hydrocephalus
June 1828	Daniel Bloxom's child	2 mos.	M	Marasmus
June 1828	Mrs. Scarber Harman	70 yrs.	F	Smallpox
July 1828	Lucretia Johnson	8 mos.	F	Diarrhoea
July 1828	Albert Peter Daily	10 mos.	M	Measles
September 1828	Hesiah West	26	M	Bilious fever
October 1828	Annabella Burton	14	F	Hydsuphalus interneus
April 1829	Da. of Wm. Draper	2 yrs.	F	Peritoneal inflammation
July 1829	Benjamin Waters	75 yrs.	M	Dropsy
November 1829	Charlotte Henry's child	5 days	F	Fits
November 1829	Asciela Brown	30 yrs.	F	Unknown

Date	Name	Age	Sex	Cause of death
February 1831	Abraham Depee	52 yrs.	M	Hernia
October 1831	John Reynolds	46 yrs.	M	Dropsy or ascites
October 1832	Daniel Bloxom's child	—	—	Stillborn
November 1832	Sarah Edwards	31 yrs.	F	Smallpox
November 1832	John Edwards's child	11 days	—	Smallpox
November 1832	James Holman's child	2 yrs	—	Lung inflammation
November 1832	Solomon Carter	29 yrs.	M	Phthisis pulmonalus
August 1836	Eliza Buntick	32 yrs.	F	Remitting fever
August 1836	Julianna Haines	6 mos.	F	Diarrhoea
February 1837	Samuel Longpoint	51 yrs.	M	Pulmonary hemorrhage
August 1837	Cornelius Sinclair	56 yrs.	M	Cholera morbus
August 1837	Roseanna Landerslay	40 yrs.	F	Fever
October 1837	Michael Butler	65 yrs.	M	Debility & disease of the bladder
October 1837	Sarah Seaton	2 yrs.	M	Measles
October 1837	Infant daughter of Isaac Smith	6 mos.	F	Diarrhoea
October 1837	Jane Singleton	65 yrs.	F	Lung inflammation
January 1838	Mary Nutts	55 yrs.	F	Remittent fever
January 1838	Samuel Swan	22 yrs.	M	Enteritis
August 1838	Martha Johnson	11 mos.	F	Lung disease
April 1839	Mary Douglass	3 yrs.	F	Convulsions
April 1839	Jemima Reed	36 yrs.	F	Parturition
June 1839	James Anderson	94 yrs.	M	Old age, born Africa
June 1839	Helen W. Keen	9 yrs.	F	Heart disorder
October 1841	Phebe A. Peters	35 yrs.	F	Sudden from habitual intemperance
November 1841	Mary Ann Prince	30 yrs.	F	Consumption
November 1841	John Becket	18 yrs.	M	Pulmonary consumption
January 1842	Mary A. Hurt	10 mos.	F	Pulmonary catarrh
January 1842	Sarah Miller	40 yrs.	F	Carcinomic uteri
January 1842	Philip F. Power	48 yrs.	M	Phthisis pulmonalis
March 1842	Sarah J. Fitterman	4 yrs.	F	Marasmus
April 1842	Mr. Collins	56 yrs.	M	Abdominal dropsy
May 1842	Mary Smith	68 yrs.	F	Haemophthisis
June 1842	Joshua Johnson	86 yrs.	M	Old age
June 1842	Pamela Jones	21 yrs.	F	Phthisis
June 1842	Anna B. Johnson	10 mos.	F	Pertussis
June 1842	Sarah Lecomb	20 yrs.	F	Phthisis pulmonalis
July 1842	Robinette Harman	9 mos.	F	Whooping cough
July 1842	Phyllis Hart	85 yrs.	F	Old age
July 1842	Elizabeth Thompson	2 mos.	F	Marasmus
September 1842	Daniel Burton	40 yrs.	M	Heart & lung disease

smallpox. James Anderson, born in Africa, lived to be ninety-four, which means he had endured the middle passage. At least two of the decedents died in the almshouse.

Tables in the project report give some occupations—washerwoman, porter, stevedore, waiter, dressmaker—and other information about church households.[14] Of 116 households that included church members in 1837, men were listed as laborers (34), seamen, plasterers, coachmen, carters, clothing dealers, waiters (15), porters, coopers, shoemakers, two preachers, and a sexton. There was an iron melter, a blacksmith, a cabinetmaker, a blacking man, a well digger, and a man and wife "in service." Women worked as washers (55), did day work (26), and were servants. There were also a couple of seamstresses, a midwife, a mantua maker, and a teacher. These were hard-working people whose incomes were small and who the burial record tells us were suffering from malnutrition.

Even though the flourishing market that supplied middle- and upper-class tables was only about five blocks away from the Eighth Street burial ground and the community it served, the psychological distances that separated black neighborhoods from white ones had increased dramatically in the first three decades of the nineteenth century. It was a period of what Gary Nash calls rising Negrophobia.[15] Prejudice and hostility toward blacks grew in intensity, along with new theories arguing that "differences between the races were innate and completely resistant to environmental modification." In 1820, according to Nash, thirteen essays were published that described blacks as "uncivilized or wild men, without our [whites'] moral sense."[16] While others have argued that it was competition for jobs that relegated blacks to the lowest rung of the economic hierarchy, Nash emphasizes the climate of anti-black thought and racial tension. In his words, "New entrepreneurs, the founders of textile mills, machine foundries, and boot and shoe manufactories, relied almost entirely on native-born and immigrant whites, freezing the city's free blacks out of the emerging industrial economy."[17]

In addition to job discrimination, there were physical attacks on blacks and black institutions.[18] Black churches were burned and in 1834 a group of whites assaulted blacks at the Flying Horses, an early carousel on South Street. After destroying the horses the assailants set upon black residents, stoning their houses. In 1835 a white crowd hurled boxes of abolitionist literature into the Delaware River with the city's mayor standing by, and in May 1838 what Nash characterizes as "a taunting white crowd several thousand strong" besieged Pennsylvania Hall, a building that had just been completed as a gathering place for abolitionists. It was in this racially charged climate that the offshoot members of the First African Baptist Church lived and died.

The earlier First African Baptist Church population was, in some ways, better off. Attacks on African Americans were less frequent in the 1820s than in the '30s, and the health of the population, it would appear, was somewhat better. The analysis of the burials from the Tenth Street First African Baptist Church was led by Tom Crist and Art

Washburn, two bioanthropologists who went on to do many subsequent projects together. Of the eighty-nine individual skeletons they analyzed, fifty-six (63 percent) were adults and thirty-three were children. Of the adults, eighteen were males and thirty-eight females. The average age at death was forty-six for males and thirty-nine and a half for females, in both cases just a little older than the later population. However, more than 16 percent of the adults from the Tenth Street site lived beyond sixty years (and were probably older than seventy), where only 18 percent had lived past fifty in the later population.[19] Children under sixteen accounted for 37 percent of the interments identified at the Tenth Street site, in contrast to 44 percent in the later cemetery. Tenth Street also included a smaller percentage of infants under six months (12 percent). Contrary to expectation, more fractures were observed in the Tenth Street group than in the later Eighth Street one, and two of the Tenth Street fractures appeared to result from gunshot wounds. X-rays showed fragments of metal still lodged in the remains of two men, one between fifty-five and fifty-nine years old and the other over sixty. Also surprising was the fact that the earlier population seemed to be less interested in expressing its African roots than the later one. John McCarthy, one of the principal investigators for both the Eighth and Tenth Street projects, became fascinated by the cultural remains that were and were not found associated with burials in both cemeteries and developed an explanation that is worth considering in some depth.

Leather shoes had been placed on or close to six of the coffin lids found in the Eighth Street cemetery, and shoe leather or leather fragments were found in three other burials.[20] Coins were found inside eight of the Eighth Street coffins, in most cases near the head. Ceramic plates had been placed on the stomach of the deceased in two burials (Figure 6.6). The only other burial-associated artifacts from Eighth Street were buttons from clothing and shroud pins. Most of the bodies had apparently been wrapped in shrouds. Fewer artifacts were associated with the Tenth Street (earlier) burials. A broken comb, probably made of whalebone, was found with a child five to six years old and a white ball clay pipe stem fragment in the coffin of a middle-aged woman

6.6. Burial with a ceramic plate in the area of the stomach.

Tom Crist and Art Washburn, Partners in Bioanthropology

By the time the Tenth Street First African Baptist Church cemetery was excavated, John Milner Associates was in need of a physical anthropologist. On the recommendation of Ted Rathbone at the University of South Carolina, the firm hired Tom Crist. Although he was only twenty-six years old and working toward a doctorate under Bill Bass, whom he calls the father of forensic anthropology, Crist took the job. He had done a bone-chemistry analysis of thirty-six African-American individuals, looking for trace elements to reconstruct their diet, for his master's thesis, and getting to oversee the analysis of a much larger population was a rare opportunity. Crist, however, was not quite ready to go it alone; his first act was to put together an oversight committee consisting of his thesis adviser, Ted Rathbone, Doug Owsley at the Smithsonian Institution, and Leslie Rankin-Hill, an African-American physical anthropologist at the University of Oklahoma who had worked on the previous African Baptist Church project. Art Washburn, who was studying at Temple University in Philadelphia, where Crist would also enroll, joined the project as a summer job and stayed for the duration.

Owsley taught them how to "score" the remains using a system originally developed by Jerry Rose for Cedar Grove, another African-American cemetery. Using the same system made the First African Baptist Church data comparable with the Smithsonian data. Another player on the project was dentist Myron Goldberg. Although he was particularly interested in the teeth, he offered to X-ray anything that needed to be X-rayed, which was fundamentally everything. Crist and Washburn were determined to create an exhaustive record. They also wanted to be sure that anyone who was interested in looking at the bones be given the opportunity. They sent out a hundred letters to professors around the country inviting them to come to Philadelphia to look at the material. Any studies finished in time would be incorporated into the report; otherwise the visiting scholars could publish wherever they wanted to. Owsley considered the data a gold mine, and any number of other outstanding physical anthropologists—Bruce Rothchild, Peer Moore-Jansen, Richard Janz, Alan Goodman, Amber McDonald, Mary Trudeau, Murray Marks—some with graduate students in tow, came to study a portion of the collection. When the bones were reburied in Eden Cemetery they had been thoroughly analyzed.

In the meantime both Crist and Washburn had finished doctorates and gone on to analyze a number of other cemeteries as a team. In 1997 they looked at 120 burials from a nineteenth-century cemetery in Wilmington, Delaware. They studied two Lutheran family cemeteries—about 80 burials—in Pawtucket, Rhode Island, and a Native American circular burial that included three or four adults and a child in Martha's Vineyard. Back in Philadelphia there was the Second Presbyterian Church cemetery on Independence Mall and the Blockley Alms House cemetery in West Philadelphia, which included 400 burials but no money for analysis. The purpose, they say, is to "look at people whose existence is not thought much about." "Each person," says Crist, "deserves to tell his or her own story. People are not like plates, which break in a limited number of ways. People are not as predictable. Everyone is different."

(forty-five to forty-nine). Fragments of mica associated with a young woman (twenty-five to twenty-nine) may have been portions of a broken mirror. There were also coins in four burials, but they were all instances in which the skeletons had been moved and reburied, and the analysts speculated that the coins were placed in the coffins at the time of reburial. In only one instance were the coins in eye sockets.[21]

McCarthy attributed a possible African meaning to all of the artifacts from the Eighth Street burials. Shoes, he said, might have been thought necessary for a journey. They have also been associated with African-American folk beliefs concerning power over spirits or good luck, and it is said that the burial of a shoe under a full moon will keep the devil away. Coins also may be associated with a journey after death, perhaps back to an African homeland. According to McCarthy, the placement of similar monetary offerings is widely documented in parts of West Africa, where it is generally associated with passage over the river of death to the afterlife.[22]

The plates on the abdomens might have been intended for use in the afterlife; alternatively, they may represent the last plate used by the deceased. McCarthy claims that in parts of the American South and in Africa it was believed that the "energy" or "essence" of the dead was embodied in the objects they last used. The last-used plate would have been buried "in an effort to prevent the deceased's spirit from harming the living." Although McCarthy does not dwell on the broken mirror, which was found in the earlier burial ground, it was suggested in the excavation report that it "had to be covered or broken lest the next person who looked into it also died."[23] It is not clear if this has an African correlate.

McCarthy has proposed that the changing position of blacks in Philadelphia accounts for the revival of African-influenced practices. In his speech at the African-American Museum in 2003 he pointed out that people of African ancestry were only about 10 percent of the city's population at the end of the eighteenth century, and in 1780, when slavery was abolished in the state, the proportion may have been as low as 4 percent. Enslaved

Africans lived in close proximity to their enslavers and households were small, including only one or two enslaved individuals and rarely more than four. In this situation Africans were encouraged to outwardly adapt to the culture of the European-descended majority. As the population grew in the early decades of the nineteenth century, Philadelphia was transformed from a colonial port into an industrial center, and cultural diversification and social distinction were part and parcel of the process. With the influx of newly emancipated slaves from the South, Philadelphia became the largest and most important center of free African-American life in the United States. Differing somewhat from Gary Nash, McCarthy argues that fierce competition for the same unskilled jobs was the cause of resentment between blacks and whites and ultimately violence. The riots that began in the late 1820s and intensified through the '30s took a toll on the African-American community, and McCarthy thinks that in response, people of African descent began to revitalize certain signs and symbols of African ethnic identity. They did what other groups have done in similar situations.[24] They strengthened their own sense of community by reviving practices that were specific to them.

For McCarthy this explains why it was in the later First African Baptist Church cemetery rather than in the earlier one that the most symbolic items were found. It is also true, however, that the later cemetery belonged to the offshoot of the original First African Baptist Church and one of the reasons for the split was resentment in the congregation of members who had "country" ways. With pressure on the African-American community, and an interest in preserving its good standing in Philadelphia, some members of the original First African Baptist Church were apparently uncomfortable with and embarrassed by their newly arrived brethren from the South. There had been name calling where "some of those coloured people have threatened to stab, or shoot, any man who dare to call them slaves," and there were fights including one instance in which one of the Simmons brothers was shot in the leg.[25] The group that left had obviously been made to feel very unwelcome, and once on their own they could practice as they pleased. It is notable that the offshoot church was not embraced by the First Baptist Church of Philadelphia. This mute evidence suggests the dissension that was prevalent in Philadelphia in this period, even within a group that was already being discriminated against.

Life in the Free Black Community

The excavation of burial grounds is, of course, about the dead, but it is also about the living. The First African Baptist Church Cemetery projects led to finding out about this lively community of free blacks, about the feistiness it took to found not one but two independent congregations, and the people who founded them. While the bones tell us more about how these people died than how they lived, other artifacts were recovered along the Vine Street corridor that speak to their lives, or at least the lives of their cultural descendants. Between 1987 and 1991 John Milner Associates monitored and conducted limited excavations on seventeen blocks during the reconstruction of the Vine Street Expressway. One of the blocks, Block 20, was the same block that was used by the First African Baptist Church congregation for its burial ground between 1810 and 1822, but after that time it became residential. In 1823 a man named William Jones created an alley that ran east from Tenth Street and north into the center of the former church property (Figure 6.7). Calling this development Liberty Court, he built seven three-story houses on the eastern side of the leg of the alley that ran north, three trinities on the south side of the east–west running street, and two trinities on the north side of the entrance off Tenth Street. Trinities are a Philadelphia phenomenon. They are tiny houses consisting of three rooms, one on top of another. African Americans occupied Mr. Jones's development, which meant that it was their privies and wells that cut through the graves of their ancestors. The artifacts from two of those privies provide a glimpse into the everyday lives of the African Americans who lived there in the 1840s.

While the upwardly mobile residents of Market Street were sipping their tea from blue transfer-printed cups and displaying their gilded monogrammed teapot for company, the residents of Liberty Court chose more colorful wares. Features 1 and 2, privies located in the rear yards of two trinity houses on the east side of Liberty Court, were not

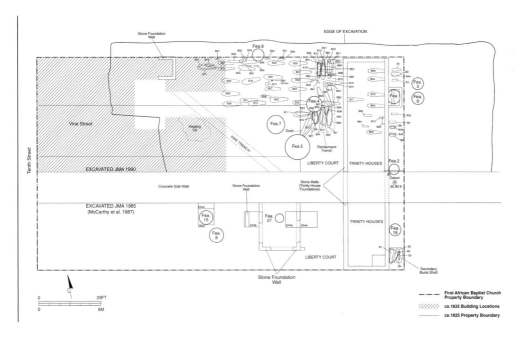

6.7. Diagram of Block 20 on the Vine Street Expressway project.

excavated stratigraphically (that is, layer by layer) due to limits on time, but the ceramic assemblages from the features revealed a distinctive taste for multicolored rather than plain or blue and white dishes. In Feature 1, for instance, eleven of the thirty-nine dishes recovered (28 percent) that were used for eating (plates of different sizes and bowls) were neither white nor blue and white, whereas the Everlys on Market Street during the same period (the 1830s) used mostly plain or blue and white dishes. For tea the difference was even greater: of the thirty-seven pieces of teaware reclaimed from the Feature 1 African-American household (or households), twenty-six (or 70 percent) were neither white nor blue and white. Nearly half (sixteen of thirty-four) of the Everlys' teas were hand-painted blue and white Chinese porcelain. The pattern for Feature 2 was a little different. Although most of the tablewares were either plain (23 percent) or blue and white (29 percent blue edge-decorated and 35 percent blue transfer printed), all thirteen of the serving vessels were multicolored. There were also some colorful teawares, with thirty-one out of seventy-eight vessels (40 percent) being neither plain nor blue and white.

In a study of ceramic assemblages recovered from colonies or former colonies of Britain, Susan Lawrence has noted significant differences.[26] Whereas the trend toward a preference for white ceramics is undeniable for America, at least among the middle class, colorful transfer-printed ceramics were preferred elsewhere (examples are drawn from Australia and South Africa, in particular). She suggests that these preferences do not mean that individuals or communities failed to "modernize"; rather, they indicate a "different cultural system at work."[27] It is likewise possible that the African-American families who lived on Block 20 in the 1830s and '40s made different choices than the upwardly mobile merchants who lived on Market Street as an expression of their own cultural system. They were also concerned with setting a respectable table, with matching plates and teawares and a variety of serving dishes, including bowls of different sizes, platters, vegetable dishes, and soup tureens, but the combinations and especially the colors would have been different than the less colorful combinations on the tables of their Market Street neighbors.

Glass artifacts associated with the Block 20 African-American households included wine bottles and case bottles, wine glasses and tumblers, but also found were salt dishes, a vase, and glass stoppers, possibly for pharmaceutical bottles. Fragments from a glass chandelier suggest that the trinity associated with Feature 1 may have been small, but it had a chandelier, and besides the chandelier there were flower pots and a ceramic figurine wearing a blue hat. The toothbrushes in the assemblage indicate a concern with hygiene; there were washbasins and, of course, chamber pots. For women there were tortoiseshell hair ornaments, perfume bottles, and a bone ring one and a half inches in diameter that might have been a pessary (a contraceptive device that has been seen on other mid-nineteenth-century sites).[28] Plenty of residents smoked; lots of clay pipes came from both

Quality over Quantity: Shoemaking in Nineteenth-Century Philadelphia

Archaeologist Helen (Linny) Schenck analyzed the leather from the Vine Street corridor project in the context of what was known about the nineteenth-century shoemaking industry. Rather than trying to compete with Lynn, Massachusetts, which was a center of shoemaking from the eighteenth century on and was specializing in cheap mass-produced shoes by the middle of the nineteenth century, Philadelphia shoemakers focused on the more lucrative quality end of the market. According to Schenck, this was possible for two reasons: high-quality raw materials were readily available in Philadelphia, and there was a supply of skilled (and willing) labor in the immediate vicinity of where the raw materials were being produced. The Northern Liberties, an industrial district just north of the Vine Street corridor, was the center for the production of Moroccan kid leather, using a technique learned from European-trained tanners in the early nineteenth century. Stronger and more supple than traditional leathers, Moroccan kid was considered more suitable for making quality shoes. The Philadelphia region's own leather was also considered superior due to the use of oak bark in the tanning process rather than the hemlock bark that was used in New York and New England. By 1857 there were twenty-five firms in the Northern Liberties that made Moroccan kid, accounting for $1 million worth of business and producing nearly one-third of the United States' total production.

Many if not most of the leather workers in the Northern Liberties were German immigrants, but African Americans were also heavily involved in the industry. In contrast to Lynn, which expanded its workforce by turning to part-time farmer-shoemakers, Philadelphia drew on its own urban population. However, the mass-produced shoes from New England were cheaper, and Philadelphia's master cordwainers attempted to control prices and regulate the quantity of lower-quality goods coming into the market. The shoes recovered from the features in the Vine Street corridor suggest that Philadelphians were not entirely faithful to their hometown product. The shoes from a privy dating to 1835–45 on Block 31, located between Fifteenth and Sixteenth Streets, included one brogue, a mass-produced pegged shoe probably from New England, as well as a handmade shoe most likely made in Philadelphia. Shoes and leather fragments from features on Block 5, located between Second and Third Streets, also included both hand-stitched and pegged examples. The shoes from Feature 1 (1850–61) were mainly hand stitched (of thirty shoe parts only two had been pegged), but all twenty-one of the shoe parts from Feature 4 (1850–67) were pegged. Toes were squared or gently rounded and heel lifts were higher than from shoes dating to the first half of the nineteenth century.

> It wasn't until 1880 that Philadelphia introduced power machinery into the shoe industry, not because the industry was backward, says Schenck, but because the machinery didn't produce quality shoes until then. As with so many things in Philadelphia, it was quality that counted most.

features, most of them with fluted bowls, the least expensive variety available in this period. No matter how limited their resources, these residents, who were mainly unskilled laborers, provided their children with toys—there were clay marbles and a doll's head—and writing slates and pencils.

The Block 20 features and others along the Vine Street corridor produced fascinating evidence relating to the leather industry. Two hundred scraps of leather were recovered from Feature 1, many of them identifiable parts of shoes. Feature 2 yielded 1,715 fragments of leather, 1,373 of them offcuts and trimming fragments. Clearly shoes were being manufactured on Liberty Court or very close by. The fragments recovered suggest that the shoemakers in the neighborhood were, like others in Philadelphia, still stitching their shoes by hand. Only 3 of the 158 recognizable examples of shoe parts from Feature 2 showed evidence of pegging. More typical were leather outsoles or fragments with stitching channels on the under surface (10) or fragments of leather soles with a unique stitching pattern of fifteen to sixteen holes per inch.

The food remains from the Block 20 features were tantalizing but too fragmentary to supply a detailed picture of what the African-American families living on the block were eating. They were definitely not having what the Everlys on Market Street, or the Turnbulls and Ogles on North Sixth, had. There were no wild birds among the bones recovered, no evidence of the kinds of things that might have served as first courses in a multicourse meal. There was fish, although the remains were not identified to the species level, and there were plenty of clams and oysters. The meat in the diet of these residents appeared to basically come from domesticated cows, pigs, and sheep. In both Features 1 and 2 there were significant numbers of bones from pigs' heads, and evidence of butchering on these bones indicated they were being consumed.[29] There were also pigs' feet and lots of vertebral and rib fragments. The few chickens identified appeared to be whole, suggesting they may have been raised on the lot.

What cannot be discerned from the excavated remains is how these people felt about the ancestors that lay buried beneath their backyards. Is it only our present perspective that makes it seem peculiar that people would be comfortable living on top of a graveyard? Block 20 is not unique in this respect. The African Burial Ground in New York

City was also covered and built over in the nineteenth century, and there was evidence there, too, of privy pits knowingly being dug right through graves (Figure 6.8). Although no bones were arranged in a skull and crossbones pattern in New York, piles of bones were found next to the pits that disturbed them. Space was at a premium in both cities in the nineteenth century, and workers were increasingly crowded into tightly packed neighborhoods. Perhaps the need for a place to live was more important than what had come before. Or, perhaps, there was comfort in living near the ancestors. We will never know for sure, but we do know a little bit more about the people who worshipped at the First African Baptist Church, and those who later lived on top of their graves, than we did before the excavations began. In death and in life African Americans in nineteenth-century Philadelphia developed distinctive ways of doing things. At least some of their burial customs referred to their African roots, and instead of choosing the same dishes as their European-American neighbors they chose more colorful ones. As discrimination against them increased, it would seem, African Americans found ways to express their solidarity with the others in their own community.

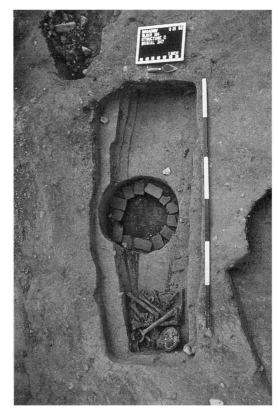

6.8. Privy cut through a grave site at the African Burial Ground in New York City. (Photograph by Dennis Seckler)

CHAPTER SEVEN

On the Waterfront

Like so many cities in the United States, Philadelphia destroyed its historic waterfront in the rage to connect to the interstate highway system in the 1970s. Bypassing the downtown, I-95 follows the course of Water Street, historically called Swanson, which ran along the riverbank. When the highway was built, though, there was more land between Water Street and the Delaware River because the old wharves had been filled in to create land extending out into the river. Many of the buildings that were taken down for the highway stood on this "made" land, and buried beneath them were remnants of the wharves that once served the thriving port of Philadelphia (Figure 7.1).

Two archaeological projects that postdate the construction of I-95 exposed remnants of the early waterfront. One, to the north of Vine Street in an area known as the Northern Liberties and currently experiencing a renaissance, revealed the remains of several eighteenth-century wharves and an early-nineteenth-century slipway, a kind of track that allowed boats to be dragged out of the water for repair. The second, to the south of South Street in an area known historically as Southwark and now connected with the Penn's Landing development along the river, exposed the remains of five wharves and numerous features related to nineteenth-century domestic occupation. Both of these projects, one done in 1987 and the other in 1988, produced dramatic results, but they have gone unappreciated for different reasons. Work on the site of the slipway, commonly called the Hertz Lot, was not reported until 2006 although it got a good deal of publicity while it was being investigated. Results from the Meadows Site, just south of Penn's Landing, are buried in a not easily accessible technical report that was completed in 1993.

New threats to the old waterfront make it particularly important to remember what wasn't destroyed by the construction of I-95. With the coming of casino gambling—two casinos are proposed on the banks of the Delaware—the development of Penn's Landing is again in the news, and postponed plans for a world

7.1. The waterfront bordering the Delaware River, on land created with fill. The Hertz Lot excavation is in the foreground; the Benjamin Franklin Bridge is at far right, and Pier 19 faces the east side of Delaware Avenue and stretches out into the river.

trade center have resurfaced. Three men with a special interest in the area where the slipway was found—the Hertz Lot—are making an effort to prevent the site from being developed by the Penn's Landing Corporation, but the corporation, which has had a hard time coming up with a workable development plan for its prime real estate, cannot fail forever. There is plenty to worry about and the three men, calling themselves the West Shipyard Group, are preparing for battle.

I met these men—Stuart Harting, Andy Sackstetter, and James Quilligan—at a picnic in 2000 or so. They were already thinking about making the Hertz Lot into an archaeological park and they wanted to share their ideas with the archaeological community. Quilligan, who lives in the neighborhood, which is familiarly known as River's Edge, took us on a walking tour. The neighborhood consists of several blocks tucked up against the embankment of I-95 on the river side (Figure 7.2). A remnant of Front Street still runs along the edge of the bluff in this location, the highway having been built slightly to the west. This is the only area where the bluff that William Penn envisioned would forever support his "green country town" still exists, and there is a staircase dating to the eighteenth century that goes down to the land below (Figure 7.3). A line of old rowhouses clings to the east side of Front Street, some apparently including parts, at least, of their eighteenth-century fabric. This is one of several pockets of houses that survived the construction of I-95, but all of them are unpleasantly close to the highway.

Although it is clear why Quilligan and Sackstetter are both interested in preventing major development on the Hertz Lot—their houses overlook the site—Harting's interest is a little more mysterious. He is a developer who once owned the lot immediately to

7.2. *River's Edge neighborhood in relation to the Hertz site area, which is visible between Delaware Avenue (foreground) and Water Street. The River's Edge houses face Water Street and the Hertz Lot; on the other side, Front Street (mostly hidden behind the buildings) sits just below Interstate 95 near the top of the photograph and is crossed at right by Callowhill Street.*

(left) 7.3. Staircase down the original bluff.

the north, where the trade center is slated to be built. Developer or not, he exudes an interest in Philadelphia's history and claims to want to leave something behind besides the many properties throughout the city he and his partner have developed. His vision is to set up a long-term archaeological research program that would investigate the portion of the Hertz land that was not touched by the work in 1987. The location includes West's Shipyard, which was constructed in 1676, six years *before* William Penn arrived, and possibly the Penny Pot House, a tavern—supposedly the city's first. Besides research, the group envisions historically themed activities, exhibits, and probably businesses—a sort of Colonial Williamsburg in the making. First, however, they need to convince enough politicians that their vision is a legitimate basis for assuming control of the land.

With a grant from Stuart Harting in 2006, John Milner Associates finished a draft report on the 1980s archaeological investigation of the Hertz Lot, to provide the group with some ammunition. The excavation was directed by Carmen Weber, then the city archaeologist for the Philadelphia Historical Commission. When she left the commission in 1988, the report had been drafted, but it was never produced. Once its component parts were relocated, JMA put them together. Weber considers the excavation a kind of climax to her career. She no longer does archaeology, which is too bad because she was very good.

7.4. Meadows Site showing an area excavation. The I-95 embankment is in the background; the upright pilings supported a nineteenth-century wall that covered an earlier wharf, visible as cross timbers on either side. (Courtesy of Ed Morin)

The other waterfront site, known as the Meadows, was excavated by another talented archaeologist, Ed Morin, who was then working for Louis Berger and Associates. Morin had investigated several waterfront sites in lower Manhattan in the 1970s and brought his experience to bear in Philadelphia. He knew you couldn't learn what you needed to know if you didn't move lots of dirt, and he designed the excavation to horizontally expose large areas (Figure 7.4). This was a departure from the usual test trenches and individual excavation units, but it was appropriate to the task and produced stunning results. But first, to the Hertz Lot.

Quilligan's Walk Through River's Edge

James Quilligan moved from West Philadelphia to River's Edge in 1998. A political economist who focuses on international monetary policy and has contacts all over the world, Quilligan took an immediate interest in his tiny adopted neighborhood. Of the three members of the West Shipyard Group, Quilligan played the role of historian. Walking up Front Street, he brought the old neighborhood into focus.

Callowhill Street crosses Front where Pool's Hill used to be and just beyond a creek (Pegg's Run), a kind of "spiritual center," he said. The present-day Willow Street follows the course of the filled-in creek. There used to be a gate at Front and Noble Streets, and when the British controlled the city during the Revolutionary War they wouldn't let anyone in. Delilah's Den now stands on the site of Daniel Pegg's house, which Quilligan claimed was there before Penn arrived and which Penn wanted, but couldn't persuade its owner to relinquish.

The first bridge over the creek was built in 1747, the second in the 1820s. The creek went all the way to Twelfth Street, and some people thought it should be continued as a canal to the Schuylkill River, but the railroad made the connection instead. The

Modern-day re-creation of the Penny Pot House.

Willow Street Station, unfortunately replaced by a twentieth-century warehouse, was on the west side of Front Street, and from the station a traveler walked to the Vine Street Landing (immediately south of the Hertz Lot) to catch the ferry to New Jersey.

Slater's Wharf was alongside Callowhill Street or along the creek. A man named Breton owned it after Slater and built himself a mansion, which stood until the middle of the twentieth century. It was probably the oldest house in the neighborhood at that time, because in 1850 a huge fire had burned all the houses along Front Street south of Callowhill—as many as 247 of them—bringing fire companies from as far away as Baltimore and New York. Perhaps that's when the market on Callowhill disappeared. It was in the swale (now under I-95) to the west of Front Street. Taverns and brothels lined Callowhill on the other (water) side of Front.

Gleaned from a number of sources and sifted through Quilligan's memory, what was most extraordinary about his walk through the neighborhood was that there was nothing left to see of all this—nothing, except in your mind's eye. Another resident, however, has built a piece of the past from his own imagination. Al Johnson, an architect who first bought the block where Quilligan lives, thinks his house stands on the site of the old Penny Pot House tavern. In its honor, he built a facsimile of the tavern at the top of his house. He, too, wants to know what still lies beneath the Hertz Lot, and from his version of the Penny Pot he will have a very good view.

The Hertz Lot

The Hertz Lot, named for the car rental company that maintained offices there in the 1970s, consisted of open parking space and two standing structures. The tract covered an area that historically encompassed eight properties that stretched 250 feet between Front Street and the river (Figure 7.5). James West ran his boatyard on the southernmost of these properties, where, according to his account book (1676–1705), he bartered the repair of vessels for goods, such as cider and beer, items undoubtedly used to stock the Penny Pot House tavern. James's son, Charles, who took over from his father in 1701, was a boat builder. A document from 1740 describes an agreement with John Reynells to build "a Square Stern Ship or Vessell . . . [with a] Fifty-five foot Keel . . . Twenty one foot Breadth."[1] To the north of West's shipyard in the eighteenth century was William Rakestraw's ropewalk and a series of shipyards, one owned by Michael Hewlings, another by William Taylor, and still another by the Lynn family. By the beginning of the nineteenth century the Lynn parcels were owned by Isaac Hazlehurst, and Samuel Shoemaker owned the lot bordering Callowhill Street at the northern end of the block. Weber's archaeological test trenches spanned the Taylor and Hazlehurst properties.

Initial test trenches uncovered the interior of a bulkhead wall eight to nine feet below the present surface along the northern edge of the property that belonged to Taylor's boatyard in the 1760s (Figure 7.6). The bulkhead ran parallel to the shoreline and was constructed of pine timbers, some with the bark still attached, connected with half-lap joints (Figure 7.7 illustrates joinery techniques). The fill inside the bulkhead was a mixture of gray and brown sand and gravel, which Weber speculated had come from nearby undeveloped areas along the Delaware shoreline. Among the few diagnostic artifacts

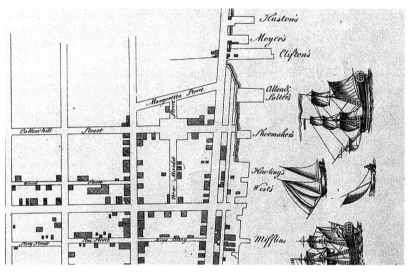

7.5. *Detail from the Clarkson and Biddle map of 1762. The eight historic properties that made up the Hertz Lot in the eighteenth century fell between Shoemaker's Wharf (at the foot of Callowhill Street) and West's Wharf (just above Vine Street).*

found was a square lead token, marked with an "X." According to Ivor Noel Hume, these tokens were used as merchandise counters in waterfront business transactions during the eighteenth century.[2]

A second bulkhead that was uncovered ran perpendicular, rather than parallel, to the shore, and appeared to be an extension to the earlier wharf. It consisted of five courses of timbers also held together with half-lap joints, and connected to the earlier wharf with a "dead man" that in turn was held together with a wooden treenail or peg. The fill inside this later bulkhead was also gray and brown sand and gravel mixed with eighteenth-century ceramic sherds and a few nails. A layer of black silt topped with oyster shells covered the sand fill. The black silt, which apparently constituted the wharf surface, included more artifacts, bricks, cobblestones, non-local limestone, and flint nodules. Weber thought the material probably came from ship ballast acquired in England and the tropics.[3] The ceramic sherds from this fill dated later in the eighteenth century than those found inside the earlier bulkhead, and there were also machine-headed nails and a flat brass button that were manufactured in the early years of the nineteenth century. An early-nineteenth-century slipway, or ship's way, was attached to the late-eighteenth-century wharf and extended toward the river (Figure 7.8). It was the slipway that was the most important find on the Hertz Lot site.

According to *The Compact Edition of the Oxford English Dictionary,* a slipway is "a sloping way leading down into the water, a slip." *The Mariner's Dictionary* from 1805 defines a slipway as "a place lying with a gradual descent on the banks of a river, or harbor, convenient for ship-building." Weber thought the definition from *The Modern System of Naval Architecture,* published in 1865, fit the slipway found on the Hertz Lot best:

7.6. Bulkhead at the northern edge of Taylor's boatyard.

(right) 7.7. Joinery techniques. (From Weber 2006, redrawn by Rob Schultz)

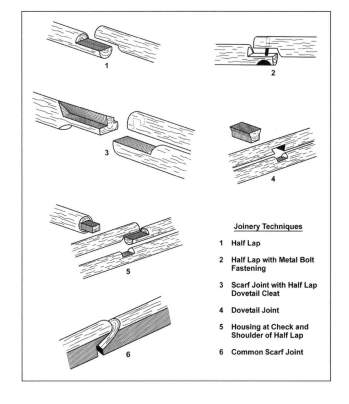

Joinery Techniques

1   **Half Lap**

2   **Half Lap with Metal Bolt Fastening**

3   **Scarf Joint with Half Lap Dovetail Cleat**

4   **Dovetail Joint**

5   **Housing at Check and Shoulder of Half Lap**

6   **Common Scarf Joint**

7.8. The slipway.

The lower line of support, or ways, forms nothing more than a kind of railroad, serving to conduct the ship into the water. They are laid perfectly smooth, even, parallel, and continuous, down the shore into the water; but, as they have heavy weight to carry, and may have great pressure to endure, they have to be laid on good foundation, and have to be carefully maintained there by cross pieces, which keep them perfectly parallel to one another. If the bottom be rock, or even good gravel, the ways, of them-selves, being stout logs of 18 inches to 2 feet square, will sufficiently carry the weight; but, if not, the ways must rest on transverse logs of timber, to embrace a large surface of ground, and great precaution must be taken to lay the ways straight, to keep them in their place true, and to carry them up strong and sound.[4]

As described in Weber's report, the Hertz Lot slipway consisted of two parallel wooden tracks, or ways, situated between two bulkheads or walls that sloped down to the water. Built with hand-hewn, finished pine timbers, the construction technique for the slipway differed from those used in the eighteenth-century wharves, and it was recorded by the Historic American Engineering Record (HAER). One side of the way was anchored against the exterior of the eighteenth-century wharf bulkhead, but the other side stood nine feet away and consisted of a three-course bulkhead wall held together with common scarf joints and wrought-iron spikes. The wall ended approximately seventy-five feet from the top of the slipway, and the eighteenth-century bulkhead continued toward the river.[5]

The excavation exposed 83 feet of the slipway, including the top, or shore end. Elevation readings, taken at 10-foot intervals, showed that it had a slope of 1 vertical foot to 15.6 feet horizontally. The slope became shallower nearer the river. The presence of a sewer conduit precluded excavating the slipway all the way to its lower end, but the geologic borings conducted prior to the excavation revealed that it extended at least 5 feet beyond the portion exposed by the dig.

A supporting timber that may have served as a footway rested along each side of the slip. This squared timber was part of the bulkhead construction on the north side, where striations, probably from rope wear, were still visible. There were ten uprights along the south side that were attached with iron spikes to the earlier wharf bulkhead (Figure 7.9). The footway sat against the bottom of these uprights, and as it ascended out of the river, it rose above the surface of the

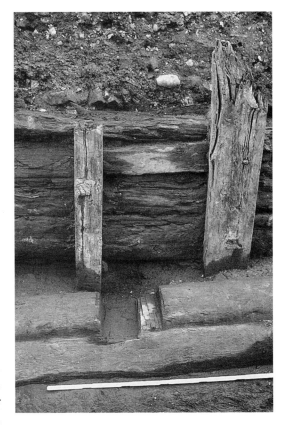

7.9. Late-eighteenth-century bulkhead and slipway uprights.

eighteenth-century wharf. Three timbers had been extended end to end to produce a continuous footway on either side. The timbers were interrupted approximately 5 feet from the end of the way and stopped altogether 2.5 feet from the end.

The two tracks, or ways, sat between 2.4 and 3.2 feet apart. They were attached to the bottom of the footways and supported by transverse timbers up to 3 feet in diameter. The excavation uncovered three support timbers. Grooves in the rounded beams that composed the ways demonstrated that they formed the base for some type of carriage or cradle, which supported vessels as they came out of, or slid into, the river. Reuse of the running ways was evident in the unevenness in the grooved track and a repair in one area.

A very dark gray sandy silt filled the bottom of the slip. The silt contained a good deal of organic material, including wood refuse, and artifacts. Weber interpreted this deposit as harbor bottom, probably created by tidal action along the river that washed material up into the bottom of the way. The artifacts recovered from the silt thus relate to the period during and immediately after the use of the slipway. They included eighteenth-century ceramic sherds—creamware, pearlware, Chinese porcelain—some handwrought nails and spikes, in addition to well-preserved leather, mainly shoes, some wooden objects, and datable copper and brass buttons. The buttons spanned the period from 1790 to 1830, providing the best available dates for when the slipway was in use. Copper nails, a wooden and brass boat-maker's rule, a wooden-handled chisel, and hair used as caulking reflected the slipway's function in the repair of boats.

The distance between the ways suggested that the vessels the slip accommodated were probably no more than fifty feet long. Weber and her colleagues speculated that they were the kinds of sloops or small schooners that sailed the Delaware River and smaller streams ferrying goods and passengers across the river or to larger vessels moored farther out, although they occasionally plied the coastal and even trans-Atlantic trade.[6] The Hertz Lot slipway would have provided an efficient means for repairing these small, ordinary vessels and was very likely a successful business venture. The question is whose business was it and who designed the slipway?

According to Weber's research, the earliest known reference to a way similar to the one uncovered at the Hertz Lot was one that Commodore John Rodgers designed for the Navy Yard in Washington, D.C., for hauling up the frigate *Potomac*.[7] Rodgers recommended that the United States Navy build marine railways, or inclined planes, to use in repairing its fleet. In 1823, President James Monroe supported Rodgers's proposal, but he also noted that to date no docks or ways had been built.

In 1827 the fledgling Franklin Institute in Philadelphia created a committee to report on the American Marine Rail-way, patented as "the Rail-way Dock" by John Thomas, a naval architect with twenty years of experience as a shipwright in the naval dock yards at Plymouth, England. Construction of this railway by Thomas for a group of merchants in New York City occurred in the years 1826–27. The committee report states:

> The object of the rail-way dock, is to take the ship, as by surprise while afloat, and before she loses the support of the water, to surround her with other supports, give her keel a firm foundation, her bilge a cradle, and her bends a general and substantial shoring. Without the least change of figure from what she had in the water, she is taken out of it, and being put in complete order, is gently returned to her element.[8]

Thomas's marine railway dock used iron rails for the ways and a specially designed cradle to support a vessel upright. Thomas referred to the inclined-plane slip invented by Thomas Morton, constructed in Scotland and used for flat-bottomed vessels, as a prototype for his railway.

The Franklin Institute's committee deemed a marine railway "convenient, expeditious & economical, for the small class of ships of war." They found it "peculiarly adapted to alluvial soils, such as the shores of most of our southern harbours" and "far more economical for our mercantile marine than the old custom of heaving down" (tipping a ship over on its side).[9] However, it is not absolutely clear that the slipway on the Hertz Lot was a true marine railway.

Early-nineteenth-century documents for the property do not refer to the slipway. Weber, however, speculated that it was built by Thomas Leiper. Leiper was an interesting man with his fingers in many pies. With connections in Virginia, he amassed a fortune in the tobacco business. His ledger book covering the years 1803–13 details various transactions with Robert Gamble, who appears to have been his factor in Richmond.[10] There are also mentions of tobacco dealings in Baltimore, Washington, New Orleans, Kentucky, and Tennessee. He apparently had a tobacco warehouse at 9 North Water Street as early as 1774 and eventually moved to Market Street, where he was known as a snuff manufacturer.[11] Much of his correspondence complains about the quality of the tobacco he was receiving, although one suspects that the objections had as much to do with negotiating a good price as with judging the actual product. While he was receiving tobacco from the South, he appears to have been supplying curbstone to various southern cities. An entry on January 20, 1807, for instance, reads, "I am informed [a certain part] is to be paved and curbed next year. My quarries on Crum Creek from the year 1793 to this date have supplied this city with curbstone from 8 to 12,000 feet per annum indeed what has been supplied by others the quantity has been small that it ought not to be mentioned." It was the quarry business that has relevance for the slipway.

Weber thought Leiper might have constructed the slipway because he built one of the first wooden railways in the country between 1809 and 1810. That railway, which was horse powered, carried stone from his quarry to his wharf on Crum Creek, a distance of three-quarters of a mile. Even more significant was the fact that in 1809 Leiper had an experimental track built to convince investors that the principle of a railway would work. The track was laid in the courtyard of the Bull's Head Tavern, "by Poplar Lane in the Northern Liberties"—not far from the Hertz Lot. It was sixty yards long, was graded at one and a half inches to the yard, and had a four-foot-gauge rail track with sleepers, or supports, eight feet apart. To demonstrate its effectiveness, a horse drew a loaded car weighing 10,690 pounds up the incline.[12]

Although tax records do not mention a wharf or slipway on Leiper's waterfront lot until 1835, the 1811 Paxton map identifies number 236 as "Leiper's Wharf" and the configuration on the map suggests the shape of the slipway. Leiper didn't own the property outright until 1815, but he helped establish the Bank of Pennsylvania, which controlled the property from 1810 until 1815, and Weber thought Leiper's connections with the bank might have allowed him to use it as early as 1810. His ledger book covering this period does not mention the slipway, but it doesn't mention the railway at the quarry either, which was successfully built during the same year as the demonstration, in 1809. The railway was a significant feat of engineering at the time, but apparently it was not the kind of thing Leiper bothered to include in his ledger, perhaps because it did not involve a specific business transaction.

What is particularly striking is that the Hertz Lot slipway diverges from the literature of the period, which prescribed either piles or a series of horizontal timbers akin to railroad ties, not the spaced sleepers that were exposed in the excavation. The Hertz slipway thus resembles Leiper's experimental track and wooden railway more than the design that was being recommended.

The slipway was not dismantled during the excavation and, in fact, lies beneath the parking lot that is still undeveloped. The threat remains though, as Philadelphia is experiencing a surge of development. The West Shipyard Group, working closely with the Preservation Alliance of Philadelphia, continues to negotiate for at least a temporary lease on the land that would allow exploratory archaeology in areas that were not examined in the 1980s.

Wharves in Southwark

Along with Kensington, an industrial area in north Philadelphia, Southwark was a center of Philadelphia's shipbuilding industry in the eighteenth century. The Meadows Site, which was investigated when it turned out to be in the path of ramp construction off Route I-95, encompassed five acres along sixteen hundred feet of the city's old waterfront. The site included ten historic lots between Swanson (now Water) Street on the west and Delaware Avenue on the east. According to the Louis Berger and Associates report on the project, the lots were all on "made" land east of Swanson Street, which began as a fifteen-foot-wide tract along the bank of the river.[13] Wharf construction and landfilling advanced progressively farther into the river between 1762 and 1860, when the present shoreline was reached (Figure 7.10). The archaeological challenge in this area was to recover information about early wharf construction and the evolution of the Philadelphia waterfront.

Ed Morin, who directed the work, exposed a large area rather than digging exploratory trenches because without that, he claimed, it wouldn't be possible to distinguish between wharf types. Early wharves were built either parallel to the shoreline, as was the earliest wharf found on the Hertz Lot, or projected out into the water, allowing vessels to load and unload cargo and people on two sides. They were made of timber or stone and were constructed in one of three ways. A crib wharf consisted of rough or square hewn timbers built up one on top of another in alternating rows of headers and stretchers, each notched together in "Lincoln Log" fashion, to form a box-shaped frame. A floor

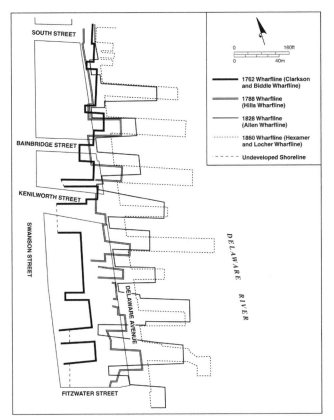

SOUTH STREET

BAINBRIDGE STREET

KENILWORTH STREET

SWANSON STREET

DELAWARE AVENUE

FITZWATER STREET

DELAWARE RIVER

0   160ft
0   40m

1762 Wharfline (Clarkson and Biddle Wharfline)

1788 Wharfline (Hills Wharfline)

1828 Wharfline (Allen Wharfline)

1860 Wharfline (Hexamer and Locher Wharfline)

Undeveloped Shoreline

7.10. Diagram of the Meadows Site between Delaware Avenue and Swanson Street, showing the outline of wharves as the shoreline was gradually extended into the river. (From LeeDecker et al. 1993)

was built up from the bottom, which allowed the crib to sink and settle into the riverbed once it was filled with ballast. When the stretcher courses were tightly fitted together so that a finer fill of mud or sand could be used to fill up and sink the crib, the wharf was referred to as a solid-filled type. A cobb-type wharf was an open crib filled with cobblestones. A grillage or raft wharf consisted of several alternating courses of headers and stretchers that were intermittently weighted with stone. Several rafts were stacked one on top of another to form a block, which was probably floated to the desired location and sunk with stone. Morin was interested in wharf technology because in New York, where he had excavated several waterfront sites in the early 1980s, a gradual change in construction techniques had been noted over time, and this was an opportunity to see whether the same held true for Philadelphia.

Because the wharves were eventually buried in the process of infilling new land, it was necessary to open large areas in order to distinguish the wharves from the overlapping courses of logs that were used to support foundations for structures built on top of them. The site covered five acres, encompassing three large areas that were mechanically

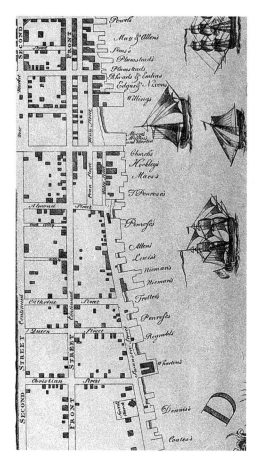

7.11. Detail from the Clarkson and Biddle map of 1762, showing named wharves along the shore. (Historical Society of Pennsylvania)

stripped. Using this method Morin identified five wharves, which were dated by referring to historical maps in combination with the recovery of diagnostic artifacts found in the wharf fills. One of the wharves appeared to be the exterior bulkhead for Lewis Wharf, shown on the Clarkson and Biddle map of 1762 (Figure 7.11). A second, mostly destroyed wharf was found farther north, apparently in the location identified on the Clarkson and Biddle map as "T. Penrose's." A more intact bulkhead was found immediately south of it in the location marked simply "Penrose's" on the map.

When it was first exposed, the Penrose bulkhead consisted of two courses of round logs and four cross logs oriented east–west. The bulkhead eventually turned out to contain seven courses of round logs (some with intact bark); it was eight feet high and forty-four and a half feet long. The logs were spliced together with half-lap joints and secured with wrought-iron barbed spikes. The tops and bottoms of each log had been hewn flat to make a tighter fit. A number of cross logs extended ten to twelve feet northward from the bulkhead's face into a series of pilings that supported a schist wall associated with a late-nineteenth-century building. The fill inside the bulkhead consisted of sand, gravel, and large river cobbles. It wasn't possible to determine whether the walls created a "closed" (crib) structure, but the presence of a southern bulkhead section and the cross logs suggested that the wharf also had a northern bulkhead.

As described by the investigators, the bulkhead was supported by a system of pilings and braces on both its eastern and western ends. At the eastern end several pilings had been placed on either side of several tieback braces to keep them from shifting. The braces were fitted to the exterior face of the bulkhead with mortise-and-tenon joints and extended approximately eight feet into the surrounding fill. Their southern ends were secured by metal pins to deadmen placed roughly parallel to the bulkhead. Like the backbraces, they were also supported on either side by pilings, creating a configuration that acted in concert with the cross logs to counteract the tendency of the fill to push the bulkhead inward.

The Penrose Wharf appeared on the 1788 John Hills map and was probably an extension of an earlier wharf in that location that was shown on the 1762 Clarkson and Biddle map. Even more dramatic than the wharf was the remnant of the Penrose Landing that was uncovered. In an area between the wharves of Isaac and Samuel Penrose, trenching uncovered a massive hand-hewn timber running north–south underneath two feet of fill. A forty-by-seventy-foot area was eventually exposed that revealed additional hewn timbers oriented in the same direction. The timbers, set in clay and an organic deposit of wood chips, had wood stakes placed at each end as a means of support. They appeared to form a series of steps that gradually descended toward the Delaware River (Figure 7.12). One-by-fifteen-foot planks were placed in a line at the northwest end of the timbers. Presumably the planks functioned as a walkway.

The Penroses were a prominent shipbuilding family. Bartholomew Penrose had carried on a shipbuilding business in Bristol, England, before emigrating to Philadelphia in about 1700. His shipyard was located on the banks of the Delaware River at Market Street. His grandson, Thomas, who was probably the owner of the wharf excavated, lived at the southeast corner of Penn and Bainbridge Streets in Southwark, but he also owned a lot forty-seven and a half feet wide to the north, the location of the wharf. Thomas made his living as a shipbuilder and merchant. He was also a leading citizen who signed the Non-Importation Agreement of 1765, served as a port warden from 1766 up to the Revolutionary War, and was one of the forty-three notable men of Philadelphia who served on the Committee of Correspondence assembled in 1774. In what may be an apocryphal story, he is credited with starting the tradition of soup houses in Philadelphia.

7.12. Penrose's Landing, reused timbers that served as steps. (Courtesy of Ed Morin)

7.13. Cannon found in upright position. (Courtesy of Ed Morin)

During a particularly severe winter when the Delaware was so deeply frozen that boats delivering firewood could not sail up the river, leaving much of the population, especially the poor, without a source of warmth, Penrose supposedly converted one of his great glue kettles into a giant soup pot. A "good stomachy soup" was prepared daily in the shipyard and served to the poor. As the story goes, Thomas's son, Charles, also a shipbuilder, presented the old glue kettle to the South House when he finally closed the family shipyard.[14]

The archaeological excavation also turned up a cannon forty feet west of Delaware Avenue on the Penrose property. It appears to have been placed in a vertical position between two north–south timbers (Figure 7.13). Ingrid Wuebber, Berger's historical researcher, found a reference to "planting a cannon" in a survey of Charles Penrose's estate in 1850. The text reads, "planted a cannon within five feet of the wharflot"—which may have been the same cannon that the dig uncovered. Planting cannons along streets near the wharves was apparently an accepted custom, and this one may have been used as a bollard or post for securing a ship's line as part of an early wharf.[15]

Another structure, referred to as the North/South Wharf, was found to the north of the Penrose property. Once the upper two to three feet of rubble fill had been removed from that area, a complex of stone piers, foundation walls, and a series of massive brick piers surrounded by deep foundation walls in the northern section appeared. The stone piers and foundation walls covered an earlier group of stone and brick walls and a number of schist piers on top of wooden pilings that had been driven into the riverbed. Further excavation in the area of the pilings revealed two abutting sections of a massive log bulkhead that formed the south and west walls of a slip. A slip appears in this location on the Hills map of 1788, and it is presumably this slip that was uncovered. Immediately south of North/South Wharf, yet another wharf was revealed, this one probably corresponding to Fisher Wharf on the Hills map.

Ambitious Acts in Early Cities

It is one thing to see representations of eighteenth- and early-nineteenth-century wharves and slips on maps of the period, but the real thing is no less than awe inspiring. The wharves uncovered on the Meadows Site make visible the vibrancy of the early water-front, as well as the engineering ingenuity that went into making the port the success that it was. Likewise, the slipway on the Hertz Lot reminds us of the work required to maintain the boats that filled the city's harbor. That all of these structures were subsequently covered over and built upon is impressive, but Philadelphia is not the only place it happened. In New York, the East River shoreline is three blocks beyond where it began, and the land alongside the Hudson River has had four blocks added. Because several excavations in New York have also uncovered the early wharf structures, it is possible to make some comparisons.

On the Assay Site in New York, which was located on Front Street just south of Wall Street and was excavated in 1984, two wharves were recorded, one referred to as North/South Wharves and the other as Baches Wharf. Both dated to the late eighteenth century and were different than anything seen in Philadelphia. North/South Wharves was filled with faggots (cord wood) in addition to cobbles, and Baches Wharf was built using a block and bridge technique. This type of wharf has not been found archaeologically elsewhere in the United States, but it has been described for wharves along the Hudson River. As observed on the Assay Site it consisted of a series of small cobb-wharf "blocks" that were set at intervals and connected by heavy timber spans or "bridges" placed above the waterline.[16] Other wharves have been excavated in other cities, and three comparative tables appear in the Meadows Site report. The authors conclude that, regardless of location, most of the construction techniques used at the Meadows Site were similar to those used at other places during the same period, except for some in Massachusetts where solid fill construction was used exclusively. They did not note a decrease in the diversity of methods over time (something that had been suggested by other archaeologists) or a clustering of particular techniques during a particular time, with the possible exception of joining techniques. Choice of specific construction techniques appeared to depend on site-specific characteristics rather than building trends.[17]

Beyond the process of building the wharves and other waterfront facilities was the act of filling them in. Landfilling, too, was considered comparatively by the archaeologists who excavated the Meadows Site. Fewer artifacts were found in the landfill at both the Meadows and Hertz sites than at those of comparable age in New York, probably, the authors argue, "more due to dredging activities and tidal action of the Delaware River, along with late commercial and industrial development, than to the implementation of sanitary practices or the types of activities that occurred around the area to be filled in."[18]

The Philadelphia samples are small, and drawing any conclusions about the city's waterfront in general is dangerous. If the West Shipyard Group gets its way, though, and the Hertz Lot becomes an archaeological park, there is a chance that much more will be revealed about the evolution of the waterfront. What is perhaps most amazing about the Delaware River shoreline in Philadelphia (and probably every other city that has a highway running along its waterfront) is that anything at all is left from the past. As these shorelines are reincorporated into the urban context from which so many were removed, there is the opportunity to find out how they were constructed in the first place.

CHAPTER EIGHT

An Archaeological Walk in the Eighteenth-Century City

Although ongoing archaeology generates the same kind of interest in Philadelphia it does elsewhere, the results of archaeological projects in the City of Brotherly Love tend to be forgotten. The construction that enables the archaeological investigations in the first place transforms the sites into something so different that what was there before is difficult to remember. It is a constant process in cities, and even aboveground changes can play tricks on the memory. Stores change hands, parking lots suddenly appear, old buildings are replaced by new ones. Cities are layered cultural landscapes; it is one of the things that makes them cities. To reveal the layers is to gain a deeper understanding of the place, something archaeology does for archaeologists. The problem is to figure out how to do it for everyone else.

This chapter and the next return to archaeological sites that were excavated in the path of construction. The sites are now covered by a variety of modern buildings, from parking garages to a federal prison, but by visiting them—taking an imaginary walk—an attempt is made to peel back the layers, to see the city in all its complexity. It was a walking city, and it still is, at least to some extent. This walk begins with several blocks near the Delaware River where, indeed, the city began, and ends at the northern edge of eighteenth-century development (Figure 8.1). There are five stops on the "tour," beginning with New Market. On the ground, the first archaeological walk would take about an hour, but it can also be done in the imagination.

Stop 1: New Market

New Market, Stop 1 on the map, was the name for the shopping mall that a developer in the 1970s conceived for the block bounded by South Second Street on the west, Lombard Street on the south, Front Street on the east, and Pine Street on

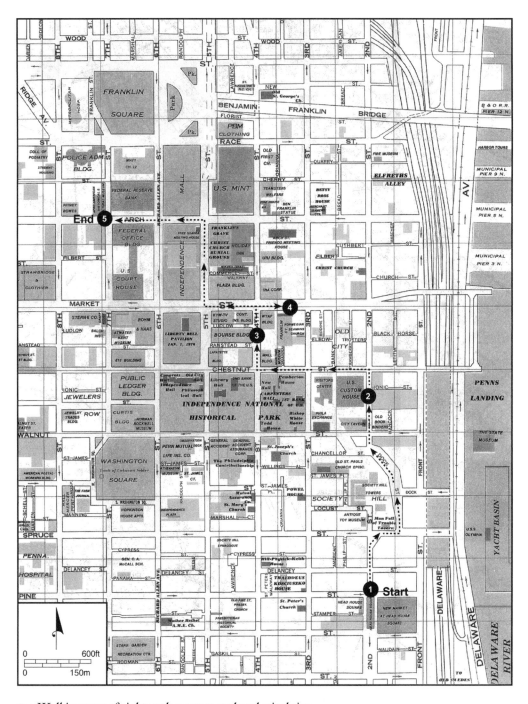

8.1. Walking tour of eighteenth-century archaeological sites.

the north, but it was also the name of the market house built on Second Street in 1745. By the 1740s the population of the city had expanded along the banks of the Delaware, and the central market on High Street was not convenient for people living north of Vine Street or south of Spruce. New markets were called for in the northern and southern parts of the city; one was built between Coates (now Fairmount) and Poplar on Second Street (later on Callowhill), and another at Second and Pine. Although the market house at Callowhill (mentioned in the previous chapter) disappeared a long time ago, the other market house has stood in one form or another since it was first built. The extant structure, restored in 1963, includes only its northern end, the southern headhouse and stalls having been demolished in 1860.[1] What's left, running down the center of Second Street, is referred to as Headhouse Square, and artisans still display their wares under the shade of its roof during the hot summer months (Figure 8.2). The original market house had sixteen stalls, eight north of Lombard Street and eight south of Lombard, but when the headhouse was added at the southern end in 1787, the number of stalls increased by twenty.[2]

The outdoor shopping mall from the 1970s did not fare nearly as well. It was already dying in the 1980s and in the mid-1990s the shoddily constructed shops were removed in anticipation of constructing a hotel on the site, a project that never came to pass in

8.2. Old Market House, Second and Pine Streets, watercolor by B. R. Evans, 1870. (Historical Society of Pennsylvania)

8.3. Barbara Liggett's map of the block she excavated at New Market, from the archaeological exhibition catalog. (The Athaenaeum of Philadelphia)

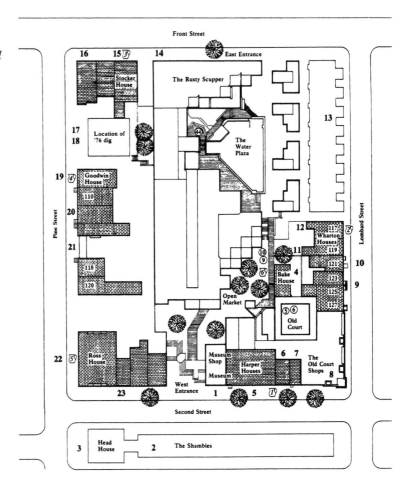

spite of its movie-star (Will Smith) backing. The failed hotel project left an empty concrete basin where the shops had been, and it remains eerily barren behind a chain-link fence. Fortunately, the 1970s shopping mall incorporated the still-standing eighteenth- and nineteen-century structures around the edges of the block, and an archaeological investigation was conducted in conjunction with construction on the block's interior. Barbara Liggett headed the excavation, which for the most part was a race with the contractors. Liggett herself characterized at least some of the excavation as "the worst type of salvage archaeology," but she also noted that "the New Market excavation analysis generated valuable information about . . . urban life that was not available from historical or other resources."[3] The area investigated was an intensely settled block, and the detailed research conducted by Betty Cosans in combination with the multitude of archaeological features uncovered produced exciting insights into the eighteenth-century city.

John Palmer's bakehouse, built in 1753 (no. 4 in Figure 8.3), still stands tucked behind the line of stores now facing Second Street. *Walk up the steps that used to lead to the mall and around to the right.* Liggett and her team excavated the cellar of the bakehouse, which measured about thirty-three feet by sixteen feet. A plank wall divided the space in half and two bricked-up entries on the southern side of the building apparently provided access to rooms on either side of the partition.[4] The lots to the south of the bakehouse on Lombard Street and to the west on South Second were vacant in the early years of the bakery's operation, and customers probably approached from both sides. You can imagine the buzz of conversation as people mingled in the yards, awaiting their turns and catching up on local gossip.

The entire eastern wall of the bakehouse was taken up by a large brick oven, hearth, and chimney. The circular domed underground oven measured twelve feet in diameter; it had three openings, two at the base, probably for removing ash, and a larger arched cavity above for inserting fuel and goods to be baked. Bakers in this period made home-prepared breads for paying customers, and they also baked commercial goods for ships' stores and for export. Palmer apparently did both.

Palmer had bought the land from Anthony Morris, one of the three men who acquired the entire block in 1738–39. Palmer's lot measured 30 feet along South Second Street and 156 feet back from the street. The bakehouse was at the rear of the lot, and Palmer did not build houses along Second Street until the 1780s, when he put up two very small frame structures, eventually numbered 473 and 475 South Second. After his death in 1800 the property was sold and a subsequent owner used the bakehouse as a blacksmith shop. Two circular mortared brick constructions, found at the west end of the bakehouse cellar, were probably footings for mounting a blacksmith's anvils. According to Liggett, a log was set upright in the center of the footing with its lower part extended several feet into the ground and the rest reaching to a comfortable height for mounting the anvil on top.

A cluster of archaeological features was found between Palmer's houses on Second Street and the bakehouse at the back of the lot. The area, now an empty expanse of concrete, was a courtyard in the eighteenth century and would have been filled with activity. There were at least two privies made out of barrels behind 423 (no. 6 in Figure 8.3). One of them, probably in use in the late eighteenth century, consisted of three barrels piled on top of one another. There was also a brick-lined oval hole in the ground that may have been for disposing of ash in this yard, perhaps from the bake oven or later from the iron forge. Only one privy was found next door at 475 (no. 7 in Figure 8.3), but on the other side of the bakehouse, behind houses built in the last quarter of the eighteenth century, there were many more.

Thomas Harper bought a 51-foot-wide lot on the north side of Palmer's property in

(top) 8.4. The Harper Houses.

8.5. Cruciform decanter. (Courtesy of the Atwater Kent Museum of Philadelphia)

1775 from Anthony Morris. He extended his land another 25 feet to the north in 1788 and built twin houses fronting on Second Street that still stand (Figure 8.4). The two sides of the building, known as the Harper Houses, are joined by an arch on the upper level that covers a narrow alley between them. There were stores behind the houses by 1790, but the archaeological evidence suggests the lots were used well before the houses were constructed, possibly for wagon parking and off-loading. The rear portions of the lots were also used for trash and waste disposal by people who lived on Lombard Street. A cluster of features, found at the southeast corner of Harper's property, had been filled before he took possession. The features included a brick-lined privy, two circular unlined trash pits, and two barrel privies, one of which (Feature 10) was undisturbed by construction and provided one of the most important collections of artifacts recovered during the New Market project. The baker, John Palmer, lived on Lombard Street and the things in Feature 10 may have belonged to him. Palmer bought one of four houses (at 115 Lombard) built by Joseph Wharton in 1743 and apparently lived there while he ran his baking business.

There were 893 artifacts found in Feature 10, among them 65 ceramic vessels and 24 glass ones. Unusual among the vessels were a cruciform decanter (Figure 8.5) dating to about 1730 and porcelain manufactured locally by Bonnin and Morris, whose short-lived factory (1770–72) was a few blocks farther south between Front and Second Streets. The food remains were analyzed in depth by Sharon Burston. Most of the bones (266 out of 284) came from a stratum described as "a dark, humic, artifact-laden trash deposit," probably nightsoil. There were bones from at least four cows, two sheep, one pig, and three chickens, including a rooster, and three cats, one of them nearly complete "with bits of fiber clinging to some of the long bones," which may have been what was left of the cat's fur.[5] The number of cats is noteworthy, but if this back lot was undeveloped in the middle of the eighteenth century and was the bevy of activity we are imagining, cats might easily have gotten in the way of wagons and would not have received formal burial.

Two of the houses that Joseph Wharton built, at 117 and 119 Lombard Street, still stand, and even though they do not include Palmer's at number 115, his house was probably quite similar. Wharton, who played a major role in the early growth of the city, was one of the first developers of the block. He bought a 51-foot-wide strip of land that extended from Front to Second Streets in 1739 and created Lombard Street along the southern edge of his property. He also contributed 40 feet of land on Second Street to create space for the market, which he and Edward Shippen built at their own expense.[6]

The Front Street side of the block was developed before New Market was conceived. As soon as Front was extended across the Dock (now Dock Street), in about 1723, Mathew Cowley and Robert Bayley began to put up rental houses. Cowley built a house on his first purchase in 1723, and by the middle of the century there were several small buildings on his holdings toward the middle of the block; these were generally rented to transients who stayed a year or two and then moved elsewhere.[7] Bayley built four frame houses farther north along the streetfront in 1729 and a brick house on the back end of the lot, which was used as a bakehouse later in the century—the second on the block. Like Cowley, Bayley also rented his houses. Still farther north were the house and shop of Francis Trumble, a cabinetmaker, and artifacts relating to his work were found in an unlined rectangular privy pit at the back of his lot.

Trumble made the Windsor chairs that were used at the State House, and it is presumably his chairs that appear in the famous paintings of the signing of the Declaration of Independence (Figure 8.6). Trumble built his house on Front Street in 1768 and lived and worked there at least into the 1780s. Although the next owner of the lot, John Stocker, replaced the house in 1791, the artifacts found in the backyard privy dated between 1759 and 1780. They were embedded in a greenish-gray clay containing numerous pockets of decayed wood, which suggested to the archaeologists that the privy had been wood-lined. Tools were recovered here, including gouges, chisels, and gravers for woodworking, as well as an iron rasp, iron spikes, and many bone and wood handles. They may very well have been the tools used to make the chairs used by the founding fathers (Figure 8.7).

The most prominent structure on the Pine Street side of the block in the eighteenth century was a Quaker meetinghouse, built on a lot left to the Society by Samuel Powell in 1747. The Quakers must have built a meetinghouse there by 1753, because the yearly meeting was held on Pine Street in the ninth month of that year. According to Liggett, the building was sixty feet long and forty-three feet deep. Two archaeological features were found along the back property line. One, a brick-lined pit, was filled in the middle of the nineteenth century, but the other, also a brick-lined pit (Feature 16), was filled

8.6. Congress Voting Independence, *a painting begun by Robert Edge Pine and completed (or copied) by Edward Savage, 1784–1801. (Courtesy of the Historical Society of Pennsylvania Collection, Atwater Kent Museum of Philadelphia)*

much earlier—probably in the 1760s and '70s—and not closed until after 1780. The soil was uniform throughout the pit, although the artifacts seemed to be stratified with the earliest at the bottom and the most recent at the top. The archaeologists speculated that the soil was placed in the pit when it was closed and filtered down through the earlier artifact deposit at the bottom.[8]

The large number of artifacts in this feature—thirty thousand in all—and the extraordinary number of faunal remains (eleven thousand bones), in particular, suggest some kind of communal feasting, although the excavators had come up with a different interpretation.[9] It seemed possible to me that meals would have been served at large Quaker gatherings, so I made an effort to find out some specifics about Quaker practice in eighteenth-century Philadelphia, especially at the Pine Street Meetinghouse. According to scholars at Swarthmore College, beginning in 1772 the Pine Street Meeting, referred to as the Hill Meeting, was the gathering place for the southern district in Philadelphia.

The monthly meetings had grown so large that it was no longer possible to bring Quakers from all parts of the city together in one group. Instead, three districts were established with each of them holding its own monthly meeting.

Monthly meetings lasted all day and attracted large numbers of people. There are no records of communal meals being served in the eighteenth century, but nineteenth-century photographs show long trestle tables piled with food, and historical references to vendors hawking food to participants in nineteenth-century meetings

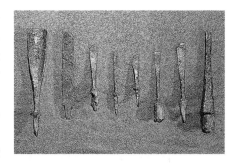

8.7. Trumble's woodworking tools. (Photograph by Murial Kirpatrick)

exist. If this was true in the nineteenth century, it seems reasonable to assume there was also a need for feeding meeting attendees in the eighteenth century, and the artifacts and bones from the Pine Street Meetinghouse privy may be the evidence.[10]

Ceramics were plentiful in the privy, including more than 9,722 sherds. Although the soil was not stratified, the analyst Betty Cosans noticed that the ceramic types at the top of the feature were from later than those at the bottom, and three general date ranges were assumed for the deposits: 1780–85, 1760, and 1755–60. The uppermost deposit contained significantly more plain creamware (33.7 percent), a type that was first available in America in the 1760s, than white salt-glazed stoneware (18.2 percent), suggesting that it was discarded well after creamware was introduced. In contrast, the deepest deposit contained only three small sherds of creamware and 36.5 percent of white salt-glazed stoneware, suggesting it was made before creamware was widely available. Since the meetinghouse was constructed in 1753 it is not surprising that there would be hardly any creamware at the bottom of the feature.

A little more than half of the ceramic vessels recovered were made of plain (undecorated) creamware. There were octagonal plates with plain rims, round plates with Royal rims, and round plates, soup bowls, and a small platter with feather rims. Conspicuously absent were any vessels with hand-painted decoration. For tea there were saucers and tea bowls, all but one of them with no decoration at all. Other vessels, including bowls of various sizes, chamber pots, tankards, and jugs, were also plain in color. The tankards had the most varied decoration, some with paneled bodies, double-twisted reed handles and sprig-molded terminals, and others with beading around the base.

White salt-glazed stonewares, which the creamwares had apparently replaced, used the same basic rim decorations in addition to more elaborate molded patterns on plates, soup plates, and platters. Nineteen pieces of white salt-glaze tableware were in the Royal shape with molded bead and reel border decoration. This apparent set included a small oval platter, seven plates, and eleven round soup plates. There were four sauceboats that didn't match the dinnerware patterns and a variety of bowls, chamber pots, tankards, tea bowls, and jugs. Again none of the vessels were painted. There was very little teaware made of creamware and none of white salt-glazed stoneware, but there were 133 vessels for tea made out of porcelain. More were English than Chinese, and the analyst classified them as plates, saucers, tea bowls, bowls, coffee cups, dessert dishes, bleeding (?) bowls, a teapot lid, and a handle. Decoration was generally hand-painted underglaze blue.

The conservative absence of decoration in the ceramic assemblage is consistent with Quaker simplicity, but the faunal remains are another thing. Sharon Burston estimated that the bones in the 1780–85 deposit represented 400 pounds of beef, 40 pounds of mutton, and 140 pounds of pork. The bones in the 1760 deposit, the largest of the three, equaled 1,200 pounds of beef, 500 pounds of calf (veal), 160 pounds of mutton, and 220 pounds of pork. In the earliest deposit there were 800 pounds of beef, 400 pounds of calf (veal), 120 pounds of sheep, and 70 to 140 pounds of pig. There was also deer—one individual in the late and middle deposits and three in the oldest. A total of 2,149 bones belonged to chickens, but there was a preponderance of head, wing, and foot bones, suggesting butchering remains rather than meals. There were also indications of butchering in the cow and sheep remains, but the majority of the bones could be identified to specific cuts.[11]

This is a lot of meat, and it appeared to Burston to have been deposited over a short rather than a long period of time.[12] She found no evidence of weathering or rodent chewing that might have indicated that the bones had been discarded on the ground and left there for some time before being put in the privy. Instead, she concluded that some of the bones were from food consumed on the site and some from elsewhere, placed here to facilitate percolation of human waste in the privy. However, another possible conclusion is that the bones were discarded after monthly meetings when lots of people gathered for daylong sessions and would have consumed lots of meals. It was also general practice to rent out the basement of meetinghouses to other groups, and these events also could have added to the accumulation of food bones. There is nothing in the bones themselves to confirm or dispute this interpretation, but the monochromatic dishes and the bones in combination are consistent with what we know of Quaker practice. Another thing found in the meetinghouse privy is more difficult to accept.

Among the animal remains in the meetinghouse privy were fifty-two bones belonging to two human infants. One of the infants was a full-term fetus, or newborn, and the other was a premature fetus, probably about seven months gestation. The remains included long bones, scapulae, pelvic parts, twenty-one cranial fragments, and nine vertebral fragments. According to Burston's analysis, X-rays of the bones showed no indication of malnutrition in the mother or mothers, suggesting that there had to be some other reason why they were found where they were, in the trash. She considered three possible

The New Market Collection and the Atwater Kent

Urban archaeology produces multitudes of artifacts that require storage space and curation in one form or another. It was already a problem in Pennsylvania by the mid-1980s, when the Atwater Kent Museum in Philadelphia and the Carnegie Mellon Institute in Pittsburgh took responsibility for managing the collections. Although the Atwater Kent didn't have space in its own facility on Seventh Street, a place was found in the basement of the Balch Institute, a museum dedicated to interpreting Philadelphia's ethnic groups, across the street. However, when the Balch needed the basement for other purposes it fell to the Atwater Kent to find an alternative. Jeffrey Ray's first task as the museum's new curator was to find that space, and it had to be free. The city's recreation department made rooms available under the seating at JFK Sesquicentennial Stadium, and hundreds of boxes of artifacts were moved there in 1985. The boxes, piled four high, were numbered by site, making the collections more or less accessible—until the artifacts were spilled out onto the floor.

On a chilly night in 1988, part of a crowd waiting to buy tickets for a Pink Floyd concert at the stadium crawled over the fence next to the steps, broke down the wooden door leading to the storage rooms, and dumped out the artifacts in order to use the cardboard boxes to build fires in the parking lot. Ray, who was on an airplane to London when it happened, did his best to rebox the artifacts by location when he returned, but site associations were basically lost. Trained in ancient history and classical archaeology, Ray compares the Pink Floyd dumping with the loss of collections from Mycenae during World War II. In that case the artifacts—the result of excavations by the British School—were stored in a warehouse in Nauplia that was bombed. When members of the British archaeological team returned, they realized that the material had lost its context, so they dumped the artifacts into the Bay of Nauplia. In Philadelphia, the collections, including the materials from New Market, were not dumped in the Delaware. Instead they were relocated to yet another offsite (and far from ideal) storage facility where they remain. A visit to the site made it clear that without records tying the numbers on the boxes (and artifacts) to the lots and features from which they came, there is no way to retrieve the context for the artifacts—making them, like the ones from Mycenae, useless.

explanations: they were the product of abortions; it was standard practice to dispose of neonatal dead or stillborns unceremoniously; or they were the result of infanticide.[13]

Abortion did not seem likely, since one fetus had reached full term and the other would have been considered viable. Abortions were conducted in the eighteenth century, but they would have been done earlier in the pregnancy. The second possibility was ruled out, because Burston found entries for neonatal deaths and stillbirths in records of the Society of Friends in Philadelphia. Premature and stillborn babies were apparently buried in the Friends Burying Ground. Although infanticide was considered murder in Pennsylvania and punishable by death, Burston concluded that it was the most likely explanation for the presence of the infant remains. She hypothesized that sometime after 1750 and most likely in the early 1780s, one or two women gave birth to infants, one full term and one two months premature. She (or they) either murdered them or concealed their births and deaths in order to avoid stigma, threat of persecution, damage to reputation, and possible loss of employment. Who the women were, or even if they were Quakers, obviously cannot be determined, but they were more than likely attempting to hide out-of-wedlock births. While well-to-do members of society might successfully conceal such pregnancies, women of lesser means had fewer opportunities and were more likely to suffer economic hardship as well as loss of respect. Clearly the women who disposed of these babies were willing to risk death if they were found out.

A selection of the artifacts recovered at New Market was exhibited at the Atwater Kent Museum of Philadelphia in 1978, with an exhibition catalog published by the Athenaeum of Philadelphia, and the collection was entrusted to the Atwater Kent for safekeeping. In the mid-1980s the Atwater Kent Museum and the Carnegie Mellon Institute in Pittsburgh were designated as repositories for urban archaeological collections. It was a good idea that unfortunately was never fully realized.

Stop 2: Area F

Fifty years before he shared ownership of the New Market block, Anthony Morris bought two lots on Front Street very near the dock. The lots lay between Front Street on the east, Walnut Street on the south, Second Street on the west, and Chestnut Street on the north. The dock (now Dock Street) was just south of Walnut. Morris built his house on Front Street twelve feet north of the house that belonged to Thomas Lloyd, the man who sold him the land. Already a businessman at age twenty-eight, Morris sold one of his two lots to Alexander Beardsley, who built his house to the north of Morris's. Within four years Morris had developed the twelve feet between his house and Lloyd's into an alley that stretched all the way to Second Street. First known as Morris's Alley, then as Gray's, and finally as Gatzmer Street, the alley was the first part of the Area F block to be developed, and many of the features found during the archaeological investigation were in the backyards of the small houses that were built there in the early years of the eighteenth century.

Unfortunately Gatzmer Street doesn't exist anymore in this location. A movie theater and its attached parking garage stand on the portion of the block that was once Morris's and a paved plaza with a miniature copy of the William Penn statue that sits on top of City Hall covers the old alleyway. The parking garage was built by Independence National Historical Park in anticipation of the Bicentennial, but first (in 1976) Dan Crozier and a crew from Temple University conducted an archaeological excavation beneath the basement floors of the huge nineteenth- and early-twentieth-century warehouses that stood on the site (Figure 8.8). *Unlike the New Market block, there are no standing structures to tie the archaeological features to, but if you go to the top of the parking garage you can see the waterfront and imagine the lay of the land.*

A report on Crozier's excavations was not written until 2006. Juliette Gerhardt, John Milner Associates' laboratory director and senior ceramics analyst, worked on the site as a Temple undergraduate and brought her experience and gained expertise to the task of completing the report. According to her research, the Morris, Lloyd, and Beardsley houses sat on the bluff overlooking the river. The bluff is gone now, but it is not hard to envision the busy riverfront in the days when 403 ships cleared Philadelphia every year and goods arrived from all over the world (Figure 8.9). Morris made his fortune as a brewer; his brewery was on Water Street east of his house, but he also subdivided

8.8. The warehouses standing on the Area F site before excavation began.

the alley into small building lots, and by the time he died he had sold five lots outright and ground rents to ten more. In about 1729 Patience and William Annis moved into a house on one of the small lots. Their two-story brick house measured a mere sixteen feet square. It had a front and back parlor with a kitchen behind, front and back chambers on the second floor, and a front and back garret above. William Annis was a mariner, the master of five ships: the *Hannah Hope,* the *Flaxney,* the *Betty Hope,* the *Vigor,* and the *William.* His ships crossed the Atlantic many times, putting in at London, Lisbon, Dublin, and Madeira and also visiting Jamaica, Antigua, Bonavista, and Porto Port in the Caribbean. He had a prosperous career, and eventually William and his wife owned two more houses on the alley although they remained in their small square one. It must have been crowded with material goods because many things were recovered from their privy, which was filled soon after Patience Annis died in 1748.[14]

There were Chinese porcelain rice bowls made for the Asian market and pieces of

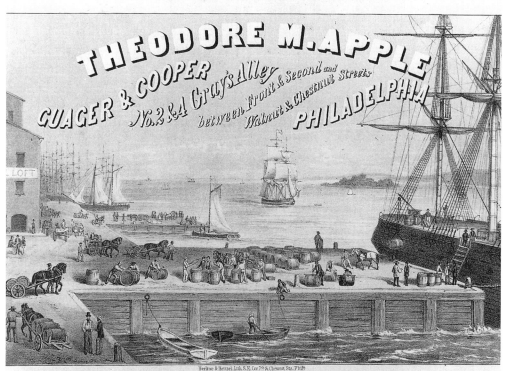

8.9. Chromolithograph advertisement for Theodore M. Apple, numbers 2 & 4 Gray's Alley, 1858; Herline and Hensel, lithographers, Philadelphia. (The Library Company of Philadelphia)

Spanish Majolica, perhaps brought back by William from his travels. The Annises owned four Chinese export porcelain tea sets and could have set the dinner table with matching Chinese export dishes. There was a cut-glass cruet, a matched set of wine glasses, champagne glasses, and an etched and painted case-style decanter (Figure 8.10). There were stoneware tankards for beer or cider and a set of posset cups for the warm alcoholic drink that was popular in the eighteenth century. Unusual in the assemblage were two pocket watches and pieces of coral, again possibly from William's travels or scavenged from

8.10. Champagne glasses from the Annis assemblage. (Photograph by Juliette Gerhardt)

ship's ballast left lying around the docks. Two stoneware chamber pots in the assemblage were made by Anthony Duche, a local potter whose factory was only a few blocks away.

A few doors east of the small Annis house, set back from the alley, was a bakehouse made of brick with an attached frame building that was probably for storing grain. Like the bakehouse at New Market there was an open courtyard in front of the bakehouse, but there were two houses, one brick and one frame, on the other side of the courtyard abutting the alley. A small passageway between them provided access to the bakehouse at the back of the lot. William Gray built the bakehouse in 1738 and lived in one of the houses, probably the brick one, with his wife and servant. Gray, who also owned the cooper shop next to his dwelling, made "bisket," which was a flat round bread, baked hard for seamen, but he only did it for ten years. By 1750 he had bought a tavern at 410 High (now Market) Street and was said to be at "the sign of the Conestoga Wagon in Market Street" that year. His wife, Elizabeth, was licensed as a tavernkeeper in 1763 and carried on after her husband's death.

Josiah Davenport of Boston apparently took over the baking business, but Mary Weyman bought the property soon after. Gerhardt speculates that it was these people, plus the inhabitants of the two houses and cooper shop on the alley, that contributed to the fill at the bottom of the privy that was excavated. The fill, which dated to about 1769, included lots of liquor bottles, especially for wine. Davenport's sideline was importing wine, and the bottles likely came from his business. Besides the bottles there were stemmed wine glasses, tumblers, tankards, mugs, two punch bowls, and a puzzle jug inscribed "WA"—the initials of William Annis, but in the wrong place at the wrong time to have been his. Most unusual of all was a coconut shell made into a cup. Clearly, the residents around the bakehouse courtyard did a good deal of drinking, but then, so did everyone else. These were exciting times when all the residents, it would seem, were carving out new businesses and ways to make money, which came with the anxiety of doing new things and making mistakes.

A second fill deposit in the privy dated to 1783, when the property was owned by Thomas Bond Jr. and tenanted by a succession of bakers and coopers. It included two glass fire extinguishers, presumably for emergencies in the bakery. Again there were lots of liquor bottles and two punch bowls with inscriptions. One playfully read: "This makes my heart Merry, while love makes it Sad, what think you to Marry, then sure you are Mad"; the other, more serious, urges "Success to the Brave." Extraordinary in this deposit were fragments of a blue and white porcelain tea set made by local potters, Bonnin and Morris. According to Alexandra Kirtley, a curator at the Philadelphia Museum of Art, these are the only fragments of a Bonnin and Morris tea set that are known to have survived.

Besides bakers and coopers, there were other craftsmen on the block. Hercules Courtney rented space in Alexander Beardsley's old house on Front Street, where he lived and worked for about fifteen years. Courtney, who came from Ireland via London, was a skilled carver and gilder, but to make ends meet, or perhaps just to make more money, he and his wife ran a tavern in the front room of their house. The privy associated with the Courtney house and shop was filled in about 1783. Besides the usual liquor bottles and drinking paraphernalia, there were remnants of the master craftsman's work, including a chunk of graphite mortar that would have been used for melting gold leaf or resins, such as the lump of yellow material identified as amber resin or a copal material known as "Demerara animi." These resins were melted and mixed with warm oil and pigments for use as a varnish on furniture, architectural trim, and coaches.[15] Two flint stones found in the same deposit may have been used for polishing and carving. There are examples of Hercules Courtney's carved furniture in the Philadelphia Museum of Art, and elaborate decorative architectural details by him have been identified in some of Philadelphia's most distinguished old houses.

After Hercules Courtney died in 1784 his wife, Mary, carried on as "beerhouse keeper," but she, too, died within a few years. A vintner, Samuel Greene, rented the Beardsley house in the 1780s, and Henry Young, a baker, was the last to occupy the house before it was taken down in 1791. The many utilitarian ceramics found in the privy may have belonged to him. Among them were butter pots, milk pans, pudding pans, and pie plates, more even than had been found associated with William Gray's bakery or with John Palmer's at New Market.

In 1790 a mathematical and optical instrument maker and optician named William Richardson lived at the other end of the block on Second Street. He was followed at the same address in 1815 by Robert Swan, who was a silversmith and umbrella maker. The three-story brick house with a two-story wood kitchen had been built by James James in 1761; Richardson paid ground rent to Pennsylvania Hospital at first but had purchased the property by 1795; Swan bought it from William Booth in 1815. Both Richardson and Swan worked at home and left evidence of their crafts in the privy associated with the property. The earliest deposit included 249 eyeglass lenses, clearly from Richardson's practice. Two crucibles, a chisel, a file, and funnels that were found may have belonged to Swan. There were also numerous pieces (fifty-seven) of cut bone and antler-horn residue, possibly left over from the manufacture of handles for flatware or umbrellas. Notable among the domestic artifacts was the number of teawares, a larger percentage of the assemblage than was found in any of the other features, and the number of tumblers, the most of all the features. It is possible that these craftsmen sold their wares out of their shops and, like Alexander Turnbull on South Sixth Street, entertained their clients in the process.

Robert Smith took down the two-story house that Alexander Beardsley had built at the end of the seventeenth century on Front Street, the same house where Hercules Courtney carved his beautiful furniture. Smith built himself a big three-story brick house with a carriage house behind it. He eventually built another stable, acquired the brick coach house and stable on the adjoining lot, and added an icehouse connected to a marble-lined subcellar at the very back of the house. Once excavated, the icehouse appeared to resemble one in the still-standing Bishop White house in Independence National Historical Park. Smith was already one of twenty-five directors for the Bank of the United States when he arrived on Front Street, and he was clearly a leading citizen throughout the thirty-one years during which he ran his business and raised a family there. Just as Richardson and, after him, Swan, operated their businesses out of their houses on Second Street, Smith operated Robert Smith and Company out of the first floor of his house on Front. He traded textiles and had connections in New York through his brother-in-law, employing relatives as agents, clerks, and accountants.

The artifacts found in the privy associated with the Smith family reflected the elite lifestyle of a successful merchant. There were at least nine tea sets, including painted and printed earthenwares, but also three sets made of Chinese export porcelain, one with elegant overglaze decoration. Ten pieces of one of the porcelain sets were decorated with the monogram "RS," indicating a special order. The Smiths also had multiple sets of tableware, all with matching serving pieces. For everyday use there was blue edge-decorated pearlware, and for company, blue underglaze decorated porcelain.

The Smiths may have been one of the last elite families to live so close to the waterfront. As the city grew westward the wealthy moved away—at least moved their homes away—from the clatter of the docks. It is even a little surprising that Robert Smith stayed into the 1820s. By 1810, it seems, many of the wealthy had houses south of Market Street on Third and Fourth Streets or even farther west.[16] Our next stop is in that direction.

Stop 3: The Bourse Garage

Whereas Robert Smith chose to live near the waterfront in the last decade of the eighteenth century, Charles Norris, another leading citizen, built his house away from the water on Chestnut Street in about 1755. *Walk along Second Street to the corner of Chestnut and turn left.* Norris's Georgian-style mansion stood midway between Fourth and Fifth Streets, where the Second Bank of the United States is now, and measured sixty feet across its facade (Figure 8.11). The roof of the brick house was surrounded by a balcony, and the outbuildings on the property included a kitchen, a washhouse, a greenhouse, and a hothouse that was one of the first in the city. The Norrises' celebrated garden extended from the west side of the house to the corner of Fourth and Chestnut Streets. According to Charles Norris's daughter, Deborah Logan, pineapples were grown in the hothouse, and medicinal herbs in the herbarium. Roses, scarlet honeysuckle, and catalpa trees grew around the edge of a terrace behind the back parlor of the mansion, and there was also a pear grove. Willow trees, evidently a gift from Benjamin Franklin, who had been the first to introduce the species to the area, were planted toward the rear of the property. Deborah Norris Logan claimed that while seated on one of the white benches in the garden, the only thing she could see beyond the wall was the State House steeple.

8.11. The Norris mansion, watercolor by B. R. Evans, 1850–1890, exact date unknown. (Historical Society of Pennsylvania)

And it is a lucky thing, because her neighbors across the street lived in considerably less elegant circumstances.[17]

It is the area across the street that was excavated when it was in the way of a hotel—the Omni—and a parking garage and movie theater attached to the back of the Bourse (Figure 8.12).[18] The Bourse is a large building now facing Independence Mall that was originally built as the Philadelphia Stock Exchange in the 1890s and has been restored as a kind of oversize food court to serve the tourist traffic on the mall. The alley that runs along the north wall of the Bourse has been there since around 1733, when Caleb Ransted erected three brick houses on his fifty-three-foot frontage along Fourth Street and reserved seven feet at the northern end for an alley—eventually widened to fifteen feet and called Ransted Alley (now Ranstead Street). The property immediately south of Ransted's on Fourth belonged to Able Noble, but he had sold the hundred-foot front-age beginning at the corner of Fourth and Chestnut Streets to John Forest, who subdivided it in 1726. John Linton, a harnessmaker, owned the parcel at the corner and John Heathcoate, a butcher, owned the lot to the north. Unfortunately most of the residents who left their material possessions in the eighteenth-century features that were excavated were renters. We do not know their names, but from the things they left behind we can guess, at least, at their occupations. Of particular interest are two individuals who lived on Fourth Street, one at the north end near the alley and the other near the middle of the block. The privy associated with the lot near the middle was filled first.

There were two major layers of fill in this privy, and although most of the domestic artifacts in both of them dated to the 1740s the upper layer also included things dating

8.12. The Bourse excavation. The Second Bank (building with columns) across the street stands on the site of the Norris mansion.

as late 1760, indicating that the privy remained open (or was disturbed) at that time. The variety of faunal remains identified in both layers was notable, but even more so was the amount of butchering waste. According to Cheryl Holt, the faunal analyst for the project, out of 2,394 faunal elements, 530 (22 percent) were cow or pig phalanges (foot bones), possibly representing as many as several hundred animals. Mandible, maxilla, molar, and skull fragments were also present. Holt thought it unlikely that several hundred cows were butchered at the site, even though a butcher (John Heathcoate) lived in the immediate vicinity and maybe even on the lot where the privy was located. Instead she and Belinda Blomberg, the author of the archaeological report, proposed that the layers with the bones were percolation fill—items that were intentionally laid down to assist in the percolation of human waste. The other artifacts found that might have related to butchering were an iron axe head and a slate hone. The hone was a rectangular piece of highly polished slate with beveled edges that was probably used to sharpen tools and cutlery.

Heathcoate was not the only one in the neighborhood in the business of slaughtering animals. Henry Dawson operated a slaughterhouse at the Fifth Street end of the block (west of the project area), which, it seems, was considered an "extreme nuisance" and was eventually shut down.[19] There was also another person in the project area whose privy contents suggest that he, too, was somehow involved in butchering or tanning or both. The privy behind the northernmost house facing Fourth Street at the corner of Ransted Alley produced 1,605 horn and/or skull fragments, 35 percent of the total faunal assemblage. Holt again speculated that the fragments represented several hundred animals. Three percent of the horn was derived from cow, but the vast majority was from sheep and goats, suggesting a possible involvement with horn works, tanneries, or slaughterhouses. There were also mandible, maxilla, and molars in this assemblage and practically no dietary debris.

The diagnostic artifacts in this privy suggest that it was filled in the 1770s, which is after an ordinance was passed in 1769 that specified allowable privy depths. Blomberg reasoned that the layer with the horn was a percolation deposit laid down to bring the privy up to the allowable depth. It is also possible that the occupant of the property was somehow involved in tanning or slaughtering. The tanneries that lined the banks of nearby Dock Creek overflowed with offal and were an increasing cause for complaint. Perhaps the Fourth Street privy was a convenient (or secret) place to get rid of at least some of the waste without adding to the already miserable conditions.

There was also evidence of bone and horn working. Two fragments of bone were found that had button blanks cut out of them, and there were sixty-four fragments of cut tortoiseshell, including two fragments of a single-sided tortoiseshell comb. Fragments of a double-sided bone comb, a bone brush handle, and a brush head were also recovered. These bits and pieces suggest that residents were involved in industrial activities, and in fact the documentary record indicates that from the mid-eighteenth century on there were all sorts of industries on the block. Anthony Duche's pottery, which operated from 1724/5 to 1762, was just seventy feet west of the project area on Chestnut Street, Jonathan Durell operated a pottery north of the project area from 1744 to 1769, and Plunkett Fleeson manufactured paper hangings and papier-mâché moldings at the corner of Fourth and Chestnut Streets.

Just one block from the statehouse, the neighborhood was also full of boardinghouses where visiting politicians stayed while Congress was in session. Mary Dickinson ran a boardinghouse a few doors up the street from the Bourse project area at 40 South Fourth Street, and Thomas Pickering, secretary of state in the Washington administration, lived in a boardinghouse at 155 Chestnut Street, a few doors to the west. Benjamin Franklin's house was around the corner, and from the top of the Bourse Parking Garage it is possible to look down into his backyard.

Stop 4: Franklin Court

It wasn't always possible to see that backyard. Franklin's grandchildren took down his house and ran a street—Orianna Street—right through the middle of the property to increase its developable value. Archaeological investigations begun by the American Philosophical Society and the National Park Service in the 1950s, however, began the long process of redefining the site and recovering as much information as possible from the structural remains and artifacts left behind by the various generations who lived there. The buildings standing on either side of Orianna Street were removed, and almost immediately the archaeologists found remnants of the eighteen-inch-wide stone foundation walls belonging to Franklin's house and a brick cellar floor. Additional excavations in the 1960s uncovered 147 features, including extensive portions of Franklin's house exterior wall foundations, interior wall foundations, cellar flooring, and subcellar features: an icehouse, a privy, and a well. In the 1970s, the eastern wall of Franklin's house was redefined and the rental properties he built along Market Street in the 1780s were investigated (Figure 8.13). The only original architectural fabric left aboveground is a tunnel that leads into the site from Market Street, but the courtyard where the house stood has been recreated and you can enter it through the tunnel just as Franklin would have done. *Walk north on Fourth Street to Market and turn right. You will find the tunnel very soon on your right.*[20]

After a heated debate over whether there was enough information on which to base a reconstruction of the house, the Park Service hired the celebrated architect Robert Venturi to design a ghost structure that would represent the building rather than recreate it (Figure 8.14). The location and dimensions of the structure are based on archaeologi-

8.13. Archaeology taking place at Franklin Court, June 1971. (Photograph by William McCullough; Independence National Historical Park)

8.14. Aerial view of Franklin Court. (Photograph by Richard Frear, date unknown; Independence National Historical Park)

cal information in combination with the documentary record. Completed in time for the Bicentennial in 1976, the ghost structure was a brilliantly innovative way to use the archaeological remnants, which incidentally are still visible through "windows" in the courtyard (the concrete hoods that can be seen in the photograph), to recreate the scale of the house without attempting to rebuild it. Quotations from letters that Franklin and his wife, Deborah, wrote during construction in 1765 are etched in the pavement. While no artifacts beyond the fragmentary foundations are on display in the courtyard, a sample of the thousands of artifacts recovered—the usual broken dishes, wine bottles, and glassware—is displayed in one of the rental houses that Franklin built on the Market Street side of his property.

In preparation for the three hundredth anniversary of Franklin's birth in 2006, referred to as the tercentenary, Patrice Jeppson, a historical archaeologist with a particular interest in archaeological interpretation and outreach, was hired to review the results of all the excavations that had been done on the site, to identify items for the Frankliniana database (a catalog of material culture belonging to or related to Franklin), and to contribute to educational outreach programs to be disseminated over the Internet. Jeppson spent a year and a half wading through reports and contemplating whether there was anything new to add to the much considered story of Benjamin Franklin by revisiting the collections. She came up with some insights that reflect our time as much as Franklin's, but they provide a good example of how the past is necessarily always viewed through the present.[21]

Jeppson was particularly fascinated by the mastodon tooth in the Franklin collection (Figure 8.15). The tooth was found in 1958 by an electrician who was working in the dirt-floored basement of one of the Market Street houses (number 316). He turned the item over to the Park Service, and a local paleontologist tentatively identified it as a specimen likely from a French fossil bed, an identification that has since been modified. For Jeppson the tooth connected her to what she calls the Natural Philosopher Franklin. "He was very interested in mastodons," she says; "his correspondence indicates he made comparative studies of mastodon teeth with elephant teeth, that he [requested] fossil specimens from the Big Bone Lick site (now in Kentucky), and that he sent and personally took mastodon specimens overseas." For Franklin, the size and presumed ferocity of the mastodon made it a symbol of the new American nation. In addition, along with other evidence of extinct animals, it contributed to the questioning of the Great Chain of Being. Franklin lived well before Charles Darwin, but scientific inquiry, in which Franklin was deeply involved, was already laying the foundations for the later scientist's theories.

Jeppson also thought the skull of a rat, on display with other artifacts at Franklin Court, was provocative. She wondered why the public found this particular artifact so fascinating. It turns out that the children's book *Ben and Me: An Astonishing Life of Benjamin Franklin as Written by His Good Mouse Amos,* by Robert Lawson, is still selling an average of twenty-three thousand copies a month

8.15. Mastodon tooth excavated in Franklin Court, 1958. (Photograph by Peter Harholdt [INDE 66583]; Independence National Historical Park)

even though it was published in 1939; in November 2004, when Jeppson did her research, it had sold thirty-six thousand in paperback. Clearly many people associate mice with Benjamin Franklin, and seeing an actual rat skull among his things makes a direct connection. The book's foreword attributes the story of *Ben and Me* to the discovery of a manuscript "while altering an old Philadelphia house," and one wonders how much Lawson knew about Philadelphia. Jeppson is careful not to equate the skull with Amos, but she argues that the object provides a useful hook for "launching any discussion or presentation about Franklin for a significant segment of the public."[22]

Jeppson's research into past projects at Franklin Court also led her to consider who did the digging. The Park Service crew in the 1960s included nine African-American laborers working under the direction of two Park Service archaeologists, one of whom, Jackson Ward "Smokey" Moore, was a Native American. Franklin, Jeppson claims, would have been interested to know it was African Americans who were digging up his property. In the later years of his life he was active in the abolitionist movement, and although he had once owned slaves, he became the first president of the antislavery movement in the New World, he opened his house to the antislavery society for meetings, and he lent his name and image to their cause.

In the 1970s the archaeological investigations at Franklin Court were directed by Barbara Liggett, the woman who did so many of the important excavations in Philadelphia around that time. As Jeppson points out, it was not only significant that a woman had been entrusted with an important element in what was then being referred to as the "sacred shrine to American Democracy" (now known as Independence National Historical Park), but her work represents some of the earliest urban archaeology that was about more than dating buildings. Liggett was interested in how people lived in the city, and her concern with matters of health and sanitation set standards for much of the urban work that followed.[23]

While other archaeologists have focused on Franklin's innovative privy with its "flushing" connection to the house and his stone-lined ice pit, it was the social context of the finds that was most important for the contemporary archaeologist Patrice Jeppson. She bemoaned the fact that the huge tercentenary exhibit mounted in Franklin's honor at the Constitution Center in 2006 used a squirrel instead of a mouse as its mascot. The missed opportunity is obvious, since images from the children's book would have been so recognizable. Those images, though, would not have fit with the elite objects chosen for display. It is Jeppson's opinion that the exhibit designers—and the consortium that sponsored all the tercentenary events—did not want to touch on the mundane side of Franklin's life or memory. They did not want Amos the mouse, or a well-used bowl with the image of Franklin that had been excavated on the site of the Constitution Center. They did not want the things of everyday existence, the things that archaeology most often produces. The mastodon tooth was included in the exhibit though, and much of what Jeppson found has been entered into the Frankliniana database.[24]

Franklin died in 1790, just about the time the city was beginning to spread westward. Unclean industries were the first occupants of outlying blocks, and an archaeological excavation conducted on the site of the Metropolitan Detention Center at Seventh and Arch Streets encountered evocative remnants of several. *Walk north on Fifth Street and turn left on Arch. The detention center sits on the southwest corner of Seventh and Arch, across the street from the African-American Museum.*

Stop 5: The Metropolitan Detention Center

Louis Berger and Associates, a firm based in New Jersey, excavated the detention center site in about 1996. According to its report, the land, characterized as gentle, wooded hills and low wetlands in the eighteenth century, sloped from north to south with the highest ground abutting Arch Street.[25] Daniel Topham operated a pottery on the low ground between 1766 and 1783. According to Berger's report, Topham used local clays, probably mined from deposits nearby. Another potter, Andrew Miller, followed him, manufacturing all kinds of red earthenware on the premises until 1840. This low ground, where the potteries were located, was preserved for a number of reasons (Figure 8.16). When the properties facing Arch Street (numbers 708, 710, and 712) were converted to commercial use in the middle to late nineteenth century, two of them (708 and 712) were not built with full basements and the third (710) was built with a relatively shallow one. This low area was seasonally wet and it was apparently used for refuse disposal by local residents and craft industries prior to its eventual development. As already mentioned, intact eighteenth-century ground surface is rare in Philadelphia, and Berger's archaeologists, under the direction of Dr. Richard Dent, smartly focused much of their efforts on excavating the midden deposits that lay on top of the ground surface.[26]

The midden covered 4,700 square feet. Using 5-by-5-foot excavation units for the most part, close to 20 percent (920.5 square feet) of it was recovered. A dense concentration of redware was found in the 100-square-foot area at the back of the 712 Arch Street property, the property where the Topham and Miller potteries had been. There was also a heavy concentration of slag in a dark-grayish-brown course sand matrix, suggesting to the archaeologists that the deposit was from a coal-fired redware kiln. In addition to kiln furniture, two vessel forms dominated the assemblage: a tall conical vessel with a hole in the constricted base and a flat-bottomed form with steep sides and pronounced shoulders. Both these vessels were used in the sugar refining process (Figure 8.17).

According to Berger's research, most of the sugar exported from the West Indies was "raw" or coarsely refined, the cane juice having been processed into coarse brown

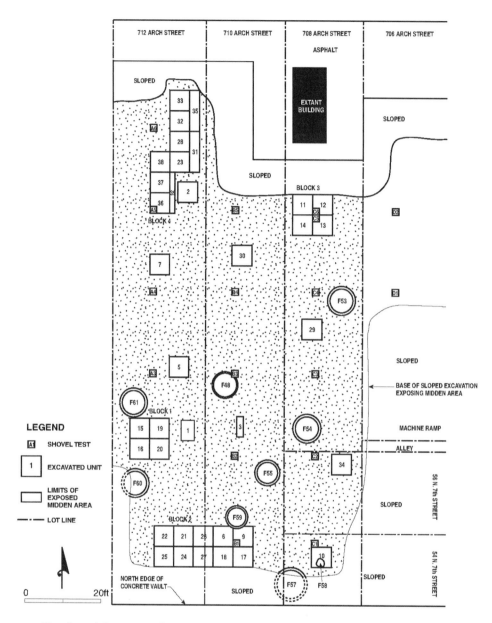

8.16. Site plan of the Metropolitan Detention Center. (From Dent et al. 1997, figure 4.18)

sugar.[27] European and North American merchants converted this into white table sugar, which sold for a considerably higher price. After the coarse sugar had been boiled in a series of vats, it was put in conical molds placed with their points down on top of syrup jars. The excess liquid drained through the holes in the bottom of the molds into the syrup jars, which had relatively small mouths and reinforced rims. The unglazed earthenware bodies of the molds allowed for evaporation of water through their walls. After the sugar was dry the molds were turned upside-down and the sugar loaves were pushed out.

8.17. Drawing of sugar mold and syrup jar, by Rob Schultz.

A total of 3,113 sherds from sugar molds was recovered from the units in Block 1 on the detention center site. The majority of the sherds had either a brushed white interior slip on a thick, coarse red-orange body or a very smoothed unslipped interior on a coarse earthenware body. The presence of mica in the clay and the relative consistency within these two types suggested to the analyst that the cones were made locally, "perhaps by Daniel Topham and Andrew Miller."[28] The fragments of the syrup jars also seemed to be local.

The excavation units in what was defined as Block 2 included a good deal of kiln furniture, probably also from the pottery of Daniel Topham, but there were also artifacts relating to a number of other industries. There were metalworking tools, including seven files, a pair of scissors, a screwdriver, a possible hand-tool shaft, three drill bits, and a punch used for engraving. Several lengths of gilded brass probably related to the manufacture of straight pins, and a piece of sheet metal with circular cuts, as well as numerous tacks and rivets, suggested the manufacture of upholstery tacks. There were button blanks made out of bone and wooden button backs that had not yet been affixed to their metal faces. Numerous leather fragments (seven hundred) and various sections of shoes and belt strap fragments were probably left by a shoemaker, and horn cores and oak bark found in the Block 1 units might have come from tanners working in the vicinity. This low-lying area appears to have been a catchall serving local industries as well as builders who worked on the block. Demolition and construction debris was found in more than one of the units.

Closer to Arch Street, the archaeologists looked for remains relating to domestic occupation. Surprisingly, they found the skeleton of a horse in a large shallow pit behind what would have been the house at 708 Arch (Unit 12 in Block 3). The ten units behind

712 Arch Street produced a more strictly domestic deposit dating to the 1760s. While the tenants who discarded these artifacts were fairly well-off in their time, wealthier households occupied grander houses in the project area in the nineteenth century, leaving the side streets—North Seventh and Filbert—to the less affluent. The segregation of neighborhoods by economic position and occupation became more prevalent in the nineteenth century, as a walk through the city of that period will show. Just a few blocks farther up Arch Street—between Eleventh and Thirteenth—a neighborhood of medical professionals was well established by 1820. It is our next stop.

CHAPTER NINE

An Archaeological Walk Through Nineteenth-Century Neighborhoods

The nineteenth century wrought too many changes to summarize here. At the beginning of the century Philadelphia was called the Athens of America, but by midcentury the city had as many problems as every other city that experienced the impact of industrialization and the explosive effects of absorbing the labor it took to do the work. From the microhistorical point of view that archaeological projects reach, there were changes in all aspects of life—from the way people set their tables to how they disposed of waste. There were changes in diet, in health care, in child rearing, in fashion, and in etiquette, to name just a few, and while not all of these are discussed here they have been explored by historical archaeologists. On this particular walk we visit a neighborhood of medical practitioners, an Irish enclave, and an institution devoted to reforming wayward women. First is Doctor's Row.

Stop 1: Doctor's Row

The Pennsylvania Convention Center takes up the two blocks between Eleventh, Race, Thirteenth, and Arch Streets. It's a sort of Gothamesque building that looks like the set for a Superman movie. The building is directly across the street from my office, which is housed in one of the old warehouse buildings that used to dominate the neighborhood. *To get there walk west on Arch Street under the overpass to the corner of Twelfth* (Figure 9.1). It's a short distance from Seventh to Twelfth, but it's a distance that took the city a long time to cover. Substantial residential development did not reach as far west as Eleventh Street until the second quarter of the nineteenth century (Figure 9.2). It began with large townhouses lining Arch Street; much smaller houses filled the spaces between the industrial buildings that had been built on the alleys to the north during the last decade of the eighteenth century.

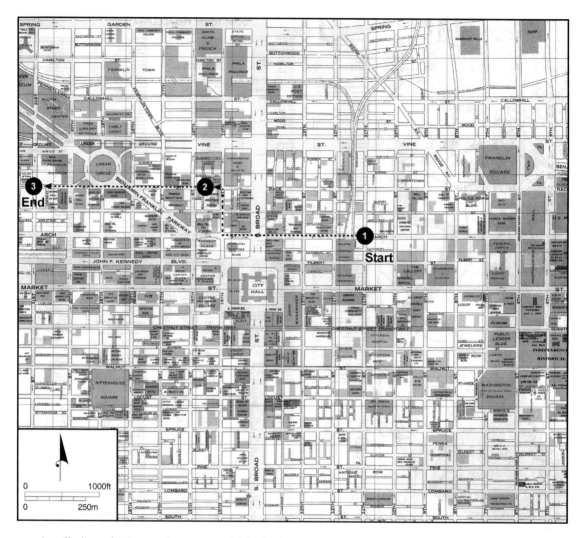

9.1. A walk through nineteenth-century neighborhoods.

Conveniently enough, John Milner Associates did the archaeological investigation for the Convention Center in 1988; Belinda Blomberg was the principal investigator. The historical research for the project discovered that between 1840 and 1870, physicians, druggists, and dentists occupied nearly every building on the 1100 and 1200 blocks of Arch Street, and Blomberg wanted to use archaeology to learn about nineteenth-century medical practice.[1] In particular, she was interested in finding out whether the doctors on Arch Street still used bleeding or bloodletting as a cure.

The famous eighteenth-century Philadelphia physician Benjamin Rush championed

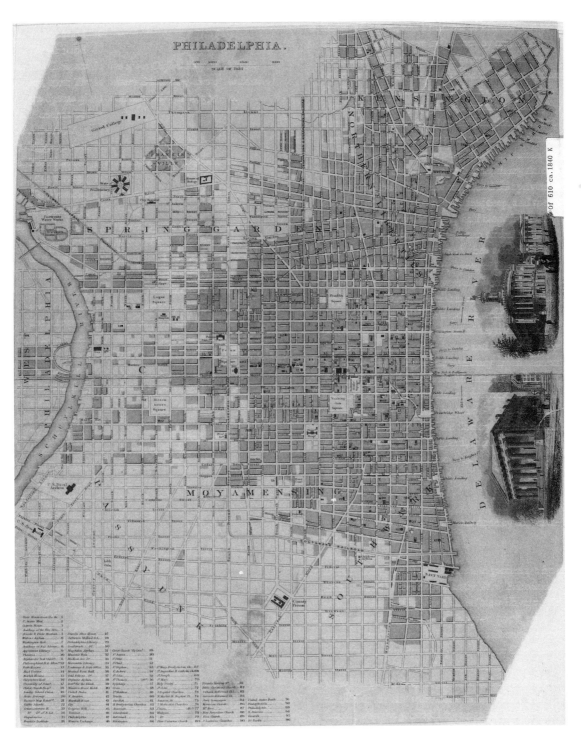

9.2. Charles Knight map of Philadelphia, 1840. (Historical Society of Pennsylvania)

bloodletting, and the practice continued to be popular up to the Civil War. Homeopathic doctors, however, were already questioning the effectiveness of this technique by 1840, and the establishment of the Homeopathic Hospital on Filbert Street below Eleventh in 1867 raised the possibility that the doctors in the neighborhood might have given up the practice entirely. Dr. Walter Williams, a pioneer in homeopathic medicine and co-founder of the Homeopathic Medical College, lived at 118 North Eleventh Street, just outside the project area, and Dr. William A. Reed, a professor of physiology at the college, lived at 1103 Arch, also outside, but very close, to the project area. Other prominent medical practitioners in the neighborhood were Dr. Robert M. Huston, emeritus professor of materia medica and general therapeutics at Jefferson Medical College; George Wood, professor of the theory and practice of medicine and clinical medicine at the University of Pennsylvania, a co-founder of the Philadelphia College of Pharmacy, and a contributor to the first edition of the *United States Pharmacopoeia;* and Dr. H. N. Guernsey, a faculty member at the Homeopathic College.

Physicians in this period had their offices in their homes, and Blomberg thought their privies might contain evidence of bloodletting. She proposed to take soil samples from primary privy deposits, that is, soil layers that related to occupation of the property, and test them for hemoglobin. While she knew that blood could derive from other sources (human waste, menstruation, or even animals), she thought a positive correlation between a doctor's presence on a property and hemoglobin in combination with the absence of such a correlation when a doctor was not present would be suggestive. As far as she knew, testing for hemoglobin had never been done in an urban archaeological context in the United States. It had, however, been used in Scotland by archaeologists who were trying to "isolate medical treatments involving bloodletting" at the Medieval Hospital at Soutra.[2]

Following the Scottish archaeologists' lead, Blomberg used a standard hemoccult test that detects hemolyzed blood in feces and produces a false positive rate only about 1 percent of the time. As described in her report, the test uses "hydrogen peroxide [which] oxidizes gum guaiac, a resin extracted from wood, to a blue colored compound in the presence of hemoglobin."[3] Multiple soil samples were tested from primary strata in privies on the Pennsylvania Convention Center site, and comparative samples were taken from other sites (the Vine Expressway and Bourse Garage/Omni Hotel) where doctors did not live.

The earliest samples to test positive came from a privy at 1107 Arch Street (Figure 9.3). The soils were from what Blomberg calls "residual primary deposits," which are the nightsoil left on the sides of the privy after it had been cleaned.[4] The artifacts from two small deposits at the base of the upper shaft of a double-shaft privy dated to the first half of the nineteenth century, but unfortunately there is no available information on who

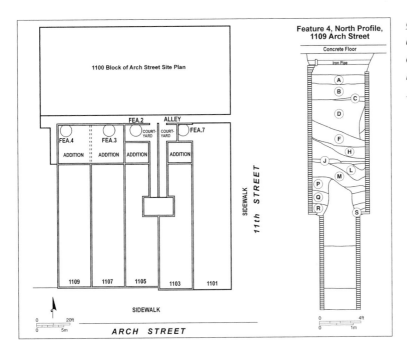

9.3. Site plan of the 1100 block of Arch Street showing the line of privies at the backs of the lots and a profile of the fill layers in Feature 4.

lived there in that period. A Dr. Reeve moved to 1107 Arch in 1850, but the privy had apparently been thoroughly cleaned during his residence, leaving no appropriate soils for testing.

Four out of six samples tested positive from strata recovered from the privy at 1103 Arch Street. The positive samples (L1–L4) came from soils characterized as a primary-percolation deposit at the base of the upper shaft of a double-shaft privy. The artifacts in this stratum included a set of blue transfer-printed pearlware plates manufactured in England by J. and R. Clewes (1818–34), whiteware/ironstone ceramics, also manufactured in England by Ridgeway and by Meir and Son (1837–97), pressed glass dishes, and Ricketts molded bottles dating to the middle of the nineteenth century. The most recent artifact from this layer was a vulcanized rubber button, not manufactured until 1851. Dr. O. H. Costil lived at 1103 Arch Street in the early 1840s, Dr. S. S. Brookes lived there from 1850 to 1855, Dr. William Reed was there until 1861, and Dr. Cooper was there in the 1870s. One would not expect Reed, as a professor of physiology, to have been practicing bloodletting, but Costil and Brookes may well have. The negative samples were from a deeper deposit in the privy.

Ten out of twenty soil samples from the privy at 1109 Arch Street tested positive for hemoglobin. These results were particularly telling because the samples that tested negative all came from strata that dated to years after which doctors lived on the property.

Privies

Since the 1950s, archaeological projects have encountered the remains of more than 319 privies in Philadelphia. This number does not count the ones found on the Constitution Center block and not yet reported. The known privies generally consist of a circular shaft made of dry-laid brick, although exceptions include a few oval and rectangular ones. There were also less permanent privies constructed of barrels piled on top of one another. The brick-lined privies that have been found vary in depth, both because many were truncated by later buildings and also because a law first passed in 1763 set standards for different parts of the city. On much of the high ground north of Market Street privies were allowed to be twenty feet deep, but in many places south of Market they could only be fifteen feet deep. The shallowest depth allowed— six feet—was for the strip of ground bordering the Delaware River. The purpose of the law was to prevent nearby water sources from being contaminated with human waste. The implications of contamination for public health were recognized early in Philadelphia, and when the law was renewed in 1769 fines were added for noncompliance. By the end of the eighteenth century there were also restrictions on how close a privy could be built to a lot boundary—not less than two feet.

The double-shaft privy appears to have been a nineteenth-century innovation that facilitated cleaning. Only twenty-one of these have been excavated in the city, most but not all of them north of Market Street. A double-shaft privy consists of a larger-diameter upper cylinder above a smaller-diameter lower one. The base of the upper shaft is typically fitted with a wooden plank floor where solid waste could accumulate, while the liquid waste drained through the floor into the lower shaft and gradually leached out into the surrounding soil. Barbara Liggett and other archaeologists have argued that the accumulations of artifacts on the wooden floors of these double shafts were put there intentionally to facilitate percolation. They also contend that artifacts were placed in the bottoms of single-shaft privies that exceeded allowable depths. Whether the artifact deposits were intentional or unintentional, these items found at the bottom of privies supply urban archaeologists with their richest artifact assemblages—indeed, with their most important data.

Of the positive samples, one from the stratum labeled S on the profile dated to the early years of the nineteenth century, five (from strata Q and P) to the middle years (1833–50), and four (from strata M and N) to later in the century (1860–85). It is not known who lived at 1109 when S was deposited, but a dentist, Joseph Parker, was there between 1841 and 1849 and a Dr. Levick was there between 1853 and 1870.

Blomberg compared the value of the ceramic assemblages recovered from the various strata in order to speculate on the occupants' economic wherewithal. Although the occupant or occupants in the earliest period had only edge-decorated plates and plain creamware bowls, which were neither fancy nor expensive in the period, their teawares were more elaborate and certainly more expensive than those recovered from the strata dating to the middle and late nineteenth century.[5] The tablewares, especially from stratum Q, however, were worth more than those in either the early or the later strata. While these rankings do not mean much by themselves, they do suggest that the dentist Parker's household was relatively well-to-do. His family owned a set of sepia transfer-printed dishes in the Regina pattern and porcelain tea and tablewares, some in the Fitzhugh pattern. The Fitzhugh would have been particularly expensive.

The only artifacts dating specifically to medical practice found in the early and middle deposits were glass test tube vials, two in stratum R (combined with S which tested positive for hemoglobin) and one in stratum Q. Thirteen pharmaceutical bottles were recovered from stratum Q, but this number could well have come from the dentist's household rather than from his professional practice. The vial from stratum R was tentatively identified as containing iodine. According to Blomberg, a lecture given by George B. Wood to the Medical Department of the University of Pennsylvania in 1842 claimed that iodine and its compounds were the only really new remedies that had come into general use since he began practicing in around 1826, suggesting that the unknown occupant of 1109 was aware of the latest products.[6]

The deposit dating to Dr. Levick's time (stratum M) included mainly plain ironstone ceramics, which were fashionable in the 1850s and '60s, and a variety of porcelain tea and tablewares. The four glass vials and a pipette in the deposit probably related to Dr. Levick's practice. The pipette would have been used for moving or transferring quantities of liquids. Even more interesting were the marked patent medicine bottles in this layer. Whether they were used in Levick's or another doctor's practice, or in their families' households, their presence suggests that even medical practitioners resorted to the less than scientifically proven cures of the day. Eight of the thirteen pharmaceutical bottles recovered were marked:

TILDEN CO/NEW YORK

. . . ARCH & 10TH STS . . .

WYETH BRO/PHILA (two bottles)

MCCIAN . . . LADR

. . . NAL (printed upside down) ARCH & TENTH STS, PHILA

/KAYS/COAGULINE

HT HELMBOLD/GENUINE/FLUID EXTRACTS/PHILADELPHIA

. . . RD/ . . . MER/ . . . NE . . . K

Charles Rosenberg, whose book *The Care of Strangers: The Rise of America's Hospital System* deals with mid-nineteenth-century medical practice, claims that doctors offered patent medicines to their patients in order to seem to be treating illnesses they did not yet understand or have any cures for. Doctors' incomes depended on patients' fees, and they needed to at least appear to be capable of treating disease.

Three (H3–H5) of the seven samples taken from the privy at 1105 Arch Street also tested positive for hemoglobin. Based on diagnostic artifacts (four coins with dates in the 1870s made into cufflinks) in the layer below H and on the artifacts included in H, the stratum appeared to date between 1878 and 1885. It consisted of nightsoil left at the bottom of the upper shaft of a double-shaft privy. The artifacts included machine-made glass dated after 1903 mixed in with generally earlier ceramics. Most of the artifacts found in this privy came from the layer directly below stratum H. Blomberg identifies this stratum as a mixture of primary and percolation fill. Although the two soil samples from that lower stratum tested negative, the date ranges for the samples, 1810–78 and 1810–60, overlap with dates when doctors were present on the property. Dr. John Wiltbank lived at 1105 Arch Street between 1856 and at least 1870, and homeopathic physician David R. Posey also lived there in 1870, but it is not clear for how long. The artifacts recovered from stratum K suggested a well-to-do household or households. Of particular note were the food remains, which included more beef and venison than any of the other privies in the project area, and greater variety including deer, pig, sheep, rabbit, squirrel, chicken, quail, duck, goose, pigeon or dove, and turkey. Possible medical artifacts found at 1105 Arch Street were thirty-three pharmaceutical bottle fragments and one glass vial.

It is uncertain who was responsible for the hemoglobin in the samples from stratum H, but Blomberg speculates that it was one of the doctors who was there before 1880 when Sarah Thomas, a widowed dressmaker, her daughter, and an Irish servant moved in. Dr. Posey is the most likely candidate, even though his being a homeopathic physician makes it tricky to explain why he might have used bloodletting, as the principles of homeopathic medicine specifically excluded it as a treatment. However, as Charles Rosenberg has pointed out, physicians needed to attract patients and they sometimes did whatever the patients wanted in order to keep their clientele. Although bloodletting was less fashionable after the middle of the nineteenth century it was, according to Rosenberg, still carried out in the 1880s.

There is, however, another possible interpretation. The same stratum that contained the positive hemoglobin samples contained cloth, pins, and buttons, all suggestive of the seamstress's trade. The blood may well have come from the all female household that occupied the property after 1880. It was, after all, the underlying stratum that dated to the years when Drs. Wiltbank and Posey were definitely in residence.

Dick Tyler, the head of the Philadelphia Historical Commission when the Convention

Center project was done, was particularly impressed with using a scientific technique to test samples recovered archaeologically to investigate a historical issue. Trained as a historian, Tyler didn't always see what you could learn from archaeology that you couldn't learn from documents. Looking for evidence of bloodletting, however, seemed worthwhile. Tyler had also been involved in the First African Baptist Church project. In that case, he immediately recognized the unique opportunity to investigate an underreported and uninterpreted population at the edge of the city. The Tenth Street First African Baptist Church burial ground, which was in use between 1810 and 1822, was just one block east and about four blocks north of where the doctors lived later in the nineteenth century. The Eighth Street burial ground, in use between 1823 and 1842, was three blocks east.

In the 1990s another historical issue was addressed by archaeologists. As more and more immigrants poured into American cities, archaeologists (and many other social scientists) turned their attention to the expression of ethnic identity. Treated as a process rather than a constellation of characteristics, the expression of ethnicity in the past was particularly approachable in urban contexts because cities had always been magnets for immigrants. By 1860, 30 percent of Philadelphia's population was foreign born, including ninety-five thousand Irish and forty-four thousand Germans.[7] They clustered in neighborhoods where housing was affordable and left remains of their lives in backyards and privies that were subsequently covered with large industrial buildings and parking lots. As the city continued to grow, the parking lots became building sites. Although not all of these sites were subject to the requirements of the National Historic Preservation Act, those that used public funding were, and plenty of urban excavations in Philadelphia and elsewhere have explored the alleys and courtyards that once housed immigrant workers. The next stop is such a neighborhood. *Walk west on Arch Street and turn right at Fifteenth. The Gateway project included a block between Fifteenth, Sixteenth, Spring, and Summer (now the Vine Expressway) Streets.*

Stop 2: An Irish Enclave

The population of Philadelphia more than doubled between 1850 and 1880, with much of the increase attributable to the influx of Irish and German immigrants. Although the immigrant groups didn't establish exclusive neighborhoods, there was some clustering with the Germans favoring the area northeast of the Old City and the Irish concentrating in the south and southwest. The Irish, however, were dispersed throughout the city, many living in the alley dwellings that were built around courtyards behind and between major streets. An excavation done in 1991 investigated one of these alley communities.[8]

The excavation included the block bound by Vine Street on the north, Fifteenth Street

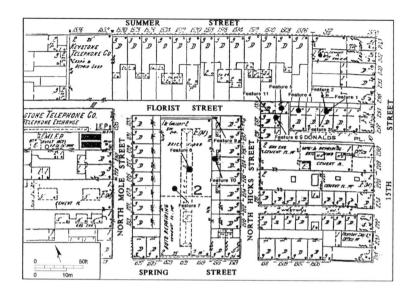

9.4 *Detail of a fire insurance map of Philadelphia produced by the Sanborn Map Company, 1916, showing the features found in the Gateway project area. (From McCarthy et al. 1994)*

(left) 9.5. *Providence Court in Philadelphia in the early 1920s, showing houses similar to those that existed on McDonald's Place in the mid-nineteenth century. (Temple University Libraries, Urban Archives, Philadelphia, Pennsylvania)*

on the east, Spring Street on the south, and Sixteenth Street on the west (Figure 9.4). When the work began most of the buildings that once stood there had been taken down. Like so many urban archaeological sites, the cleared area had been paved with asphalt and was being used as a parking lot. The earliest houses on this block were built in the early nineteenth century, but what John McCarthy, the principal archaeologist for the project, was most interested in were remains left by the Irish families who once occupied the inner courtyards. Built by developers, the courtyards were lined with two- and three-story tenements (Figure 9.5). On this block the courtyards were created by North Mole, Florist, and Hicks Streets in the middle of the block and McDonald's Place and Western Avenue on the eastern side of the block. Excavation trenches were strategically placed to test the backyards associated with these streets.

Privies were found behind 3 and 5 McDonald's Place (Features 3 and 4). Both properties were developed before 1860 and both were occupied by Irish families between 1860 and 1870. Another privy, Feature 5, was found farther west on McDonald's Place, but that property was eventually reconfigured to face the northeast corner of North Hicks Street (235 North Hicks). The contents of the privy, though, were probably associated with the Irish residents of McDonald's Place who predated the reconfiguration of the street. A well found farther to the west in what was originally an open space (eventually 231 North Hicks Street) was probably used communally, serving the McDonald's Place residents and their neighbors. The neighborhood was referred to as McDonald's Place.

There were also features in what had been the open space between North Hicks and North Mole Streets. A privy (Feature 7) found there was either associated with a lot on the east side of North Mole Street, occupied by an Irish household in 1880, or with the house that faced Spring Street at number 1521, occupants unknown. There was yet another privy (Feature 10) on the east side of the open space, probably associated with the Irish household that lived at 228 Hicks Street between 1850 and 1860. Needless to say, the density of the privies and their proximity to the backs of the houses would have created a less than pleasant living environment.

The least disturbed and richest artifact deposits associated with Irish households came from Features 3, 4, and 10, and McCarthy and his colleagues concentrated on them in their artifact analysis, although Feature 4 was eventually eliminated because of sampling error.[9] Feature 3, associated with an Irish household or households living at 3 McDonald's Place, contained several distinct layers of nightsoil. The bottom three layers were combined into one stratum because ceramic vessels within them mended with each other. Above that stratum was a layer of ash, which in turn was overlain by another layer of nightsoil. Perhaps the ash marked a change in tenants or owners of the property. The ceramics recovered from both nightsoil layers suggest they were deposited in the 1840s and '50s, probably while the privy was in use. Both the upper and lower nightsoils contained more transfer-printed ceramics than undecorated ones and even fewer edge-decorated or banded ones (Table 9.1). Highly decorated ceramics were more expensive in the mid-nineteenth century and they were also more fashionable. McCarthy speculated that the use of these ceramics by the Irish might have been "associated with ceramic display." At Five Points in New York City, a mid-nineteenth-century ceramic assemblage, from a cesspool full of artifacts relating to Irish immigrants living in a tenement on Pearl Street, also included good amounts of transfer-printed wares manufactured in Stafford-

Table 9.1. Ceramics from the Gateway Site in Philadelphia and Five Points in New York

	Gateway Feature 3, F		Gateway Feature 3, H–J		Five Points Feature J, 1850		Gateway Feature 10		Five Points Feature J, 1870	
	#	%	#	%	#	%	#	%	#	%
Hand painted	5	(5.5)	57	(9.2)	20	(10.9)	39	(21.6)	7	(5.8)
Transfer printed	49	(54.4)	268	(43.5)	84	(45.7)	6	(3.3)	27	(22.3)
Banded/dipped	14	(15.6)	90	(14.6)	1	(0.5)	4	(2.2)	1	(0.8)
Edge decorated	1	(1.1)	53	(8.6)	10	(5.4)	3	(1.6)	4	(3.3)
Plain	19	(21.1)	135	(21.9)	27	(14.7)	122	(67.4)	62	(51.2)
Porcelain	—		—		14	(7.6)	—		7	(5.8)
Other	2	(2.2)	13	(2.2)	28	(15.2)	7	(3.9)	13	(10.7)
Total	90	(99.9)	616	(100.0)	184	(100.0)	181	(100.0)	121	(99.9)

Note: The totals for Features 3 and 10 at Gateway are based on ceramic sherds. The totals for Feature J at Five Points are based on ceramic vessels.

shire. In the case of Five Points, more than half of the transfer-printed ceramics from the earliest nightsoil layer in the cesspool belonged to vessels associated with tea. Although the residents were not well-to-do, they clearly valued the ceramics that were identical to the ones they used at home in Ireland, especially for the all-important ritual of drinking tea.[10]

The artifacts found in Feature 10 at Gateway came from fills that were presumed to have been stored elsewhere on the site and redeposited in the privy when it was closed in about 1907.[11] The fills, which were analyzed together, appeared to date to the 1850s and '60s, when there were Irish residents on the property. Unlike the nightsoil layers from Feature 3, these fills included many more undecorated ceramics than hand-painted and transfer-printed ones and practically no edge-decorated and banded ones. The change to plain ceramics is consistent with trends at the time and is further evidence that the Irish were willing to invest in what was considered fashionable. This was also true at Five Points, where the most recent layer of nightsoil in the cesspool on Pearl Street also included more plain granite wares than transfer-printed ones. It is interesting that the decorated wares that did come from the Feature 10 deposit included considerably more hand-painted wares than transfer-printed ones. This may be an expression of personal taste, since the neighbors (Feature 3) had more transfer-printed vessels than hand-painted ones. The Irish assemblage from Five Points included very few hand-painted ceramics.

The food remains from Feature 3 indicate that in addition to mutton, pork, and beef, fish and fowl were consumed in some quantity (15 percent fish and 14 percent fowl in the earliest nightsoil). The majority of the meat consumed, however, came from the three major mammals: sheep, 24 percent; pig, 23 percent; and cattle 23 percent. This is different from Five Points, where the Irish seem to have consumed very little fish, even though it would have been considerably less expensive than the pork they evidently preferred. Chicken made up a very small proportion in the Irish diet at Five Points, probably because it was expensive. The chicken found in the McDonald's Place features may have been home grown, raised in backyards and slaughtered there, or maybe it was cheaper in Philadelphia.

When McCarthy and his colleagues wrote their report, there weren't any other Irish assemblages from Philadelphia to use for comparison. Instead they compared the McDonald's Place materials with what had been recovered at Liberty Court, an African-American neighborhood between Ninth and Tenth streets south of Vine. The African-American workers generally spent less on material goods, probably because they had less to spend. African Americans in Philadelphia were at a disadvantage in the middle of the nineteenth century, as they were losing jobs to newly arrived immigrants who were willing to work for even lower wages to get a foothold in their new homes. McCarthy also compared the ceramics and glass bottles from McDonald's Place with materials recovered from a feature identified as Irish-French in Paterson, New Jersey. That assemblage was analyzed by Lu Ann De Cunzo as part of her study of the Dublin section of Paterson, a neighborhood of Irish workers who came to the city in the 1840s to work in the many mills located there. The ceramics from Paterson and McDonald's Place were generally comparable.[12]

The Five Points project in New York City, reported in 2000 and explored in many publications, has thrown further light on the Irish immigrant experience.[13] Five Points was considered New York City's most notorious nineteenth-centuy slum, a characterization that has been perpetuated by such works of fiction as *The Alienist* by Caleb Carr and the Martin Scorsese movie *The Gangs of New York*. An archaeological project done on the site of a new federal courthouse in the formerly infamous neighborhood provided a glimpse into the lives of the people who really lived there—newly arrived Irish immigrants, Eastern European Jews, African Americans, and eventually Italian Americans. Like the immigrants crowded into unsanitary courtyard communities in Philadelphia, the Irish at Five Points in the middle of the nineteenth century were packed into tenement apartments. Overflowing privies and, later, school sinks (communal privies that could be flushed out) filled the small yards behind the buildings while those same yards were where children played and housewives hung the laundry to dry. The Irish in New York and in Philadelphia suffered enormous discrimination even as they displaced African Americans in the workplace. Unskilled jobs fluctuated with the season and wages were notoriously low. Women worked at home—doing outwork in the garment industry, taking in laundry, and keeping boarders—to add to family income, but even then resources were limited. What archaeological investigations in these neighborhoods have revealed is what Irish families did with those resources. In both Philadelphia and New York, families ate well, enjoying meals with lots of meat, including pork, mutton, and beef. They set respectable tables, choosing Staffordshire dishes that reminded them of home and were not much different from what the middle classes were using, although there were fewer matching sets and fewer serving pieces.

Employment opportunities were good for immigrants in Philadelphia, with three major industries—textiles, machinery fabrication, and transportation—absorbing as much labor as was available. Housing opportunities in the city were superior to New York and Boston, where there were also huge influxes of Irish immigrants. According to historian Dennis Clark, small rowhouses were built throughout Philadelphia between 1850 and 1870. These brick structures measured about sixteen by thirty-one feet; they had two stories, with two bedrooms on the second floor and a living room and kitchen on the first floor. With a cellar and gas service they sold for a thousand to twenty-five hundred dollars new and could be rented for as little as eight to fifteen dollars per month. Clark claims that between 1840 and 1851 more than 5,000 of these houses were added to the city, with another 1,535 built in 1861, 2,154 in 1862, and 2,462 in 1863. There were parts of Philadelphia that were referred to as slums, but even in those neighborhoods (Moyamensing, Southwark, Grays Ferry, Kensington, and Port Richmond) the Irish owned as well as rented homes. The Irish were "their own slumlords," according to Clark.[14]

By the end of the nineteenth century the Irish in Philadelphia were moving out of the slums and courtyards onto the main streets. They had founded mutual benefit and aid societies, fire companies, and even elite clubs for business and professional men that served them well. While we don't know how many of the residents on McDonald's Place participated in such organizations, at least one was a fireman, as evidenced by a fireman's dress-coat button lost in Feature 3 (Figure 9.6). The Irish moved up in their employment, opening small businesses and becoming manufacturers as well as professional men. As has been pointed out by Noel Ignatiev, the Irish were white, and they took advantage of their whiteness to advance in the social hierarchy.[15]

Some Philadelphians, however, were less patient for upward mobility. Among these were women who used prostitution to make a better living than they could sewing shirts or doing laundry. Philadelphia's reformers did not approve of these shortcuts to prosperity and set up institutions to teach the wayward souls other ways. The next stop on our walk through nineteenth-century neighborhoods is the site of one of those

9.6. Drawing of a fireman's coat button found in Feature 3 at number 3 McDonald's Place. (Drawn by Sarah Ruch)

institutions, the Magdalen Society of Philadelphia. *Return to Race Street and walk west to Logan Square. The Magdalen Society was where the Franklin Institute now stands on the west side of the square.*

Stop 3: The Magdalen Society

Neither the doctors on Doctor's Row nor the Irish immigrants at McDonald's Place left records of their everyday activities, but forty volumes of documents exist for the Magdalen Society. They include the society's act of incorporation, annual reports, minutes of annual meetings, minutes of Board of Managers meetings, matron's diaries, registers of asylum admissions and releases, and published tracts. For her study of the Magdalen Society of Philadelphia, 1800–1850, Lu Ann De Cunzo reviewed those records, but more important, she placed the society in the context of the culture that spawned the institution.[16] Differences between rich and poor had become pronounced by the end of the eighteenth century, and according to De Cunzo, Philadelphians of the "better" sort became convinced that "the poor as a group posed an imminent danger to the peace, order, and stability of society."[17] Bishop William White, who was the United States senior and presiding bishop of the Episcopal Church, brought together a group of leading citizens in 1800 to form a society to help women who had "been seduced from the paths of virtue, and are desirous of returning to a life of rectitude." The phrase is from the society's act of incorporation and says a great deal about the attitudes of the time.

In the first place, it assumes a natural state of moral virtue for women. Women in need of the Magdalen Society's services were believed to have "fallen" from that natural condition. It also assumes that reform is possible and that returning to a life of rectitude is desirable. Reform, according to society members, "required a repentant soul, the proper Christian instruction, and isolation from the world's temptations in an environment conducive to contemplation, revelation, and regeneration. To rejoin society as productive members, these women also needed practical skills—those of domestic economy—and disciplined habits of industry."[18] To accomplish the desired transformation the society bought a house at the northeast corner of Schuylkill Second (now Twenty-first) and Sassafras (now Race) Streets in 1807. The house looked very much like Bishop White's own house, which was located on Walnut Street between Third and Fourth. In other words, the society chose a structure that met its own standards. It hired David Love and his wife to serve as steward and matron of the Magdalen Society Asylum and waited patiently for women to seek out its services. By 1813, 54 women had passed through the asylum, and by 1850, 925 women had received its services, although fewer than one-third of them returned to a "life of rectitude" as a result of their experience.[19]

The asylum building was no longer standing when the archaeological investigation was conducted on the property. The building had been demolished by the Franklin Institute in 1977 to construct an outdoor science park, and in 1988 the institute wanted to replace the park with the Franklin Institute Science Museum Futures Center. The Clio Group was hired to conduct historical archaeological research before construction began, also monitoring the excavation of utility lines, the laying of the amphitheater's foundation, and the removal of old foundations and an underground fuel tank. Actual controlled excavation was limited to the southwest portion of the lot where the asylum's garden had been.[20] While some artifacts were recovered, De Cunzo's analysis goes well beyond the ceramic sherds found in the garden soil.

De Cunzo suggests that the society intentionally chose a site for the asylum that offered tranquility in a rural, "natural," and thus moral setting. The block at Schuylkill Second and Sassafras was about as far as could be from the Southwark section of the city. Southwark (where our eighteenth-century walk began) was described in a 1789 newspaper article as "the wrong end of the city." Houses of prostitution were supposedly concentrated in the district, and contemporaries complained that this and other poor neighborhoods were little more than "sinks of filth" and "hot beds of disease." The language is familiar. As the class system solidified in Philadelphia and elsewhere, neighborhoods developed that reflected class distinctions. For the middle and upper classes, working-class neighborhoods were places of danger. Crowded, impoverished conditions, they believed, produced disease, moral disorder, and debauchery. Since the Magdalen Society's fundamental purpose was to save fallen women from those very conditions, they sited their institution outside their reach.

The asylum was established in a garden suburb of Philadelphia, diagonally opposite Southwark. There was a large public garden between Schuylkill Second and Third (now Twenty-second and Twenty-third) Streets and another at Schuylkill Fifth and Sixth (now Nineteenth and Twentieth). A short distance to the north were the famous eighteenth-century gardens of Springettsbury, the Penn family estate, and in 1811 the city built the Fairmount Water Works, which were also eventually surrounded by gardens. Although the developed part of the city moved constantly westward, the majority of the poor remained east of Broad Street into the 1840s, thus ensuring the tranquility of the asylum's environs. The asylum itself was surrounded by gardens until some were sacrificed to the enlargement of the original house and ultimately to the construction of another building. According to society records, an addition to the original house was built as early as 1809. The addition had one large room on the first floor for manufacturing, eleven "lodging rooms" on the second, and a large, well-ventilated room on the third that was converted to an infirmary in 1819. In 1831 another addition was built that functioned as a classification building. The board thought the Magdalens needed to be classified according to "moral grades." Unrepentant new arrivals were to be segregated from those who were already on the path to reformation. A passage-way thirty-two feet long separated the classification building from the main structure. Storm damage and deterioration ultimately required that the entire complex be replaced, which was apparently accomplished in the 1850s. The image of the asylum seen here represents that building (Figure 9.7).

Interior spaces were spare. An inmate's room contained a small closet, a single bed, and a table, not much different from a prison cell or a room in a cloister. The reformers believed "worldly goods might distract the Magdalens from their otherworldly concerns. Like the nun in the cloister cell, the Magdalen must shun the world's pleasures for the life of the spirit."[21] These goals must have been particularly challenging for prostitutes, many of whom had entered the profession for the very purpose of participating in the consumer culture of the day. According to Christine Stansell's study of New York City prostitutes in the nineteenth century, women had few employment options, and prostitution was by far the most lucrative. Stansell even claims that most working-class women resorted to prostitution in times of particular need. With its rewards, they could support their children, escape from their families of birth, buy nice clothes, and generally achieve a higher standard of living.[22] Some even became wealthy and married respectable men. The board of the Magdalen Society evidently saw only the evils of prostitution and the threat that unbridled sexuality presented to society. It sought to control women who deviated from the bourgeois norm, to bring them back into the fold.

9.7. *The Magdalen Asylum, drawing made by Catherine M. Leonard from the cover of the Ninetieth Annual Report of the Board of Managers of the Magdalen Society, 1890. The drawing was prepared for the cover of Lu Ann De Cunzo's 1995 study of the Magdalen Society.*

Besides the physical environment, the society used dress to control the inmates. Described in the minutes of the Board of Managers, the uniform consisted of

> A long gown for first days, and short gown for the remainder of the week, of grave colored muslin, nankeen petticoats, white or colored cotton stockings, white muslin handkerchief, muslin cap of neat modest pattern, and neat leather shoes—and for the winter season, the addition of a linsey short gown and petticoat and woolen stockings.[23]

Smoking was prohibited after 1821, drinking was forbidden from the beginning on the premise that it led to illicit sexual activity, and all kinds of social interactions were discouraged. The skills that were taught prepared a reformed Magdalen for life as a servant or a worker in the needle trades, neither of which offered much economic security, and it is no wonder that so many returned to their old ways. From the perspective of the reformers, however, the inmates were being equipped to reenter society at a level that was appropriate. Whereas a prostitute might have attempted to rise in the class hierarchy, her life as a Magdalen ensured that she would remain at the bottom.

The archaeological materials recovered in the southwest garden of the asylum provide very little evidence for rebellion among the inmates. The seventeen pipe stems and five pipe bowls found do not suggest that much smoking took place on the premises, and the few (four) possible liquor bottles in the assemblage may just as well have been used for sweet or salad oils.[24] Inmates were not allowed cologne or jewelry and while there was no conclusive evidence of the former, two clear glass fragments of earrings or a pendant and a cobalt blue fragment of a "paste jewel" were recovered. It is, of course, not possible to determine whether these decorative bits and pieces belonged to inmates or to the matrons who oversaw the institution at various times in its history. The ceramics tell a slightly more cogent story.

A total of 271 ceramic vessels was estimated from small sherds found in a layer of tilled, organically enriched soil in the asylum's southwest garden. Of the 83 vessels classified as tableware, 22 were undecorated white earthenware (creamware or pearlware), 13 were molded white earthenware, and 13 were edge-decorated. Since this deposit of tilled soil probably included trash from the forty-year period between the opening of the asylum in 1807 and the construction of the new building in 1846, it is more than likely that inmates sat down to a table set with plain white or molded dishes in the early decades and to edge-decorated (pearlware) ones in the later decades. In either case, the table was being set as inexpensively as possible. There were also bowls made out of glazed and slipped redware, possibly used for serving food, and other bowls made of decorated porcelain. One undecorated and four molded platters plus one edge-decorated tureen were the only other serving pieces identified. The porcelain bowls—all hand painted, one blue, one under- and overglaze, and one overglaze—are difficult to explain. De Cunzo speculates that they could have been hand-me-downs from board members or leftovers from the matron's own sets of dishes.

Only 45 vessels were definitively identified as teaware, 17 of them made of porcelain including Canton, enameled, and gilded wares in a variety of polychrome floral and geometric designs. In other words, they were fancier than one would expect in an institutional setting. There were also painted and transfer-printed bowl/tea bowls, saucers, and bowl/saucers, and a variety of teapots: one glazed redware, one undecorated creamware, one with blue painted decoration, one with polychrome painted decoration, one sponge decorated, and one black basalt. Not much effort appears to have been made to match teawares, and it is conceivable that inmates had their own cups, which would have been distinguished by different designs. Of the 45 vessels relating to tea, 37 were either tea bowls, bowl/tea bowls, saucers, or bowl/saucers. Perhaps entrusting inmates with individual cups was a lesson in responsibility, a basic component in the society's mission.[25]

The archaeological investigation also looked at features of the landscape. One posthole marked the edge of the garden and another probably belonged to the fence that divided the south yard during renovations in the 1840s (coal was found in the hole). The entire yard was enclosed in a fence eight feet high as early as 1810. It had long spikes at the top, and the board thought the fence would "prevent the escape of discontented Magdalens and elude prying eyes."[26] The fence was repaired and expanded over the years, but in 1823 it was replaced with a wall. The wall was thirteen and a half feet high and fourteen inches thick, with pillars eighteen inches thick. A gateway, ten feet wide, rose twelve and a half feet high on the Sassafras (Race) Street side of the property and another smaller one was placed on the Schuylkill Second (Twenty-first) Street side. Clearly the fence, and later the wall, sent a message. As the century progressed and the philosophy of reform evolved, separation, segregation, isolation, and containment became more and more entrenched. There is no better example than Eastern State Penitentiary, which is discussed in the following chapter.

The nineteenth century was a complicated time in Philadelphia. The righteous Quaker ideology of equality had pretty much been displaced by a culture of rank, but the inclination to help the less fortunate was alive and well. The reformers, however, were confused by the social complexity of a heterogeneous population. Difference equaled deviance, and help, as we have seen, meant bringing others into line. The Irish immigrants on McDonald's Place and elsewhere in the city were part of the confusion, German immigrants were another, and newly emancipated African Americans were yet another. The city was becoming a kaleidoscope of cultures that the white Anglo-Saxon Protestant reformers were only partially able to control. There were also other stresses: cold winters, volcanic eruptions that affected the local climate, hurricanes, droughts, and fires.

Religious ritual, De Cunzo argues, was one of the ways Philadelphians tried to "bring order to a world seemingly gone awry." Although not defined as such, the regimen of the Magdalen Society had all the elements of a religious ritual. Upon entry women were separated from the environment in which they had become degraded. They entered a marginal or liminal state; their identities as sexual, independent beings were denied, they were secluded from men, dressed in drab clothing, fed dull meals on dull dishes, encouraged to spend quiet time alone in their sparely decorated rooms, and trained to do tedious work. Each day began with Bible reading before breakfast and ended with Bible reading before bed, with the Sabbath set apart by even more extensive time for contemplating scripture. Through the ritualized routine, the society believed, these women would be transformed. They would be ready to reenter the world outside the walls of the asylum as productive God-fearing human beings. The trouble is, it didn't work, or at least it worked for only a small proportion of the women who spent time as inmates. The strategy wasn't successful, De Cunzo says, because the women didn't see themselves as sinful, immoral, un-Christianlike, or wicked. They didn't need the asylum to learn how to live or what to believe, although some were willing to use it as a respite, an alternative to prison or the almshouse, and an escape from unhappy family situations, abusive men, and the competitive pressures of the economy. The women had different cultural values and weren't susceptible to those underlying the society's rituals, no matter how well-meaning.[27]

An alternative to bringing the wayward under control was escaping from them altogether. As the nineteenth century progressed, the city spread out horizontally, with the well-to-do removing themselves completely from the Old City to the communities of the Main Line, Chestnut Hill, and beyond. As economically, ethnically, and racially distinct neighborhoods became more established, their residents became invisible to one another, a feature that has lasted into the present.

CHAPTER TEN

The Legacy of William Penn
and the Power of the Past

Philadelphia's archaeological past, the past we walked through in Chapters 8 and 9, is not easy to see. Even the brick outlines of eighteenth-century buildings that were taken down when Independence National Historical Park was created in the 1950s do little to suggest the vibrancy of the early city. But the archaeological process of finding buried remnants of Philadelphia's past is ongoing, and it is amazing how often the process encounters the legacy of William Penn. Two projects done in 2005–6 met with the "proprietor" in very different ways. The first, in Franklin Square, touched on Penn and his direct descendants who, in the spirit of religious freedom, rented and ultimately sold the square to a church for use as a burial ground. The second, at Eastern State Penitentiary, traced the route of an escape tunnel from one of the original cell blocks that belonged to the extraordinary architectural creation that was intended to inspire repentance, an approach to prison reform that interested Penn a century before the penitentiary was built. It is not only through the physical design of Philadelphia that the proprietor is still with us; it is also through many of the ideals on which he founded the colony.

Franklin Square

One of the things that fascinates me about living in Philadelphia is that I am walking through the city that William Penn and Thomas Holme imagined in 1683. With one exception, the five squares in their original plan are still very much intact. City Hall fills Center Square, but Washington Square, at the southeast corner of the plan, has recently been refurbished and remains the open public space that was intended. Rittenhouse Square and Logan Square (now actually a circle), neither of which had been laid out in Penn and Holme's time because the city didn't extended that far west yet, mark the western corners of the original plan, and Franklin Square, originally known as Northeast Square, has just recently become a kind of mini-amusement park with a beautifully restored fountain at its center. A grant from the state of Pennsylvania to Philadelphia in 2005 called for (and funded) a refurbished, enlivened Franklin Square as well as storytelling benches throughout Independence National Historical Park. Under an umbrella organization called Once Upon a Nation, storytelling began in the summer of 2005 and construction in the square was under way by the following spring.

Although Franklin Square was one of the original five squares, it had been neglected by the city since the construction of the Benjamin Franklin Bridge in 1926. The fast-moving traffic on and off the bridge made the square difficult to reach, and its location outside the mainstream of tourist activity on Independence Mall left it to local habitués in need of someplace to hang out. The square was considered run-down and dangerous even though crowds of preschoolers used its dilapidated playground daily. The opening of the Constitution Center at the northern end of Independence Mall (catty-corner to the square) brought increased activity to the immediate vicinity and plans were made to convert the square into a place for family recreation. The initial design, developed in

10.1. The Franklin Square Fountain, lithograph printed by J. Childs & Company, 1851.

FOUNTAIN IN FRANKLIN SQUARE

2005, included a carousel, a historically themed miniature golf course, an updated playground, food kiosks, decorative flags, and, most important of all, a restored fountain. The fountain in the middle of the square was a showpiece in mid-nineteenth-century Philadelphia. A nineteenth-century observer described "40 jets of water [falling] into a marble basin which was guarded from intrusion by an iron railing round the top"; a lithograph from the early 1850s shows a lacy wrought-iron fence below the iron railing with trees planted decorously around its edge (Figure 10.1).[1]

Before the fountain, and well before the square became a public park, the land was used for other purposes, among them as a burial ground for the First German Reformed Church. Rev. George Michael Weiss and four hundred members of the church came to Philadelphia from the Palatinate region of western Germany in 1727. By 1741 they had bought a lot at the southeast corner of Fourth and Sassafras (now Race) Streets for their church, but the lot was not big enough to accommodate a burial ground. Philip Bohme, the church's pastor at the time, and Jacob Siegel, an elder, requested the use of land in Northeast Square, for which they agreed to pay fifty pounds sterling and a yearly quitrent of five shillings. It appears that the request went originally to Thomas Penn, the proprietor's son, who issued a warrant to Benjamin Eastburn, Pennsylvania's surveyor general. As of 1742 the church was using a plot of ground that began 100 feet west of Sixth Street and extended another 150 feet to the west to bury their dead. Bounded by Vine Street on the north, the burial ground extended 306 feet to the south (Figure 10.2). In 1763 the church bought the original plot from John Penn, the proprietor's grandson, and rented additional ground as the need arose.[2]

Although it seems peculiar that a church would be granted land in one of the squares reserved for public use, portions of Southeast (now Washington) Square were also rented out in the eighteenth century. As early as 1704 William Penn himself set aside the area as a potter's field and stranger's burial ground. The city took possession of Southeast Square in 1706, but it did not attempt to take control

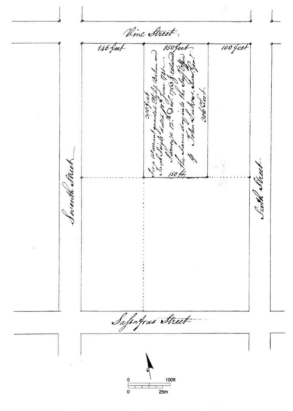

10.2. Plat of the original burial ground, 1741. (From the records of Old First Reformed Church of Philadelphia)

of Northeast Square until the end of the eighteenth century. In 1797 the City Council decided the lease to the church was illegal and resolved to enter suit for the recovery and possession of the ground. Nevertheless, the church held on and it wasn't until 1836 that the Supreme Court of Pennsylvania "concluded that the church congregation had no right to the land, that the 1741 grant from Governor Thomas Penn and the subsequent proceedings were illegal, the Penn family having no title to the land."[3]

The descendant congregation, still known as Old First Church, is well aware of the history of its original burial ground and also of the previous construction projects that have disturbed burials. A sewer was laid from the southwest corner to the northeast corner of the square in 1915, and a subway was dug under the southern portion in the 1930s. A few of the headstones found during these previous projects are displayed in the church narthex (Figure 10.3). Many more headstones were supposedly tipped over and covered with fill when the area was landscaped to create a public square in 1836. According to a manuscript history of the graveyard in the Genealogical Society of Pennsylvania, "very few if any of the bodies were removed. The gravestones were laid flat upon the graves and the whole covered with earth to a depth of several feet."[4] Archaeologists monitoring the new construction could therefore expect to encounter headstones lying on top of the burials they marked.

According to church records, as many as thirty-one hundred bodies were buried in the square during the ninety-five years it was in use.[5] Among them were the early ministers of the church, including Rev. Michael Schlatter, who served as pastor of the combined

10.3 Workman with headstones excavated during construction in 1915.

German Reformed congregations of Germantown and Philadelphia from 1747 to 1755, and Dr. Casper Dietrich Weyberg. Weyberg ministered to the Continental troops during the Revolutionary War and was briefly imprisoned for preaching to Hessian soldiers and advocating independence. The descendant congregation was interested in having their headstones if they were found, as well as several others belonging to ministers important in the church's history. On the advice of the archaeological consultant to the project, Once Upon a Nation initiated discussions with the church regarding the disposition of any headstones or burials that were found during construction. By the time work began an agreement was in place that specified lines of communication, how headstones would be moved to the church if they were found, exactly how burials would be excavated if they needed to be removed, how the human remains would be analyzed, and where they would be reinterred. The agreement, or protocol as it was called, followed the format of previously developed compacts for other burial grounds disturbed by construction. It thus sought to ensure that human remains were treated with dignity and respect and in accordance with the wishes of the descendant congregation.[6]

Once Upon a Nation hired John Milner Associates to monitor construction in 2006. Besides the burial ground, the powder magazine for the City of Philadelphia was located on the other side of the square during the Revolutionary War. In the mid-1970s during preparations for the bicentennial, Jeff Kenyon, an archaeologist employed by the University Museum of the University of Pennsylvania, found at least one foundation wall belonging to the magazine, but no thorough investigation had ever been conducted.[7] In spite of the possibility that the planned construction would disturb remains of the powder magazine as well as the burial ground, there was no discussion of canceling the project. With the exception of the miniature golf course, most of the ground-disturbing activities took place outside the area of the burial ground. The golf course, however, was well within its bounds. Alexander Bartlett served as the archaeological monitor for the project. He had spent a year monitoring construction activities in Independence Square and had become expert at fitting in with construction crews and gaining their respect. At Franklin Square he learned everyone's name, bought coffee for the crew when it was his turn, and marshaled so much trust that the workers not only stopped the minute they uncovered something possibly significant, they stopped for things that weren't significant as well. Bartlett was on the site ten hours a day, six days a week for about two months.

The first few weeks were slow; a cobble surface, first interpreted as the floor of an outbuilding—a possible kitchen—appeared under the playground on the west side of the square, but when the cobbles began to show up everywhere else another interpretation was required. We thought they might have related to the use of the square for cattle and horse auctions in the early 1800s, or maybe they were just the first layer of fill that had been placed on the ground before it was developed as a park. The ground was suppos-edly swampy in the eighteenth century and cobbles would have provided percolation at the base of the thick (almost two feet) layer of fill, mostly brick and chunks of mortar mixed with sandy soil that lay above them. The cobbles were not present on the east side of the square where the burial ground was, which suggests they were laid down while the burial ground was still in use.

Construction around the fountain was dramatic; the whole infrastructure was re-moved to prepare for the installation of a new one. The fountain marked the center of the square, and we knew the oldest part of the burial ground began just to the northeast of it. In fact, a mid-nineteenth-century document claimed that the reverends Steiner, Winkhaus, Weyberg, and Hendel lay "east of the sparkling jets of the fountain, a few feet from the edge of the circular gravel walk," and that Schlatter was some distance to the north "about midway between [the fountain] and Vine Street."[8] The first headstone un-covered was found near the northeast corner of the square, possibly outside the bounds of the original burial ground, but a 1797 map shows the area to the east and south of the original bounds to have been "encroached upon" by that year.

The burial dated to 1793, the year of a fierce yellow fever epidemic in Philadelphia. A husband and wife had apparently died of the fever within days of each other. The inscrip-tion on their impressive seven-foot-long headstone read:

In memory of
John George Weibel
Was born April the 10th, 1754
And departed this life October the 11th
1793 Aged 39 years 6 months & 1 day

Also

Charlotte Weibel
Wife of John George Weibel
Who departed this life October the 26th
1793. Aged 33 years.

The stone continued with verse in German, translated here by Barbara Blomeier, the wife of one of the pastors of the congregation's partner church in Germany:

I rest here by my husband's side,
Who short time before me was a prey of illness
In those days of horror.
To me immediately after his going away

> Death seemed through harsh grieving
> As only a sinner's bed.
>
> He waved me with seriousness to the grave.
> Thus I with my pilgrim's staff
> Refused his solemn waving.
> I looked upon the end of the journey
> Gave my spirit in Jesus's hands,
> And Jesus rewarded me with the crown.

Neither Weibel is listed in the church records, but the death of the minister, Rev. Winkhaus, from the same epidemic created a gap in the recordkeeping, which was not resumed until February of the following year.[9]

More headstones followed quickly on the first find. The next three, however, were out of place, appearing to create a kind of retaining wall (Figure 10.4). The fill on one side of the wall differed from the fill on the other, suggesting an intentional landscaping effort. The stones belonged to Philep [*sic*] Ulrich, aged sixteen, who died on July 28, 1785; Jacob Miller, also sixteen, who died November 13, 1788; and Mary Schnider, twenty-seven, who died December 18, 1782. Because the stones were out of place there was no way to connect them with the specific coffin outlines that were found nearby. While the documentary record for this historic burial ground was unusual in that no one even claimed to have moved all the bodies, the record still did not tell the truth. The stones were not simply laid on top of the graves, as claimed; they, or at least some of them, had been reused as curbing for a system of paths, more evidence for which was found in the area of the proposed golf shack.

The footprint of the golf shack measured about twenty-two feet square. The first bucketful the backhoe removed from the area hit yet another upturned headstone, then another, and then another. Bartlett managed to direct the backhoe so that the line was uncovered without moving any of the stones, which were only inches below the present ground surface. Once mapped, they appeared to outline a serpentine pathway, presumably created after the city took back the land in the 1830s (Figure 10.5). The fill on one side of the

10.4. Retaining wall made of headstones dating to the 1780s uncovered in 2006.

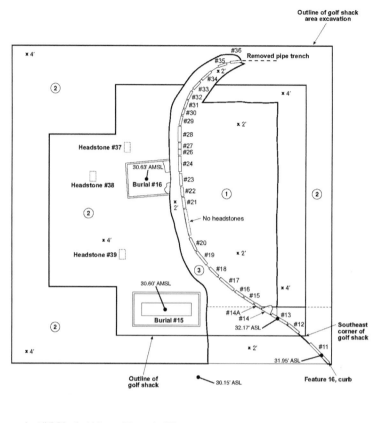

10.5. Diagram of a portion of the curved walkway uncovered in 2006. (From Yamin et al. 2007)

stones was capped with red gravel as if for a path, while the fill on the other side was hard-packed rubble. A watercolor rendering of the square dating to 1824 shows a series of curving walkways in the park, and although there is no way to know whether the exact design was ever realized, the serpentine line of gravestones is suggestive (Figure 10.6).

The hard-packed rubble outside the walkway covered two large vaults (Figure 10.7). The fancier one had a marble lid with beveled edges. A portion of it was covered by the walkway, but the visible part of the inscription read:

10.6. *Watercolor rendering of Northeast (Franklin) Square, designed and drawn by William Rush, 1824. (The Library Company of Philadelphia)*

(right) 10.7. *The two vaults now hidden beneath the golf shack.*

In Memory of
Mrs. FRANCES MAAG
wife of
Mr. HENRY MAAG
who departed this life
September 16
in the year of our Lord
1774
Aged 54 years
Also of
Mrs. SARAH MAAG
Second Wife of Mr. HENRY MAAG
Who departed this Life
July 5th in the Year of our Lord
1783
Aged 55

One wonders if Mr. Maag sacrificed the space reserved for himself to his second wife or whether he waited until the second wife died to bury the first one.

The second vault, also with a beveled lid, did not include an inscription, although a pecked rectangular area in the middle of the lid may have held a brass nameplate. We, of course, wondered if this was the burial place of Michael Schlatter, the minister who was supposedly buried halfway between the fountain and Vine Street. A few datable ceramic sherds found in the rubble fill right above the sarcophagi were consistent with the time the city repossessed the land.

These finds presented problems for the construction. Some of the uprighted head-stones had to be removed, but the vaults were left in place and are now covered by the ticket booth and equipment storage area for the miniature golf course. Representatives of Old First Church were curiously undisturbed by all of this. Although they originally wanted to remove a selection of headstones to their church for display, representatives of Fairmount Park, now custodians of the land for the city, opposed removing anything from the site. Park personnel argued that out of respect for the dead, headstones should be left as close to their original locations as possible. They also noted that a state law specified that historic headstones could only go to an "accredited museum," which the church was not.[10] Taking this news in stride, Nancy Donohue, the archivist for Old First Church and the person who was most closely involved with the project, continued to visit the site, to record the headstones uncovered and consult with the archaeologists. She also wrote a letter to the state requesting museum status in order to prepare for the eventuality of finding a headstone associated with one of the early ministers. For that, the church would mount a fight and wanted to be ready.

During the last week in May 2006 human bones began to turn up in a sewer trench. The first bones found had been previously disturbed, but a second group was associated with a coffin outline. Suspecting there might be more undisturbed graves within the remainder of the trench alignment, Bartlett directed the contractor to remove dirt only down to the depth where graves were likely to be present. We then troweled the surface to look for coffin outlines. Three were found, all oriented east–west in a line cross-cutting the trench. Fortunately the contractor was able to reroute the pipe into an already disturbed area, allowing the bones to rest in peace.

More headstones, this time in situ, were found in the drainage trench that crossed the center of the proposed miniature golf course, and still more were found in another trench farther north. These were earlier, some with dates in the 1760s, and most included inscriptions in old German. There was apparently a dispute in the church about whether to retain German as the language of service or adopt English. The argument was reflected in the fact that some names on headstones dating to the 1770s had been anglicized, while the same names retained their German form in the church records.

Although not all of the burial ground was exposed during the Franklin Square project, enough was revealed to establish the reality of this piece of Philadelphia's past. It is a part that is not widely known, but it adds to the picture of the heterogeneous colony that welcomed people from many different religious denominations. Even though they were found out of place, it did not seem right to just bury the eighteenth-century headstones that served as curbing for a nineteenth-century walkway. We thought they might be incorporated into a kind of memorial garden that would recognize the burial ground and add interest to the refurbished park. The problem was to convince Fairmount Park of the idea. Bill Zumsteg, the ever amiable logistics director for Once Upon a Nation, was in favor of the garden; Donohue wrote the proposal, and Zumsteg confronted park officials.[11] He was turned down, and the stones—all fifty-four of them—were buried without ceremony in a place where other stones had been left in situ. The human bones, however, were treated differently.

Portions of two skeletons were removed from the sewer trench before it was rerouted. Physical anthropologist Dr. Arthur Washburn analyzed the remains, both of which appeared to be young adult females. They were reburied in a small ceremony presided over by Rev. Jeff Shanaberger, the present minister of Old First Church. He and Nancy Donohue, the church archivist, carefully placed the bones in a grave dug in front of the historic marker for the burial ground (Figure 10.8). Although this reburial ceremony was considerably less elaborate than others in which archaeologists have participated in recent years, it served the purpose. It is only odd that the marker is so close to the miniature

10.8. Nancy Donohue and Rev. Jeff Shanaberger reburying the bones recovered in the sewer trench. (Photograph by Alexander Bartlett)

10.9. Mayor John Street at the podium and Governor Ed Rendell, lower right, celebrating the reopening of Franklin Square, August 2006. (Photograph by Alexander Bartlett)

golf course. The refurbished park opened in August 2006 with a very different kind of ceremony, this one presided over by Governor Rendell and Mayor Street (Figure 10.9). No mention was made of the First Reformed Church burial ground.

Eastern State Penitentiary

As just described, Philadelphia's squares may have been refurbished and reinterpreted, but they remain where they were originally intended and the symmetry they create still anchors the city's plan. Penn's vision permeates the city in other ways as well. Although Eastern State Penitentiary was built many years after the founding of Philadelphia, the philosophy behind it was not very different from the founder's own. Along with other Quakers, Penn opposed the severe corporal and capital punishment that were being used in Britain in the seventeenth century. He considered imprisonment an effective alternative, and the penal code he adopted for the colony in 1682 declared the offender's reform to be more important than his punishment.[12]

Conditions in prisons, however, were pretty dismal in the eighteenth century, and a group of progressive Philadelphians—again, mostly Quakers—concerned themselves with their improvement. Soon after the Revolutionary War the Philadelphia Society for Alleviating the Miseries of Public Prisons was formed, including in its membership such luminaries as Benjamin Franklin and Benjamin Rush. The society embraced the Quaker penal philosophy, which stressed individual rehabilitation through solitary confinement coupled with religious instruction, hard work, and prison visitation. The well-meaning reformers proposed to build a "true penitentiary," that is, "a prison designed to create genuine regret and penitence in the criminal's heart." Although the Commonwealth of Pennsylvania did not embrace the idea for another thirty years, the construction of Eastern State Penitentiary in 1829 represented the physical realization of these principles. The penitentiary would not simply punish, it would move the criminal toward spiritual reflection and change. To do this, prisoners were kept isolated from one another. Each had his own cell with his own exercise yard where he remained isolated from all but the most minimal contact with other human beings (Figure 10.10).[13]

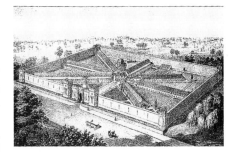

10.10. Eastern State Penitentiary, drawing by Samuel Cowperthwaite, convict number 2954, showing John Haviland's radial design; lithograph published by P. S. Duval and Company, 1855. (The Library Company of Philadelphia)

Several architects competed for the design of Eastern State, with John Haviland winning out over William Strickland, who had designed many of the most distinguished buildings in Philadelphia. According to Norman Johnston's study of Eastern State Penitentiary, Haviland's radial design was similar to many county prisons that were being built in Britain. The architect claimed that he selected the hub-and-spoke arrangement to promote "watching, convenience, economy, and ventilation." The watching, or surveillance, was done from the hub in the middle out of which the seven cell blocks radiated. Each cell required its own exercise yard, flush toilet, and source of heat and ventilation. The toilets were a particular challenge in this era since indoor plumbing was only beginning to be widely introduced. They emptied into pipes that led directly to a central sewer located under the corridor floors. Haviland modeled the exterior of the prison after jails that had been created in England during the decade before he left for America. With its Gothic turrets and forbidding metal gate, it was surely as successful a deterrent to crime as a container for criminals.[14]

Because of this history, and probably even more because it is such a visually extraordinary structure, Eastern State Penitentiary was designated a National Historic Landmark in 1965 while it was still in use. In 1971 the prison closed and the virtually abandoned building began to deteriorate. When Sally Elk became executive director of the historic site in 2000, the forbidding structure was in a state that only photographers could appreciate.[15] Elk had been interested in the site since the 1980s when she was working at the Philadelphia Historical Commission. The city owned the building, but turned it over to the Redevelopment Authority in 1984 to seek proposals for commercial use. Alarmed that such an important landmark might become condominiums or, worse, a shopping center, leaders in the preservation community formed a task force to prevent the sale. As an employee of a city agency, Elk found herself in a difficult position. She couldn't publicly take a stand, but finally even the director of the Historical Commission, Dick Tyler, supported preservation and, under pressure, Mayor Wilson Goode took the building off the market.

With the support of a Pew Foundation grant, a Historic Structures Report was completed for the building in the 1990s and a succession of organizations ran tours. By the end of the decade, though, there was a need for an executive director. Elk had the relevant master's degree, hands-on experience, and connections in the preservation community. She took charge of bringing the building back to life, and with Sean Kelly as program director, the site has become a major historical attraction in Philadelphia, especially at Halloween.

Kelly saw entertainment potential in the prison's creepy long corridors. He went to a Halloween conference and in no time dreamed up an event that takes full advantage of the eerie building. Visitors are "admitted" to prison; they wind through crumbling corridors and thirteen rooms haunted by actors playing resident spooks. The event attracts seventy thousand people a year, but it isn't Kelly's only brainchild. He has also exploited events in the prison's history, including the escape of twelve prisoners in 1945. Willie Sutton, the celebrated bank robber who was incarcerated at Eastern State from 1934 to 1946, was among the twelve escapees and even though the tunnel was dug by someone else its association with Sutton is what attracts attention. In 2000, on the fifty-fifth anniversary of the escape, Kelly staged a reenactment of the prison break on the embankment above Fairmount Avenue where the tunnel exited, and in 2005, in anticipation of the sixtieth anniversary, he hired archaeologists to locate the actual exit from the tunnel, to define the alignment across the prison yard, and determine whether the tunnel was still open.

Finding the tunnel's exit was not exactly a challenging archaeological problem. Photographs taken immediately after the escape showed guards stooping around the hole in front of the prison wall (Figure 10.11). Putting an excavation unit in the right place was simply a matter of counting the stones in the wall and laying it out. We hit a rectangular stain that appeared to represent the closed-up exit from the tunnel at a little more than one foot below the present surface, but there was also another hole that cut through the nice neat rectangular one. The 2000 reenacters, it turned out, had dug themselves a hole to theatrically pop out of that cut right into the one dug by the prisoners. Fortunately the actors left what to them looked like a lackluster assemblage of artifacts behind.

Among the artifacts were a 1945 nickel and fragments of a Sealtest milk bottle that also dated to 1945. Additional milk bottle fragments, melted glass, mesh-reinforced safety glass, and soda bottle glass were also recovered. The prison authorities claimed to have filled the tunnel with ash from the incinerator after the escape, and the melted glass suggested this was at least partially true. The most personal object found in the vicinity of the tunnel's exit was a miniature figurine of Saint Joseph, patron saint of workers, travel-

10.11. Guards outside the penitentiary wall near the exit from the escape tunnel. (Temple University Libraries, Urban Archives, Philadelphia, Pennsylvania)

ers, pioneers, and craftsmen. An Ilco key fragment in the assemblage appeared to have been rolled or flattened and may have served as someone's good luck token.

Finding the tunnel's entrance was a considerably greater challenge than finding its exit. The entrance was in Cell 68 at the end of Cell Block 7. The cell belonged to Clarence Klinedinst in 1945. He was a mason and plasterer, skills he used inside the prison as well as outside. When he replastered Cell 68 he left a portion of the wall open, camouflaging it with a false panel made of cement. A laundry basket, hung over the panel, successfully hid the tunnel entry even from a close inspection by guards right before the escape (Figure 10.12).[16]

Klinedinst began the tunnel alone but was joined by a cellmate, William Russell, sometime during the year. (By the 1940s prisoners were no longer kept strictly in isolation.) Klinedinst and Russell worked at night, "after lights were out." One of them stayed in the cell while the other dug, and they fooled the guards by putting the head of a dummy made from plaster of paris in the bed of the one who was down in the hole. According to Klinedinst's testimony after he was caught, they put the dirt "down the

10.12. *Guard inspecting the entrance to the escape tunnel. (Temple University Libraries, Urban Archives, Philadelphia, Pennsylvania)*

(below) 10.13. *Ingling's diagram of the escape tunnel. (Eastern State Penitentiary)*

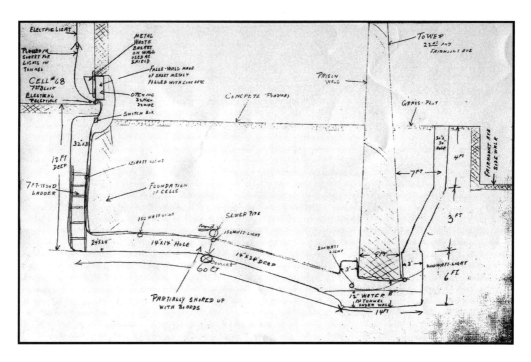

hopper" (toilet) and hid stones under the bed until they got a chance to bury them in the prison yard. Once the tunnel reached the middle of the yard, the dirt was deposited directly into a brick sewer pipe that ran perpendicular to, and under, the tunnel's alignment. Cecil Ingling, the prison overseer, was sent down into the tunnel to record it after the prison break. He claimed "the hole leading into the sewer was kept sealed, except when in actual use, for the purpose of preventing escaped gas from the sewer from filling the tunnel."[17]

According to Ingling's drawing, the tunnel went through the wall behind the laundry basket and cut back under the cell floor before it headed down to a depth of twelve feet

10.14. Ground-penetrating radar grid in the prison yard outside Klinedinst's cell.

(right) 10.15. Matt Harris augering into the tunnel below.

(Figure 10.13). It crossed under the yard, a distance of ninety-seven feet, and then dipped down to fifteen feet to get under the perimeter wall. It wasn't hard to know where to look for the entry to the tunnel—again, there were photographs—but to reach the vertical shaft was another matter. Two days with a jackhammer got just far enough into the wall to see where the tunnel began, but it was not possible to go farther. David Thomas, the JMA employee who did the demolition work, hypothesized that the tunnel entrance was most likely filled with at least four feet of reinforced concrete at the top and ash below that.

The next step in the project was to define the exact route of the tunnel across the prison yard and determine whether any portion of it still remained open. We used ground-penetrating radar for this task. A grid measuring ten by twenty meters was laid out centered on the outside wall of Klinedinst's cell (Figure 10.14). Geoarchaeologist Bill Chadwick then dragged the antenna back and forth along the grid lines to produce vertical sections at one-meter intervals, the expected width of the tunnel. Although the radar signal seemed to be blocked between three and five feet below the surface, two faint anomalies at the appropriate depths were interpreted as potentially relating to the escape tunnel. We used an auger to test those locations.

With an audience made up of Eastern State Penitentiary Historic Site personnel, the press, and a few members of the public, archaeologist Matthew Harris began augering in the location closest (about twenty-one feet) to the cell block wall (Figure 10.15). Once the pavement had been removed, the auger encountered about four feet of soil mixed with crushed brick fragments, oyster shells, bone fragments, mortar, and large quantities of schist, probably fill relating to the construction of the building in the 1830s. Beneath it was silty clay with coal flecking, material laid down to level the ground when the prison was built. This consolidated fill continued to a depth of just more than twelve feet, the depth where the tunnel should have been, but beneath it was undisturbed subsoil. The silty clay was either all that remained of the collapsed tunnel or the hole wasn't within the tunnel alignment at all. Needless to say the audience was disappointed and the archaeologists were just a little embarrassed. But there was a chance to redeem themselves. The next morning, with no one watching, two archaeological technicians augered a hole in the second location that hit a void, which they immediately recognized as a section of tunnel that had not collapsed.

The void began eight and a half feet below the surface and extended to about ten and a half feet. The sediment on the floor of the tunnel was loose, probably as a result of the augering. To look into the tunnel we rented a sewer camera—an Electric Eel Sewer Snake, to be exact. These cameras, which look like microphones with a lens in the top, are made for detecting problems in sewer pipes, transmitting an image from belowground to a computer-controlled monitor. An audience again gathered as Harris lowered the camera into the tunnel. At first the camera showed only the floor of the tunnel, but by manipulating the lead it was possible to move it along the tunnel toward the outside wall of the prison, and suddenly the jumbled remains of wooden shoring appeared. It didn't show much, but it was enough to confirm that at least a portion of the tunnel was still open.

The small diameter of the tunnel and the fact that it seemed to pass through barely consolidated sand made the feat of building it seem even more phenomenal. The site chosen for Eastern State Penitentiary naturally sloped from north to south. Before construction began in 1826 fill was used to level the ground, and it is likely that the tunnel cut through this fill material rather than undisturbed subsoil, a fact Klinedinst would not have known. Clearly he and his partner were taking their lives in their hands, as were the ten other guys who went out with them on April 3, 1945. Willie Sutton latched on to the group at the last minute, but when he wrote his autobiography seven years later, he claimed the tunnel was his own creation. Sutton, who refers to Clarence Klinedinst as "Kliney," calls him his "first recruit." Because Kliney had the outside cell, Sutton says, he planned to go through its wall, which was "5 feet thick," and "then start digging directly down." He told Quentin Reynolds, to whom he dictated his autobiography, "We would have to go 30 feet [down]. I knew that the prison wall itself extended 25 feet beneath the surface of the ground and that it was fourteen feet thick at the base."[18] These figures were all exaggerated. In addition to Kliney, Sutton claims to have recruited six men to do the work during the inmates' yard periods. According to Sutton, prisoners were not forced to go outside during the recreation period and could remain in their cells. Even if that was true for others, it seems unlikely that Willie Sutton, who by that time in his criminal career had broken out of other prisons, would be left to his own devices during recreation period and positively inconceivable that he could have gotten away with directing a crew of a dozen to dig a tunnel under the noses of penitentiary personnel. According to Sutton, he doubled the work force after six months. At least he is honest about being caught. He was one of several prisoners who were apprehended moments after they emerged from the tunnel. Sutton, of course, added a flourish by saying he was shot at several times, probably not true.

10.16. The plaster-of-paris head and artifacts recovered from the tunnel after the escape. (Temple University Libraries, Urban Archives, Philadelphia, Pennsylvania)

With one exception, none of the men stayed out very long. Klinedinst himself was caught within hours and his cellmate, William Russell, made the mistake of visiting his old girlfriend whose father was a policeman. He resisted arrest and was shot seven times. Four other escapees stole a parked milk truck and drove around until they literally ran into a police car. And still another inmate, James Grace, hid out in a nearby city park, but got so cold and hungry that he came back to the prison gate asking to be readmitted. Only one prisoner remained on the outside. The transcribed testimony of the recaptured inmates recounts their experiences, and other documents describe what the guards found in the tunnel. There were three blue shirts, a pair of underdrawers, a large mason's trowel, a nine-inch knife with a three-inch blade, a two-cell flashlight, a homemade ice pick, a toy gun, and three flattened tin cans that were used for digging (Figure 10.16). The men apparently abandoned their possessions, including clothes, and emerged in broad daylight covered with mud. This might have been all right if they had gone out when Klinedinst finished the tunnel at midnight, but Russell had insisted on waiting until morning, which clearly did not work to the escapees' advantage.[19]

The tunnel had electricity, which was ingeniously hooked up to an outlet in Klinedinst's cell. Although the Electric Eel did not pick up any evidence of this system, more powerful cameras brought in the next year did. In 2006, Elk and Kelly wanted to use archaeology again to celebrate the sixty-first anniversary of the tunnel break. This time we came with fancier remote-controlled camera equipment. Using a high-resolution zoom camera and a robotic crawler, along with high-intensity gas-discharge lamps, the arch of the tunnel and its relationship to the remaining pieces of wooden shoring that

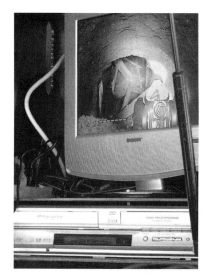

10.17. Image transmitted by the robot crawler from inside the tunnel, April 2006.

once supported the arch could be seen more clearly (Figure 10.17). Although most of the shoring appeared to be out of place, one piece seemed to be in its original position. The wood was painted the same green as was used elsewhere in the penitentiary. The only visible thing that might have been used for digging was a shaped piece of plaster lying on the floor of the tunnel. Hanging off one of the pieces of shoring above it was an electrical wire with a split connection at the end, finally tangible proof of the electrical system Klinedinst had rigged up. Paltry though this evidence may seem, it was exciting to onlookers. Criminals do not inspire awe for their criminal acts, at least not in most of us, but they appear to gain a whole different status when they try to get out. The physical proof of those attempts is awe inspiring. Like feats of athletic prowess celebrated in the Olympics or the circus, prison breaks demonstrate the courage and ability to accomplish acts that seem humanly impossible.

The Power of the Past

These two projects—Franklin Square and Eastern State Penitentiary—connect us to the past in a different way than written documents do. They have a kind of power that is hard to define, maybe because it is inherent in their materiality. No matter how mundane, the buried record—the archaeological record—is tangible evidence that things were different in the past. Sometimes intended, sometimes not, peoples' actions and accomplishments leave a physical signature that cannot be denied. The tangible evidence unexpectedly found on the president's house site has demonstrated exactly how powerful that record can be. Although the finds are nothing more than stone foundations for small portions of the long-gone house where the first two presidents of the United States lived while the federal government was seated in Philadelphia, the foundations have generated a conversation about race rarely seen in a public forum (Figure 10.18).

The excavation, or at least preparations for it, began in April 2007. A company called URS, working closely with the National Park Service, shored the half-acre site that once held the house where George Washington and John Adams lived, and began to remove the fill overlying the cellar foundations of the three buildings that postdated the president's house on the site. Once below the cellar floors they found more foundation walls relating to the earlier house than anyone knew existed. First was a wall running north–south that marked the western edge of the kitchen and its northwest corner (visible in

10.18. Foundations uncovered on the president's house site, 2007. The foundations relating to the president's house lie under later nineteenth-century foundations. (Independence National Historical Park)

the middle of Figure 10.18); the eastern wall appeared to be directly under a later wall. Within the two, at one end, was a deep, rectangular stone-enclosed space that might have been a wine cellar or cold storage. It was not known that the kitchen had a basement, but it clearly did and there was another wall that belonged to an underground passage between the kitchen and the front portion of the house. The first foundation fragment discovered belonging to the front portion of the house was a short segment of its back, or south wall (in the foreground, far right). Behind this wall was a kind of stone smear in a semicircular shape. Once the smear was fully exposed it became clear that it was the foundation for the bow window that Washington had installed at the back of the reception room where he received dignitaries and the public. These fragments, elegantly uncovered by the archaeological team, represent two worlds: the world of the elite—Washington and his family—and the world of the enslaved Africans who were also part of his household. Just feet apart, the tangible evidence of the kitchen where the slaves worked and the reception room where Washington held court attests to the reality of the terrible contradiction that plagued the early years of the republic, and thousands of people came to watch the process of uncovering it.

10.19. Dr. Cheryl LaRoche talking to visitors on the president's house site. (Independence National Historical Park)

Before the digging even began the Park Service built a viewing platform at the edge of the excavation area (Figure 10.19). The platform was crowded with visitors every day. School classes came, Independence Historical Park tours passed through, but mainly just interested people—all ages, all races—hung on the words of the archaeological interpreters. They asked many questions and had lots to say. Most important, says Cheryl LaRoche, a member of the archaeological team, were the discussions of race between blacks and whites. The viewing platform, she says, broke down the barriers that often prevent people from talking about this emotionally charged subject. By beginning with the fragments in the ground they could contemplate and talk about slavery, its implications in the past and its impact on the present.[20]

The public interest generated by the project was so great (three hundred thousand people visited the excavation) that the oversight committee for construction of the memorial didn't know how to proceed. Some members wanted to leave the foundations in place as a substitute for a memorial; others thought some portion of the archaeology should be incorporated into the memorial design or, perhaps, the memorial's design should be completely rethought. No one was certain whether it was the foundations themselves that ignited the interest or the process of uncovering this hidden part of our shared past. It was not completely clear whether the foundations alone, that is, without the archaeologists at work, would have the same impact; besides, as Karen Warrington, a member of the oversight committee, emphasized, if the memorial were just the foundations, the opportunity to tell more complex stories would be lost. "The project," she wrote, "must tell the stories of the intelligence and strategies utilized by blacks to escape the horror of slavery, and the role of the many free blacks who lived near the President's House in nineteenth-century Philadelphia. . . . These stories must be told because they inform all of us: those who are the descendants of the enslaved and those who benefited from the commerce of slavery."[21] The memorial design team, Kelly/Maiello, was asked to develop four alternatives, three of them incorporating some remnant of the archaeological fabric. The alternative that places a glass box over the small part of the excavation where the corner of the kitchen, the passageway, and the bow window foundations are visible was accepted and announced to the public on December 13, 2007. This plan connects the original memorial design with its video screens for telling stories to the authentic remnants of the house. The aboveground design is reinforced by the belowground remains.

In a lecture at one of the early public sessions devoted to the president's house project, Fath Davis Ruffins, curator of African-American history and culture in the Division of Home and Community Life at the Smithsonian's Museum of American History, made a distinction between the past and history. The past, she said, is everything that came before; history is the fragments we have selected to recognize. This book has done some of that, but the selections have not been merely subjective. The archaeological projects discussed here were not conducted because of someone's particular academic interest or as a result of fashions in research. They were conducted because planned construction threatened to destroy significant remains of the past or, in the case of the president's house and the James Dexter site, because construction would hide pieces of the past we haven't paid enough attention to. The projects took us (and others) to places, and especially people, we otherwise would not have known. This kind of archaeology adds the unintentional to history. It adds the people we stumble upon because construction in the present is about to take place where they lived, or worked, or were buried.

We began with the excavations on Independence Mall because they are the most recent large archaeological projects that have been conducted in the city. More is forthcoming though. A privy belonging to an early almshouse is under investigation in south Philadelphia, and testing on the site of an expansion of the Convention Center between Thirteenth and Broad Streets has just been completed. More people will emerge from these studies, people whose names we don't even know yet and whose things will lead us to stories of their uncelebrated lives. There will also be more politics, more challenges, and more archaeologists. The past is in Philadelphia's future. We just don't know where it will lead.

Notes

Chapter 1. Beneath the Symbolic Surface

1. Narrative is the historian's method, the way to create coherence out of strings of supposed facts. For historians Joyce Appleby, Lynn Hunt, and Margaret Jacob (1994, 263), "the flow of time does not have a beginning, middle, and end; only stories about it do," and historians, they say, "should attend to the pervasive appeal of stories." Much earlier Hayden White (1981, 1) found in narrative "a solution to the problem of general human concern, namely, the problem of how to translate knowing into telling, the problem of fashioning human experience into a form assimilable to structures of meaning that are generally human rather than culture-specific." Simon Schama's tale of George Parkman's murder in 1849 and the Harvard professor who was accused of the crime, as told in *Dead Certainties* (1991), is a wonderful example of the limits of knowing the past even after all the evidence is marshaled into the most complete story possible. Schama weaves the bare facts of the case into a tale that evokes the feeling of mid-nineteenth-century Boston, the class tensions characteristic of the period, and the strong personalities of the major players. His sources are primary documents, but he also invents thoughts and conversations for his characters in order to transport the reader into the complexity of the case. Once there we recognize how impossible it is to know what really happened. The narrative uses everything that is known, but ends in ambiguity, as knowing the past always must. "We are doomed to be forever hailing someone who has just gone around the corner and out of earshot," says Schama (1991, 320).

2. The attempts by archaeologists to present their results in a more narrative rather than technical format surely relates to postmodern developments in other fields during the 1980s and 1990s. In 1997 Mary Praetzellis organized a session at the Society of Historical Archaeology's annual meeting titled "Archaeologists as Storytellers." The contributors to the session and to the subsequently published volume (*Historical Archaeology*, vol. 32, no. 1, 1998) used storytelling to bring to life people encountered on archaeological projects: from a feisty mother of ten in seventeenth-century Boston who managed to divorce her adulterous second husband to late-nineteenth-century bakers of Italian bread in the California Mother Lode. Storytelling reflects a movement away from an elitist control of knowledge. As American society and scholars have paid more attention to class, racial, ethnic, and gender differences, an adequate portrait of the past needs to include all kinds of people. Although archaeologists have access to things people leave behind, the things by themselves—sets of dishes, glass bottles, pins and needles—don't mean much unless they are connected to peoples' lives. Storytelling is a hermeneutic method of weaving the artifacts together with everything else we know—from primary documents, secondary sources (especially by historians), landscape analysis, anthropological theory, and anything else that seems relevant. The stories are a way of finding out what we know and, equally important, what we don't know, which, in many cases, leads to new questions and new avenues of research.

3. Greiff (1987) recounts the process and players involved in creating the park. "The principal goal for

the planners," she says, "was to teach the values of the founding fathers" (x). They proposed putting Independence Hall in a "proper setting by removing unsightly buildings that were long out-moded and have ceased to be useful" (46). Mires (2002) explores the changing meanings of Independence Hall and the Liberty Bell at length. She contrasts the mobility of the bell with the stability of Independence Hall and looks at the roles of both of them in forging public memory.

4. Wood 1991.

5. Wolf 1975, 123.

6. Glassie 1982, 86.

Chapter 2. Hudson's Square: The Middle Block of Independence Mall

1. The historian for Independence National Historical Park, Anna Coxe Toogood, completed historical overviews for the eighteenth-century occupation of all three blocks that make up Independence Mall. Her history of the middle block (known as Block 2) was completed in 2000 and is the source of the basic facts about Hudson's life. Toogood's work in general and her willing counsel were invaluable throughout the archaeological effort. Frederick Tolles (1948, 10–11), a historian of Quakerism, believed that Penn envisioned "a land peopled largely by Friends, brought by the Spirit into a state of perfection like that of Adam before the fall, [that] would thus become a second Eden. The coercive functions of the state could be expected to wither away from disuse, and a holy community of love and peace under the sway of God's Spirit would come into being on the banks of the Delaware." The idea that New World merchants, who did not generally have the landed estates that were identified with elites in the Old World, created legitimacy in other ways is discussed in depth in Goodwin 1999.

2. The federal Occupational Safety and Health Administration (OSHA) publishes and enforces regulations guiding safety procedures on construction sites. Among them is a restriction on digging any deeper than four feet without shoring the sides of the excavation or stepping them back at a slope

no greater than forty-five degrees. If there is not enough space to use the stepping method, which was the case on Block 2, it is necessary to devise a secure shoring system. The wooden boxes were designed, built, and installed by a specialized contractor. Tommy Williams was the machine operator for this stage of the project.

3. Prince 1977.

4. The letters quoted in the vignette include: letter from William Simmons to James McHenry, April 18, 1799, in Syrett, ed., 1961–87, 23:45n; letter from President John Adams to James McHenry, in ibid., 23:486n; letter from Alexander Hamilton to President George Washington, in ibid., 18:304; letter from William Simmons to James McHenry, March 19, 1800, in ibid., 24:314. The information on Simmons's dismissal is from Pitch 1998, 68. According to this account, Simmons had joined the fight against the British at Bladensburg during the War of 1812 and claimed to "have saved James Madison from falling into enemy hands" (97).

5. Elkins and McKitrick (1993) discuss the tensions between Federalists and Republicans in general, and Rosswurm (1994) discusses class relations in the Federal period in Philadelphia. Faler (1974, 367–94) describes alcohol use in the eighteenth century.

6. Syrett, ed. (1961–87, 13:465) was my source for comparative salary information.

7. Coxey Toogood supplied the location of the War Department in 1799. Mrs. Barbara Beckley Chaney of Sun City West, Arizona, began a correspondence with me on January 12, 2002, after reading an article in the *Philadelphia Inquirer* in which I mentioned the privy of William Simmons. She enclosed a picture of Simmons in uniform, a picture of his home near Coshocton, Ohio, and a letter written by her great aunt that provided some basic biographical information. Additional material she supplied included an addendum and index to *Postal History, Coshocton County, Ohio, 1805–1864,* with several mentions of Simmons, in June 2003.

8. All references to Adam and William Everly in city directories were checked. These included Wilson 1825, DeSilver 1830, 1833, 1835, and 1836, and McElroy 1839 and 1850.

9. Information on the history of comb manufacture came from Doyle 1925. The references to Philadelphia appear on pp. 25–30. The direct quote is from p. 341.

10. The memoir is reprinted in Collins and Jordan 1941, which calls the memoir "a peculiar publication."

Chapter 3. An Icon and an Icehouse: The First Block of Independence Mall

1. Toogood 1985.

2. Washington's query to Morris appears in a postscript to a letter dated June 2, 1784, the main body of which deals with securing a job for George Washington's brother's son. Morris found no position for the nephew in Philadelphia, but recommended him to an associate in New York. The major portion of his response, dated June 15, 1784, is a detailed description of the icehouse. Both letters appear on the Library of Congress Web site.

3. Toogood (2001, 87) discusses Morris's penchant for modern conveniences. Morris's Schedule of Property from 1797 lists the mills, in Morris c. 1769–c. 1821. Westcott (1877, 360) repeats Watson's description of "Morris's Folly."

4. Parsons 1893; Lawler 2002.

5. The specific information about George Washington's slaves is from Edward Lawler's Web site, www.UShistory.org.

6. Toogood (2001, 87) describes the addition of a well to the backyard.

7. Among Gary Nash's books are *Class and Society in Early America; Forging Freedom: The Formation of Philadelphia's Black Community, 1720–1840;* and *First City: Philadelphia and the Forging of Historical Memory.*

8. Articles that appeared in the *Philadelphia Inquirer:* Acel Moore, "For Whom Did the Liberty Bell Toll," April 14, 2002; Stephan Salisbury, "Liberty Bell's New Home Will Address Slavery," May 14, 2002; Stephan Salisbury, "Liberty Bell's Symbolism Rings Hollow for Some," May 26, 2002; Acel Moore, "As Liberty Bell Flap Continues, a Slave Memorial Is Suggested," June 2, 2002; Stephan Salisbury, "At Liberty Bell, Protesters Push for Excavation of Slave Quarters," June 11, 2002; Stephan Salisbury, "A Visitor's Innocent Query Spurs Historic Revelations," July 3, 2002; Stephan Salisbury, "A Protest Today Seeks Memorial to Slaves," July 3, 2002; Acel Moore, "Park Service's Promise on Slave Flap Is Doubted" November 3, 2002; Stephan Salisbury, "Planners Rethink Slavery, Liberty Project," December 25, 2002; Jillian McKoy, "Tour Aims to Stop 'Lies' About Slavery in Philadelphia," July 3, 2003; Stephan Salisbury, "A More Perfect Philadelphia Story," December 21, 2003. Also, Dinitia Smith, "Slave Site for a Symbol of Freedom," *New York Times,* April 20, 2002.

9. Interview with Michael Coard conducted by Rebecca Yamin, April 9, 2007.

10. Additional research has not been able to confirm the identity of the African-American cook in the portrait now hanging in the Liberty Bell Center. Personal communication, Anna Coxe Toogood, 2005.

11. Joseph A. Slobodzian, "Independence Mall Slavery Memorial Gets Federal Funding," *Philadelphia Inquirer,* September 6, 2005, reported that a federal grant of $3.6 million was in place "to fund the President's House project at Sixth and Market Streets near the entrance to the Liberty Bell Center." The article went on to say that with the $1.5 million in matching city funds promised in 2003 by Mayor Street, there was enough to complete the project that "some say could become the nation's most significant symbolic attempt to come to terms with more than three centuries of slavery and its legacy."

12. As described in Foner 1999, 162.

13. Stauffer 2002 is a study of the friendship and unlikely alliance among four men, two of them white and two of them black: Gerrit Smith, John Brown, Frederick Douglass, and James McCune Smith. The direct quotes from the letter were taken from the version reprinted in Foner 1999. However, quotes from the same letter cited in John Stauffer's book are even more radical. Stauffer (2002, 163) writes, "The document advocated a massive slave rebellion: it urged all slaves to revenge themselves against their masters; to resist them 'unto death' and kill them if necessary; and to confiscate their money, horses, and other property. 'You are pris-

oners of war in an enemy's country' that was 'un-
rivaled for its injustice, cruelty, meanness,' Smith
proclaimed in his black voice, 'and therefore by
all the rules of war, you have the fullest liberty to
plunder, burn [and] kill.'" The discrepancy cannot
be explained unless the version published by Douglass in his newspaper, *North Star,* and included in
Foner was toned down for public consumption and
Stauffer had access to the original.

14. Much of the specific information on the convention
is from Humphreys 1994. The editorial quoted was
in the *Madison County Whig,* published in Cazenovia, August 14, 1850 (microfilm, Cazenovia Public
Library). The response to the editorial appeared
in the August 28 edition of the same paper. The
picture of the church where the convention began
appears in Grills 1993, 56.

15. A second paragraph on the wayside recounted other
"famous and infamous" people who lived on the
site, including Governor John Penn, British general
Sir William Howe, General Benedict Arnold, and
Revolutionary financier Robert Morris. The third
paragraph noted that a more elaborate house was
built for the president, but neither Washington nor
Adams wanted to live there. The wayside was next
to the sidewalk in front of the women's rest room
that stood on the site of the president's house before the recent renovations began.

Chapter 4. Artisans in a Changing World

1. Blumin (1989, 36) claims this unresolved contradiction arose from the fact that "the social degrada-
tion of manual work circumscribed the status of
all artisans, but the independence of many, and
the prosperity of a few, strained the very idea of a
clearly differentiated set of social levels." Quoting
Eric Foner, Blumin goes on to say, "Philadelphia's
artisan culture was pervaded by ambiguities and
tensions, beginning with the inherent dualism
of the artisan's role on the one hand, as a small
entrepreneur and employer and, on the other, as a
laborer and craftsman." Gordon Wood (1991, 278)
makes the same point, and Sean Wilentz (1984)
discusses the effects of the "market revolution" on
artisans.

2. Wall 1994; Yamin 1997.

3. U.S. Census 1810; Hibbard 1943 lists Thomas
Ogle's many wives.

4. The receipts were found in the Butler Family Papers
that reside at the Winterthur Library. Wainwright
(1982, 277) mentions Ogle and Watson's carriage
works.

5. Powell 1993, 4.

6. Powell 1993, 148, 257, 260, 265.

7. William Rorabaugh (1979, 151) argues that drinking
was seen as an expression of independence in the
post-Revolutionary period and was not stigmatized
or believed to interfere with productivity.

8. Powell 1993, 259.

9. The ceramics were analyzed by Juliette Gerhardt
for the project and the glass was analyzed by Alexander Bartlett. Both are John Milner Associates
employees.

10. Wood 1991, 306.

11. Klein, Friedlander, and Cohen 1987.

12. Stafford 1800; Poulson 1811–30, vol. 70; Duroff-
Barone 1991.

13. General information on the cabinetmaking business in the first quarter of the nineteenth century is
from Heckscher 1964 and Catalano 1972.

14. Arky (1952) mentions Alexander Turnbull Jr.'s
newspaper.

15. Calvert 1992, 76.

16. Calvert 1992, 103, quoting from a contemporary
source.

17. Wainwright (1982, 275) mentions these contests two
pages before he describes the "city's famous coachmaker, William Ogle."

Chapter 5. "We the People": The Free Black Community, Native Americans, and the Celebration of the Constitution

1. Inga Saffron, the *Inquirer's* architecture critic, described the NCC in "A Perfect Union of Elements,"
Philadelphia Inquirer, July 4, 2003.

2. Feldman (2003) celebrates the efforts of University
of Pennsylvania graduate Joe Torsella. Emily Bittenbender (interviewed by Rebecca Yamin, June 15,
2005) told me that one of the first things Torsella
asked her to do when he hired her was to study

Section 106 of the National Historic Preservation Act, the law that mandates cultural resources investigations.

3. Crist, Mooney, and Abbot 1999.

4. Crist, Mooney, and Abbot 1999, Appendix 1. Racial mixture in the neighborhood is discussed on p. 17.

5. Interview with Tom Crist and Art Washburn conducted by Rebecca Yamin, August 8, 2006.

6. Interview with Jed Levin conducted by Rebecca Yamin, June 28, 2005.

7. See Cantwell and Wall (2001) for a description of the archaeological projects that were done in New York City in the 1980s and early 1990s.

8. Bittenbender interview.

9. Interview with Douglas Mooney conducted by Rebecca Yamin, June 10, 2005.

10. Personal communication, Tom Crist, November 13, 2006.

11. The descriptions of the features are from Mooney interview. The field records were not available for examination and no report has been written. James Deetz discusses Parting Ways in the most recent edition of his classic, *In Small Things Forgotten* (1996, 187–252). The study of Yaughan and Curriboo plantations is in Wheaton and Garrow 1985, 239–59.

12. Armstrong 1985, 261–87. Artifact descriptions are from Mooney interview. The artifacts were not available for study.

13. Yentsch (1994, 188–95) discusses "material expressions of black identity." LaRoche (1994, 3–20) studied the beads associated with seven of the four hundred burials excavated at the African Burial Ground in New York City.

14. Deetz (1996, 237) includes a drawing of Colono Ware shapes. He also gives Richard Polhemus credit for being the first to claim that Colono Ware was made by African Americans rather than Native Americans and Leland Ferguson credit for proposing the term Colono Ware to designate the pottery. It had formerly been called Colono-Indian pottery because of its assumed association with Native Americans. Polhemus compared examples of Colono Ware found in South Carolina with pieces from Nigeria and Ghana. Ferguson (1991, 36) sub-

sequently compared the Colono Ware from sites in South Carolina and concluded that "the foodways of eighteenth-century African American slaves in South Carolina were quite similar to those of West Africa and significantly different from those of European-Americans of the same time period."

15. The historical record of the neighborhood is covered in Toogood 2004. She discusses the African Americans on Cresson Alley on pp. 30 and 36.

16. The artifacts recovered from the barrel were described by Doug Mooney in a lecture at the Living History Center and Archaeological Laboratory in Independence National Historical Park on October 14, 2006. Jed Levin also showed me some of the artifacts on November 3. The still incomplete site report was not available for review.

17. African-American houses in backyards are discussed in Nash 1988, 167. Toogood (2004, 30) discusses Catherwall's purchase of Smith's property and also describes (p. iv) the participation of Catherwall and Smith in the 1783 address to the Continental Congress petitioning the nation's new leaders to discourage the slave trade. Lapsansky (1997, 11) describes the requirement that Philadelphia Friends give up their slaves, and Nash (1988, 62) discusses the emancipation law.

18. Soderland 1985, 11–12, 185. See Nash 1988 for an in-depth discussion of the emergence of the free black community and the founding of black institutions.

19. Toogood provided me with a photocopy of Cresson's journal. The original is in the Pennsylvania Historical Society. He describes the uprising in Hispaniola on p. 156.

20. Cresson 1877, 140–42, 146.

21. Doug Mooney described the shell midden and associated artifacts in the June 10, 2005, interview. He and Jed Levin, however, were much less sure about a Native American association in November 2006 when I visited them in the lab.

22. Mooney interview.

23. The prehistoric finds at the Sheraton Society Hill Hotel site are reported in McCarthy and Roberts 1996. The Bookbinder site was briefly described in a lecture by Drew Kenworthy on October 14, 2006, at the Living History Center and Archaeological Laboratory, Independence National Histori-

cal Park. I discussed the site further with Doug
Mooney on November 3, 2006.

24. Direct quotes from Cresson 1877, 107, 119, 148, 157,
172. There are references to construction on his
properties throughout Cresson's diary.

25. Artifact descriptions from Mooney interview and
lectures.

Chapter 6. Life and Death in the Nineteenth-Century City

1. In the very beginning of the book Cary acknowl-
edges Phil Labsansky at the Library Company of
Philadelphia for "leading [her] to the story of Jane
Johnson in William Still's *The Underground Rail-
road,* 1872, available in reprint from Ayer Company
Publishers, Inc., New Hampshire."

2. Unless otherwise attributed, much of the information in this section was drawn from an interview
with Dan Roberts, conducted by the author on
March 10, 2005. The first FABC project is generally described in Parrington and Roberts 1984. The
direct quotes are from the transcription of a talk
Roberts presented at the African-American Museum in Philadelphia on the occasion of the rites of
ancestral return dedication ceremony in honor of
the ancestors originally interred in the Eighth and
Tenth Street First African Baptist Church cemeteries, October 18, 2003.

3. Crist et al. 1996, 13.

4. Pitts in Crist et al. 1996, 13, citing Nash 1988; Du
Bois 1967.

5. Crist et al. 1996, 15.

6. Crist et al. 1996, 26.

7. Parrington and Roberts 1984, 28.

8. See Cantwell and Wall 2001, chapter 16, for a discussion of the African Burial Ground project.

9. Exact quotes are from a transcript of the October
18, 2003, talk, on file, John Milner Associates, Inc.,
Philadelphia.

10. The site of the Eighth Street cemetery had been
declared eligible for the National Register of Historic Places and mitigation was required in compli-
ance with the National Historic Preservation Act
as a result of federal assistance for the construction
of the proposed office building. The building was
never built.

11. Parrington et al. 1987, 71.

12. Summary information presented here is from Crist
et al. 1997, which relied on an unpublished disserta-
tion by Leslie M. Rankin Hill, Department of Anthropology, University of Massachusetts, 1990, and
an article by Jennifer Olsen Kelley and J. Lawrence
Angel, 1987.

13. The following information comes from Parrington
et al. 1987, 96–98.

14. Table 3 in Parrington et al. 1987.

15. Nash 1988, 223.

16. Nash 1988, 144.

17. Nash 1988, 144.

18. Nash 1988, 273–77.

19. Crist et al. 1997, 30.

20. Parrington et al. 1987, 72.

21. Crist et al. 1996, 246.

22. Included in the transcription of John McCarthy's
talk at the African-American Museum in Philadelphia on the occasion of the rites of ancestral return
dedication ceremony in honor of the ancestors
originally interred in the Eighth and Tenth Street
First African Baptist Church Cemeteries, October
18, 2003.

23. Crist et al. 1996, 246.

24. McCarthy 1997 includes a thorough discussion of
these ideas.

25. Pitts in Crist et al. 1996, 23–24.

26. Lawrence 2003, 20–33.

27. Lawrence 2003, 21.

28. A similar artifact was found in the Rocks in Syd-
ney, Australia, and subsequently identified at Five
Points in New York City. The interpretation was
suggested by archaeologist Graham Wilson on the
Rocks project. He found a description in Michelle
Perrot's *History of Private Life,* for an "occlusive
pessary" that consisted of "membranes of rubber
encircled by rings of bone" (Karskens 1999, 174).

29. The food remains from the Vine Street Expressway
Corridor project were analyzed by David Landon,
now at the University of Massachusetts, Boston.

Chapter 7. On the Waterfront

1. Historical Society of Pennsylvania, Miscellaneous
Business papers, Gratz Collection, Case 15, Box 20.
Research by Carmen Weber.

2. Weber 2006, 16.

3. Weber 2006, 16.

4. *The Compact Edition of the Oxford English Dictionary*, 1971; *The Mariner's Dictionary*, 1805; *The Modern System of Naval Architecture*, 1865, 395–96.

5. Weber 2006, 18.

6. Allen 1986, 33, 37.

7. Weber 2006, 33.

8. *The Franklin Journal and American Mechanics' Magazine* 3 (1827):74.

9. *The Franklin Journal and American Mechanics' Magazine* 3 (1827):84–85.

10. Leiper 1803–13, reviewed by the author at the Historical Society of Pennsylvania. Weber referred to the recently acquired Thomas Leiper account books, but did not review them for her report because they had not yet been indexed. They still aren't indexed, but because they are chronological the relevant years were examined.

11. Thomas Leiper Railroad Papers, twelve-page article in the Leiper Railroad folder, Historical Society of Pennsylvania.

12. Thomas Leiper Railroad Papers, twelve-page article.

13. LeeDecker et al. 1993, 3:31.

14. The story of the glue kettle and soup for the poor is from a footnote in Leach 1903, 39.

15. LeeDecker et al. 1993, 4:26.

16. LeeDecker et al. 1993, 6:11.

17. LeeDecker et al. 1993, 6:8–17.

18. LeeDecker et al. 1993, 6:32.

Chapter 8. An Archaeological Walk in the Eighteenth-Century City

1. Liggett 1978, 19.

2. Liggett 1981, 38.

3. Liggett 1981, 6.

4. Liggett 1981, 32.

5. Burston in Liggett 1981, 193.

6. Liggett 1978, 9.

7. Liggett 1981, 12.

8. Liggett 1981, 108. Information about the Pine Street meeting is from Shel Avery at the Quaker Information Center and from Chris Densmore and Pat O'Donnell at Swarthmore College, July 2006.

9. Barbara Liggett, and a number of Philadelphia archaeologists who were influenced by her, believed that the artifact-rich deposits often found at the bottoms of privies were what she called percolation fill. The artifacts might come from offsite rather than onsite, or they might be a mixture of both, but instead of intentional or unintentional discard she argued that they were placed in the bottom of shaft features to facilitate percolation of human waste or to fill the shaft up to the depth regulated by law after 1769. This law stipulated that privies could be no more than twenty feet deep, and specific depths were set for every half block from the surface of the nearest north–south street. In the area of Front and Dock Streets they were permitted to be only six feet deep; north of High Street depths up to twenty feet were allowed. Patrice Jeppson (interview, December 21, 2006) has made the point that even if the deposits were not for percolation Liggett was ahead of her time in thinking about environmental issues and how they were confronted in an eighteenth-century urban context.

10. Archaeological evidence for communal meals has been recognized elsewhere and was described for a site in Lower Manhattan by Marie-Lorraine Pipes at the annual meeting of the Society for Historical Archaeology in York, England, in 2005.

11. Burston in Liggett 1981, 204–13.

12. Burston in Liggett 1981, 216.

13. Burston 1982.

14. Gerhardt 2006, 66–67.

15. Gerhardt 2006, 77. Analysis was done by conservator Lori Aument.

16. Westcott 1877, 483.

17. Details about the Norris house and garden are from Caleb Crain, *American Sympathy: Men, Friendship, and Literature in the New Nation* (New Haven: Yale University Press, 2001), 17. Toogood (1998, 57) quotes Deborah Norris Logan's recollections reproduced in Charles Peterson, ed., "Before Our Time," *The American German Review*, April 1951, 6–7.

18. John Milner Associates conducted data recovery on this site in July 1988. Belinda Blomberg et al. (1990a) was the principal investigator. In spite of intensive nineteenth-century development, the excavation revealed numerous (nineteen) archaeological features in the northwest corner of the project

area, and the Philadelphia Historical Commission recommended data recovery of the six shaft features that predated the nineteenth century.

19. Toogood 1998, 58.

20. See Cotter et al. (1992, 92–96) for a general description of the work at Franklin Court. According to Patrice Jeppson (interview, December 21, 2006), the first archaeological excavation was sponsored by the American Philosophical Society (APS) on the 250th anniversary of Benjamin Franklin's birth. The APS provided laborers (from the Laborer's International Union Local 57), and the National Park Service (NPS) supplied archaeologist Paul Schumacher to direct the effort. Jeppson summarizes the results of the three phases of excavation at Franklin Court—1953, 1960s, and 1970s—in her 2005 report.

21. Much of the information relating to Jeppson's study is from Jeppson 2004 and from an interview with her held on December 21, 2006. Jeppson's 2005 report was also consulted.

22. Jeppson 2004, 5.

23. Jeppson 2004, 7.

24. The consortium consisted of the Philadelphia Museum of Art, the Franklin Institute Science Museum, the Library Company of Philadelphia, the American Philosophical Society, and the University of Pennsylvania.

25. Information on the project is from Dent et al. 1997.

26. Nineteen brick-shaft features were also identified; five were excavated.

27. Dent et al. 1997, 5:109.

28. Dent et al. 1997, 5:112.

Chapter 9. An Archaeological Walk Through Nineteenth-Century Neighborhoods

1. Blomberg et al. 1990b, 5.

2. Blomberg et al. (1990b, 42) cites three reports by Brian Moffat and Gordon Ewart (1988 and 1989) which describe their work at the Medieval Hospital at Soutra, Lothian Region, Scotland.

3. Blomberg et al. (1990b, 43) cites as her source for the test Smith-Kline Diagnostics, "Hemoccult Slides and Tape Product Instructions," Product Development Department, San Jose, CA, 1981.

4. The features on the 1100 block are described in Blomberg et al. 1990b, 33–49.

5. Blomberg et al. (1990b) calculated index values for the ceramics from Feature 4, which are presented in table 14 of her report. George Miller first presented the idea of economic scaling in a paper published in *Historical Archaeology* in 1980 and revised in 1991. By studying merchants' and manufacturers' wholesale pricing records for various years, Miller was able to determine how much more certain ceramic types cost than the cheapest (plain creamware) available at the time. The index value for an assemblage is calculated by multiplying the comparative value of each ceramic type as presented by Miller by the number of vessels of each type in the assemblage, adding the various types, and dividing by the total number of vessels to achieve an average, referred to as the index value.

6. Blomberg et al. 1990b, 96.

7. Burstein 1981, 179–86.

8. Information is drawn from McCarthy et al. 1994.

9. McCarthy et al. 1994, 59.

10. Henry Glassie recorded a wonderful example of using transfer-printed dishes for display in the small village he studied in Northern Ireland in the 1970s. In *Passing the Time at Ballymenone,* he explores the meanings locked in Mrs. Cutler's "dresser of delph" (Glassie 1982, 363). The transfer-printed platters that lined the top shelf ranged from early-nineteenth-century English blue willow patterns through late-nineteenth-century pale English china and Belleek with its green, white, and gold decoration. The "delph is not to use," explained Mrs. Cutler. "No. It is for passin on to people that won't use it." This practice in 1970s Ireland surely draws on an old tradition, and it is not unlikely that the Irish took this and similar customs to their new homes in America and elsewhere.

11. McCarthy et al. 1994, 59.

12. De Cunzo 1982.

13. Yamin, ed. 2000; Yamin, ed. 2001; Reckner and Brighton 1999; Griggs 2001; Yamin 1997.

14. Clark 1973, chapter 3. The direct quote is from p. 43.

15. Ignatiev 1995.

16. De Cunzo 1995.

17. De Cunzo 1995, 13. According to De Cunzo, by 1800 the wealthiest 0.5 percent of the city's taxpayers owned more taxable property than the bottom 75 percent.

18. De Cunzo 1995, 25.

19. De Cunzo 1995, 1.

20. Lu Ann De Cunzo was director of archaeological services for the Clio Group when the excavation took place and was the co-author of the final report (1989) on the project. Her 1995 publication is a much more developed study that grew out of the original project. De Cunzo is now an associate professor at the University of Delaware and the president of the Society for Historical Archaeology.

21. De Cunzo (1995, 36) cites David Rothman, *The Discovery of the Asylum: Social Order and Disorder in the New Republic,* rev. ed. (Boston: Little, Brown, 1990).

22. Stansell 1987.

23. De Cunzo 1995, 48.

24. De Cunzo 1995, 77.

25. Recent archaeological work at the Cypress Street almshouse (between Pine and Spruce and Third and Fourth Streets) has produced a large assemblage of artifacts relating to life in the almshouse from the early 1730s to the early 1760s. Among the artifacts recorded by Mara Kaktins, a Temple graduate student who is investigating the site, are a spoon and a bowl with initials scratched into them (personal communication, David Orr, June 2007). Inmates apparently did identify their own eating paraphernalia in this institution. While Magdalens may have been discouraged from marking their dishes, they very well could have claimed certain distinctively decorated dishes as their own.

26. De Cunzo 1995, 81. The quote is from Magdalen Society records.

27. De Cunzo 1995; the discussion of ritual may be found on pp. 125–33. The direct quote is from p. 127.

Chapter 10. The Legacy of William Penn and the Power of the Past

1. Jackson 1932, 695.

2. Research for the Franklin Square project was conducted by Douglas McVarish and Courtney Clark, both John Milner Associates employees. The results were reported in McVarish, Yamin, and Roberts 2005. Sources relevant to the early years of the church included Anonymous 1927, Jackson 1932, and Lyons 2001.

3. Anonymous, n.d., newspaper clipping.

4. McVarish et al. 2005, 5; Spiese 1903.

5. Personal communication, Nancy Donohue, 2006.

6. Yamin 2006. This protocol was based heavily on John Milner Associates' experience with other burial ground projects, including the African Burial Ground in New York City and the First African Baptist Church burial grounds in Philadelphia. Dr. Thomas Crist was largely responsible for developing the procedures for excavating burials included in the Franklin Square protocol.

7. Kenyon 1975.

8. McVarish et al. 2005, 4. The quote is from Harbaugh's *Life of Schlatter.* In its entirety it reads, "Directly east of the sparkling jets of the fountain, a few feet from the edge of the circular gravel walk, under the green sod, lie the Revs. Steiner and Winkhaus, and Dr. Weyberg and Hendel, the aged. Directly north of this spot, about midway between it and Vine st., lies Rev. Michael Schlatter; around these leaders of the Lord's host, far and near—a silent congregation now!—sleep thousands of those to whom they once ministered the holy ordinances of the church, and the precious instructions and consolations of the Gospel."

9. Personal communication, Nancy Donohue, May 2006.

10. As a compromise the park allowed that headstones could be removed to the church if a "replicate" was made of a "durable material (plastic or vinyl)" and "reburied in the square in, or near, its original location"; e-mail from Mark A. Focht, executive director, Fairmount Park Commission to Bill Zumsteg, logistics director, Once Upon a Nation.

11. Personal communication, Nancy Donohue, 2006.

12. Johnston 1994, 21.

13. Johnston 1994, 26.

14. Johnston 1994, 32.

15. The following information came from an interview with Sally Elk conducted by Rebecca Yamin on July 12, 2006.

16. Johnston 1994, 35.

17. Johnston 1994, 36.

18. Willie Sutton's autobiography, as told to Quentin Reynolds, was published as *I, Willie Sutton* in 1953. The paperback version with the alternative title came out the same year.

19. After the escapees were apprehended and returned to the penitentiary, they were all interviewed. The transcriptions of their testimony, including Klinedinst's, are on file at the Eastern State Penitentiary in Philadelphia. They were reviewed before beginning the hunt for the tunnel.

20. Cheryl LaRoche, who spends two days a week on the site, was quoted in Stephan Salisbury, "Slavery Laid Bare: A Historic Platform for Dialogue on Race," *Philadelphia Inquirer,* May 20, 2007. LaRoche also worked on the African Burial Ground project in New York City.

21. Karen Warrington, "Tell Slaves' Story Truthfully," *Philadelphia Inquirer,* December 14, 2007.

References

Allen, Jane E. 1986. "Lying at the Port of Philadelphia: Vessel Types, 1725–1775." Unpublished manuscript. Philadelphia Maritime Museum.

Ames, Kenneth L. 1992. *Death in the Dining Room and Other Tales of Victorian Culture.* Philadelphia: Temple University Press.

Anonymous. 1927. "Men and Things: Penn's Dedication of Northeast Square to Public Use Is Recalled." *Philadelphia Evening Bulletin.* April 7.

Appleby, Joyce, Lynn Hunt, and Margaret Jacob. 1994. *Telling the Truth About History.* New York: W. W. Norton.

Arky, Louis H. 1952. "The Mechanics Union of Trade Association and the Formation of the Philadelphia Workingmen's Movement." *Pennsylvania Magazine* 76:142–76.

Armstrong, Douglas. 1985. "An Afro-Jamaican Slave Settlement: Archaeological Investigations at Drax Hall." In *The Archaeology of Slavery and Plantation Life,* edited by Theresa A. Singleton, pp. 261–87. New York: Academic Press.

Blomberg, Belinda, Philip Carstairs, Glenn A. Ceponis, and Cheryl A. Holt. 1990a. "Archeological Investigations at the Site of the Bourse Garage/Omni Hotel at Independence Park, Philadelphia, PA." Prepared for Bourse Garage Associates and the Kevin F. Donohoe Company, Inc. John Milner Associates, Inc.

Blomberg, Belinda, with contributions by Philip J. Carstairs, Patrick O'Bannon, Diane Newbury, and Cheryl Holt. 1990b. "Archeological Data Recovery in the Vicinity of Twelfth and Arch Streets at the Site of the Pennsylvania Convention Center, Philadelphia, PA," ER 84-0265-101. Prepared for Philadelphia Industrial Development Corporation, Philadelphia. John Milner Associates, Inc.

Blomberg, Belinda, Helen Schenck, Philip Carstairs, George Cress, and Thomas A. J. Crist. 1996. "Archeological Monitoring and Data Recovery of the Vine Expressway Corridor (I-676) L.R. 67045. Philadelphia, PA." Prepared for Gaudet and O'Brien Associates/Urban Engineers, Inc., and the Pennsylvania Department of Transportation. John Milner Associates, Inc.

Blumin, Stuart. 1989. *The Emergence of the Middle Class: Social Experience in the American City, 1760–1900.* New York: Cambridge University Press.

Burstein, Alan N. 1981. "Immigrants and Residential Mobility: The Irish and Germans in Philadelphia, 1850–1880." In *Philadelphia: Work, Space, Family, and Group Experience in the Nineteenth Century,* edited by Theodore Hershberg. New York: Oxford University Press.

Burston, Sharon Ann. 1982. "Babies in the Well: An Underground Insight into Deviant Behavior in Eighteenth-Century Philadelphia." *Pennsylvania Magazine of History and Biography* 106 (2):151–86.

Butler family papers. Winterthur Library, Wilmington, Delaware.

Calvert, Karin. 1992. *Children in the House: The Material Culture of Early Childhood, 1600–1900.* Boston: Northeastern University Press.

Cantwell, Anne-Marie, and Diana diZerega Wall. 2001. *Unearthing Gotham: The Archaeology of New York City.* New Haven: Yale University Press.

Cary, Lorene. 1995. *The Price of a Child.* New York: Alfred A. Knopf.

Catalano, Kathleen Matilda. 1972. "Cabinetmaking in Philadelphia, 1820–1840." Master's thesis, University of Delaware, Newark; on file at the Athenaeum, Philadelphia.

Clark, Dennis. 1973. *The Irish in Philadelphia: Ten Generations of Urban Experience.* Philadelphia: Temple University Press.

Clarkson, Matthew, and Mary Biddle. 1762. *A Plan of the Improved Part of the City of Philadelphia.* Philadelphia: Clarkson and Biddle.

Collins, Herman LeRoy, and Wilfred Jordan. 1941. *Philadelphia, A Story of Progress.* New York: Lewis Historical Publishing.

Cotter, John L., Daniel G. Roberts, and Michael Parrington. 1992. *The Buried Past: An Archaeological History of Philadelphia.* Philadelphia: University of Pennsylvania Press.

Crain, Caleb. 2001. *American Sympathy: Men, Friendship, and Literature in the New Nation.* New Haven: Yale University Press.

Cresson, Caleb. 1877. "Diary of Caleb Cresson, 1791–1792." Printed from his original manuscript for family distribution by Ezra Townsend Cresson and Charles Caleb Cresson.

Crist, Thomas A. J., Douglas B. Mooney, and Martin B. Abbot. 1999. "Archaeological Sensitivity Study of the National Constitution Center Site, Block 3, Independence Mall, Independence National Historical Park, Philadelphia, PA." Kise, Straw and Kolodner, Philadelphia.

Crist, Thomas A. J., Reginald H. Pitts, Arthur Washburn, John P. McCarthy, and Daniel G. Roberts. 1996. "A Distinct Church of the Lord Jesus: The History, Archeology, and Physical Anthropology of the Tenth Street First African Baptist Church Cemetery, Philadelphia." Prepared for Gaudet & O'Brien Associates/Urban Engineers, Incorporated, Philadelphia. John Milner Associates, Inc.

Crist, Thomas A. J., Daniel G. Roberts, Reginald H. Pitts, John P. McCarthy, and Michael Parrington. 1997. "The First African Baptist Church Cemeteries: African-American Mortality and Trauma in Antebellum Philadelphia." In *In Remembrance: Archaeology and Death,* edited by David A. Poirier and Nicholas F. Bellantoni, pp. 21–49. Westport, Conn.: Bergin and Garvey.

De Cunzo, Lu Ann. 1982. "Households, Economics, Ethnicity in Paterson's Dublin, 1829–1915: The Van Houten Parking Lot Block." *Northeast Historical Archaeology* 11:9–25.

De Cunzo, Lu Ann. 1995. "Reform, Respite, Ritual: An Archaeology of Institutions; The Magdalen Society of Philadelphia, 1800–1850." *Historical Archaeology* 29 (3):1–164.

Deetz, James. 1996. *In Small Things Forgotten: An Archaeology of Early American Life.* New York: Doubleday.

Dent, Richard J., Charles H. LeeDecker, Meta Janowitz, Marie-Lorraine Pipes, Ingrid Wuebber, Mallory A. Gordon, Henry M. R. Holt, Christy Roper, Gerard Scharfenberger, and Sharla Azizi. 1997. "Archaeological and Historical Investigation, Metropolitan Detention Center Site (36 PH 91), Philadelphia, Pennsylvania." Prepared for U.S. Department of Justice, Federal Bureau of Prisons, Washington, D.C. Louis Berger and Associates, Inc.

DeSilver, Robert. 1830; 1833; 1835; 1836. *DeSilver's Philadelphia Directory and Stranger's Guide.* Philadelphia.

Doyle, Bernard W. 1925. *Comb Making in America: An Account of the Origin and Development of the Industry for Which Leominster Has Become Famous.* Compiled and privately published by Bernard W. Doyle.

Du Bois, W. E. B. 1967. *The Philadelphia Negro: A Social Study.* New York: Schocken. Originally published, 1899.

Duroff-Barone, Deborah. 1991. "Philadelphia Furniture Makers, 1800–1815." *Antiques Magazine* 139 (5):982–95.

Elkins, Stanley, and Eric McKitrick. 1993. *The Age of Federalism: The Early American Republic, 1788–1800.* New York: Oxford University Press.

Faler, Paul. 1974. "Cultural Aspects of the Industrial Revolution: Lynn, Massachusetts, Shoemakers and Industrial Morality, 1826–1860." *Labor History* 15:367–94.

Feldman, Kathryn Levy. 2003. "The House That Joe Built." *The Pennsylvania Gazette,* pp. 32–37. November–December.

Ferguson, Leland. 1991. "Struggling with Pots in Colonial South Carolina." In *The Archaeology of Inequality,* edited by Randall H. McGuire and Robert Paynter, pp. 28–39. Oxford: Blackwell.

Fitts, Robert K. 1999. "The Archaeology of Middle-Class Domesticity and Gentility in Victorian Brooklyn." *Historical Archaeology* 33 (1):39–62.

Foner, Philip S., editor. 1999. *Frederick Douglass: Selected Speeches and Writings,* abridged and adapted by Yuval Taylor. Chicago: Lawrence Hill.

Frey, Carroll. 1926. *The Independence Square Neighborhood.* Published by the Penn Mutual Life Insurance Company, Philadelphia.

Gerhardt, Juliette. 2006. "Life on the Philadelphia Waterfront, 1687–1826: A Report on the 1977 Archeological Investigation of the Area F Site, Philadelphia, Pennsylvania." Prepared for Independence National Historical Park. John Milner Associates, Inc.

Glassie, Henry. 1982. *Passing the Time at Ballymenone.* Philadelphia: University of Pennsylvania Press.

Goodwin, Lorinda. 1999. *An Archaeology of Manners: The Polite World of the Merchant Elite of Colonial Massachusetts.* New York: Kluwer Academic/Plenum.

Greiff, Constance M. 1987. *Independence: The Creation of a National Park.* Philadelphia: University of Pennsylvania Press.

Griggs, Heather J. 2001. "Go gCuire Dia Rath Blath Ort (God Grant that You Prosper and Flourish): Social and Economic Mobility Among the Irish in Nineteenth-Century New York." *Historical Archaeology* 33 (1):87–100.

Grills, Russell A. 1993. *Upland Idyll: Images of Cazenovia, New York, 1860–1900.* Louisville: Harmony House.

Heckscher, Morrison H. 1964. "The Organization and Practice of Philadelphia Cabinetmaking Establishments, 1790–1820." Master's thesis, University of Delaware, Newark; on file at the Athenaeum, Philadelphia.

Hibbard, Francis Charles. 1943. "A Comparison of the Ogle Records of Blandena Ogle and Frances Charles Hibbard." Manuscript, on file, Historical Society of Pennsylvania, Philadelphia.

Humphreys, Hugh C. 1994. "Agitate! Agitate! Agitate! The Great Cazenovia Fugitive Slave Law Convention (1850) and Its Rare Daguerreotype." *Madison County Heritage,* no. 19.

Ignatiev, Noel. 1995. *How the Irish Became White.* New York: Routledge.

Jackson, Joseph. 1918. *Market Street, Philadelphia: The Most Historic Highway in America, Its Merchants and Its Story.* Philadelphia: Historical Society of Philadelphia.

Jackson, Joseph. 1932. *Encyclopedia of Philadelphia.* Harrisburg: The National Historical Association.

Jeppson, Patrice. 2004. "Not a Replacement, but a Valuable Successor . . .": A New Story from Franklin's Mansion in Colonial Philadelphia." Paper presented at the Society for American Archaeology annual meeting, Montreal, Canada.

Jeppson, Patrice. 2005. "Historical Fact, Historical Memory: An Assessment of Archaeological Evidence Related to Benjamin Franklin." The Benjamin Franklin Tercentenary Consortium, Philadelphia.

Johnston, Norman. n.d. *Escapes from Eastern State Penitentiary.* Philadelphia: Published by Eastern State Penitentiary Historic Site.

Johnston, Norman, with Kenneth Finkel and Jeffrey A. Cohen. 1994. *Eastern State Penitentiary: Crucible of Good Intentions.* Philadelphia: Philadelphia Museum of Art for the Eastern State Penitentiary Historic Site, Philadelphia.

Karskens, Grace. 1999. *Inside the Rocks: The Archaeology of a Neighborhood.* Alexandria, NSW, Australia: Hale and Iremonger.

Kenyon, Jeff L. 1975. "Preliminary Investigation of the Franklin Square Powder Magazine in Philadelphia." Report on file, Philadelphia Historical Commission.

Klein, Terry H., Amy Friedlander, and Jay Cohen. 1987. "Cultural Resource Investigation of the Barclays Bank Site, 75 Wall Street, New York City." Prepared for London and Leed Corporation and Barclays Bank. Louis Berger and Associates, South Orange.

Lapsansky, Emma Jones. 1997. "Philadelphia Friends and African Americans, 1680–1900: An Introduction." In *For Emancipation and Education: Some Black and Quaker Efforts, 1680–1900.* Essays prepared for Awbury Arboretum and the Germantown Historical Society, pp. 7–17.

LaRoche, Cheryl J. 1994. "Beads from the African Burial Ground, New York City: A Preliminary Assessment." *Journal of the Society of Bead Researchers* 6:3–20.

Lawler, Edward, Jr. 2002. "The President's House in Philadelphia: The Rediscovery of a Lost Landmark." *The Pennsylvania Magazine of History and Biography* 126 (1):5–95.

Lawrence, Susan. 2003. "Exporting Culture: Archaeology and the Nineteenth-Century British Empire." *Historical Archaeology* 37 (1):20–33.

Leach, Josiah Granville. 1903. *History of the Penrose*

Family of Philadelphia. Philadelphia: Published for private circulation by Drexel Biddle Publisher.

LeeDecker, Charles H., Edward M. Morin, Ingrid Wuebber, Meta Janowitz, Marie-Lorraine Pipes, Nadia Shevchuk, Mallory Gordon, and Diane Dallal. 1993. "The Meadows Site (36PH35) Archaeological Data Recovery Program, I-95 Completion Project, Philadelphia, Philadelphia County, Pennsylvania." Prepared for Pennsylvania Department of Transportation Engineering District 6-0 and the Federal Highway Administration and Urban Engineers, Inc. The Cultural Resource Group, Louis Berger and Associates, Inc.

Leiper, Thomas. 1803–13. Thomas Leiper Ledger Book. On file, Historical Society of Pennsylvania.

Leiper, Thomas. Folder, Thomas Leiper Railroad Papers. The Historical Society of Pennsylvania. The folder includes an unattributed twelve-page article; an article by Lawrence W. Sagle, "Thomas Leiper's Railroad," vol. 3 4(, February 1943; and an article by Robert Patterson Robins, "A Short Account of the First Permanent Tramway in America," *Pennsylvania Magazine of History and Biography,* Philadelphia, 1897.

Liggett, Barbara. 1978. *Archaeology at New Market Exhibit Catalogue.* The Athenaeum of Philadelphia.

Liggett, Barbara. 1981. "Archaeology of New Market, Excavation Report." On file, John Milner Associates, Inc., Philadelphia.

Lyons, Matthew. 2001. "Background Note in Old First Reformed Church Records, 1741–1976." Collection 3010. Inventory on Historical Society of Pennsylvania Web site: www2.hsp.org/collections/manuscripts/o/ofrc3010.htm.

McCarthy, John P. 1997. "Material Culture and the Performance of Sociocultural Identity: Community, Ethnicity, and Agency in the Burial Practices at the First African Baptist Church Cemeteries, Philadelphia, 1810–1841." In *American Material Culture: The Shape of the Field,* edited by Ann Smart Martin and J. Ritchie Garrison, pp. 359–79. Winterthur: Henry Francis du Pont Winterthur Museum; distributed by University of Tennessee Press, Knoxville.

McCarthy, John P., and Daniel G. Roberts. 1996. "Archaeological Data Recovery Excavation at the Site of the Sheraton Society Hill Hotel, Front and Dock Streets, Philadelphia, Pennsylvania." Prepared for Rouse and Associates, Philadelphia.

McCarthy, John P., Billy R. Roulette Jr., and Thomas A. J. Crist, with a contribution by Lisa D. O'Steen. 1994. "Phase IB/II and III Archeological Investigations at the Philadelphia Gateway Development Parcel: An Archeological Perspective on Philadelphia's Nineteenth Century Irish-American Community." Prepared for Realen Gateway Development Associates, L.P. Realen Gateway Development Corporation, 1235 Westlake Drive, Suite 350, Berwyn, PA 19326. John Milner Associates, Inc.

McCullough, David. 2001. *John Adams.* New York: Simon and Schuster.

McElroy, A. 1839. *McElroy's Philadelphia Directory for 1839.* Printed by Isaac Ashmead and Co., Philadelphia.

McElroy, A. 1850. *McElroy's Philadelphia Directory for 1850.* Printed by Isaac Ashmead and Co., Philadelphia.

McVarish, Douglas C., Rebecca Yamin, and Daniel G. Roberts. 2005. "An Archeological Sensitivity Study of Franklin Square, Philadelphia, Pennsylvania." Prepared for Once Upon a Nation, Philadelphia. John Milner Associates, Inc.

Miller, George L. 1980. "Classification and Economic Scaling of Nineteenth-Century Ceramics." *Historical Archaeology* 14:1–40.

Miller, George L. 1991. "A Revised Set of CC Index Values and Economic Scaling of English Ceramics from 1787 to 1880." *Historical Archaeology* 25 (1):1–25.

Mires, Charlene. 2002. *Independence Hall in American Memory.* Philadelphia: University of Pennsylvania Press.

Moffat, Brian, and Gordon Ewart. 1988. "The First Report into the Medieval Hospital at Soutra, Lothian Region, Scotland, Volume II." S.H.A.R.P., Edinburgh, Scotland.

Moffat, Brian, and Gordon Ewart. 1989. "The First Report on Researches into the Medieval Hospital at Soutra, Lothian/Borders Region, Scotland, Volume III." S.H.A.R.P., Edinburgh, Scotland.

Morris, Robert. c. 1769–c. 1821. "Promisarry [*sic*] notes, bills of exchange, Robert Morris Business papers," E-27, Box 1 (H437). Historical Society of Pennsylvania.

Nash, Gary B. 1970. *Class and Society in Early America.* Englewood Cliffs: Prentice Hall.

Nash, Gary B. 1988. *Forging Freedom: The Formation of Philadelphia's Black Community, 1720–1840.* Cambridge: Harvard University Press.

Nash, Gary B. 2002. *First City: Philadelphia and the Forging of Historical Memory.* Philadelphia: University of Pennsylvania Press.

Parrington, Michael, and Daniel G. Roberts. 1984. "The First African Baptist Church Cemetery: An Archaeological Glimpse of Philadelphia's Early Nineteenth-Century Free Black Community." *Archaeology Magazine,* November–December, pp. 27–32.

Parrington, Michael, Daniel G. Roberts, Stephanie A. Pinter, Janet C. Wideman, with contributions by David A. Sashiell, Gail T. Frace, and Robert C. Baldwin. 1987. "The First African Baptist Church Cemetery: Bioarcheology, Demography, and Acculturation of Early Nineteenth Century Philadelphia Blacks." Prepared for the Redevelopment Authority of the City of Philadelphia.

Parsons, Jacob Cos, editor. 1893. *Extracts from the Diary of Jacob Hiltzheimer of Philadelphia, 1765–1798.* Philadelphia: William F. Fell.

Paxton, J. A. 1811. *Plan of the City and Its Environs.* Philadelphia: J. A. Paxton.

Pitch, Anthony S. 1998. *The Burning of Washington: The British Invasion of 1814.* Annapolis: Naval Institute Press.

Poulson, Zachariah. 1811–30. *Poulson's American Daily Advertiser.* Philadelphia: Zachariah Poulson.

Powell, Richard E., Jr. 1993. *Coachmaking in Philadelphia: George and William Hunter's Factory of the Early Federal Period.* Winterthur Portfolio 28:4.

Praetzellis, Adrian, and Mary Praetzellis, editors. 1998. "Archaeologists as Storytellers." *Historical Archaeology* 32 (1).

Prince, Carl E. 1977. *The Federalists and the Origins of the U.S. Civil Service.* New York: New York University Press.

Reckner, Paul E., and Stephen A. Brighton. 1999. "Archaeological Perspectives on Class Conflict and the Rhetoric of Temperance." *Historical Archaeology* 33 (1):63–86.

Reynolds, Quentin. 1953. *Smooth and Deadly (I, Willie Sutton): The Personal Story of the Most Daring Bank Robber and Jailbreaker of Our Time.* New York: Popular Library.

Richardson, Edgar P. 1982. "The Athens of America, 1800–1825." In *Philadelphia: A 300-Year History,* edited by Russell F. Weigley, pp. 208–57. New York: W. W. Norton.

Roberts, Daniel G., and David Barrett. 1984. "Nightsoil Disposal Practices of the Nineteenth Century and the Origin of Artifacts in Plowzone Proveniences." *Historical Archaeology* 18 (1):108–15.

Rorabaugh, William. 1979. *The Alcoholic Republic: An American Tradition.* New York: Oxford University Press.

Rosswurm, Steve. 1994. "Class Relations, Political Economy, and Society in Philadelphia." In *Shaping a National Culture: The Philadelphia Experience, 1750–1800,* edited by Catherine E. Hutchins. Winterthur: Henry Francis du Pont Winterthur Museum.

Schama, Simon. 1991. *Dead Certainties (Unwarranted Speculations).* New York: Alfred A. Knopf.

Scull, Nicholas, and George Heap. 1754. *An East Prospect of the City of Philadelphia.* London. Engraved print.

Soderland, Jean R. 1985. *Quakers and Slavery: A Divided Spirit.* Princeton: Princeton University Press.

Soderland, Jean R. 1994. "The Quaker Vanguard: Philanthropy in Eighteenth-Century Philadelphia." In *Shaping a National Culture: The Philadelphia Experience, 1750–1800,* edited by Catherine E. Hutchins, pp. 129–42. Winterthur: Henry Francis du Pont Winterthur Museum.

Soderland, Jean R. 1997. "Radical and Conservative Friends in the Fight Against Slavery." In *For Emancipation and Education: Some Black and Quaker Efforts, 1680–1900,* pp. 18–25. Essays prepared for Awbury Arboretum and the Germantown Historical Society.

Spiese, George W. 1903. "The Burial Ground." In *First Reformed Church of Philadelphia Records. Compiled by the Genealogical Society of Pennsylvania.* Vol. 1. The Historical Society of Pennsylvania.

Stafford, Cornelius William. 1800. *Directory for the City of Philadelphia.* Philadelphia: William W. Woodward.

Stansell, Christine. 1987. *City of Women: Sex and Class*

in New York, 1789–1860. Urbana: University of Illinois Press.

Stauffer, John. 2002. *The Black Hearts of Men: Radical Abolitionists and the Transformation of Race.* Cambridge: Harvard University Press.

Syrett, Harold C., editor. 1961–87. *The Papers of Alexander Hamilton.* 27 vols. New York: Columbia University Press.

Tolles, Frederick B. 1948. *Meeting House and Counting House: The Quaker Merchants of Colonial Philadelphia.* Chapel Hill: University of North Carolina Press.

Toogood, Anna Coxe. 1985. Map Reconstruction of Early Philadelphia in 1787. On file, Independence National Historical Park.

Toogood, Anna Coxe. 1998. "Historic Resource Study, Independence Mall, The 18th Century Development, Block Two, Market to Arch, Fifth to Sixth Streets." Cultural Resources Management, Independence National Park, Philadelphia.

Toogood, Anna Coxe. 2001. "Historic Resource Study, Independence Mall, The 18th Century Development, Block One, Chestnut to Market, Fifth to Sixth Streets." Cultural Resources Management, Independence National Park, Philadelphia.

Toogood, Anna Coxe. 2004. "Historic Resource Study, Independence Mall, The 18th Century Development, Block Three, Arch to Race, Fifth to Sixth Streets." Cultural Resources Management, Independence National Park, Philadelphia.

Wainwright, Nicholas B. 1982. "The Age of Nicholas Biddle, 1825–1841." In *Philadelphia: A 300-Year History,* edited by Russell F. Weigley, pp. 258–306. New York: W. W. Norton.

Wall, Diana diZerega. 1994. *The Archaeology of Gender: Separating the Spheres in Urban America.* New York: Plenum.

Weber, Carmen A. 2006. "An Examination of Philadelphia's Early Waterfront Through the Archeology of the Hertz Lot, Edited and Compiled by Rebecca Yamin." John Milner Associates, Inc., 1216 Arch Street, 5th Floor, Philadelphia, PA.

Westcott, Thompson. 1877. *The Historic Mansions and Buildings of Philadelphia, with Some Notice of Their Owners and Occupants.* Philadelphia: Porter and Coates.

Wheaton, Thomas R., and Patrick H. Garrow. 1985. "Acculturation and the Archaeological Record in the Carolina Low Country." In *The Archaeology of Slavery and Plantation Life,* edited by Theresa A. Singleton, pp. 239–59. New York: Academic Press.

White, Hayden. 1981. "The Value of Narrativity in the Representation of Reality." In *On Narrative,* edited by W. J. T. Mitchell. Chicago: University of Chicago Press.

Wilentz, Sean. 1984. *Chants Democratic: New York City and the Rise of the American Working Class, 1788–1850.* New York: Oxford University Press.

Williams, Susan. 1996. *Savory Suppers, Fashionable Feasts: Dining in Victorian America.* Knoxville: University of Tennessee Press.

Wilson, Thomas. 1825. *Philadelphia Directory and Stranger's Guide.* Printed by Thomas Wilson and William D. Vandary, Philadelphia.

Wolf, Edwin, 2nd. 1975. *Philadelphia, Portrait of an American City.* Harrisburg: Stackpole.

Wood, Gordon S. 1991. *The Radicalism of the American Revolution.* New York: Vintage.

Yamin, Rebecca. 1997. "New York's Mythic Slum: Digging Lower Manhattan's Infamous Five Points." *Archaeology Magazine* 20 (2):44–53.

Yamin, Rebecca, editor. 2000. *Tales of Five Points: Working-Class Life in Nineteenth-Century New York.* Six volumes. Prepared for Edwards and Kelcey Engineers, Inc., and General Services Administration.

Yamin, Rebecca, editor. 2001. "Becoming New York: The Five Points Neighborhood." *Historical Archaeology* 35 (3):1–135.

Yamin, Rebecca. 2006. "Protocols for the Treatment of Human Remains and Archeological Excavation. Franklin Square, Philadelphia, Pennsylvania." Prepared for Once Upon a Nation. John Milner Associates, Inc.

Yamin, Rebecca, Alexander B. Bartlett, and Nancy Donohue. 2007. "Leaving No Stone Unturned: Archeological Monitoring and the Transformation of Franklin Square, Philadelphia, Pennsylvania." Prepared for Once Upon a Nation. John Milner Associates, Inc.

Yentsch, Anne Elizabeth. 1994. *A Chesapeake Family and Their Slaves: A Study in Historical Archaeology.* New York: Cambridge University Press.

Index